Key Words in context

Thematischer Mittelstufenwortschatz Englisch

von
Rosemary Hellyer-Jones
und Philip Hewitt

Ernst Klett Sprachen
Stuttgart

Key Words in context
Thematischer Mittelstufenwortschatz Englisch
von Rosemary Hellyer-Jones und Philip Hewitt

Bildquellen:
Punch Library, London: pp. 71, 76, 80, 100, 183
www.cartooonstock.com, Lansdown Mews, Bath, Avon: pp. 60 (Bryant, Adey), 126 (Gerard Whymann)

1. Auflage   1 ⁶ ⁵ ⁴ ³ | 2013 12 11

Alle Drucke dieser Auflage können im Unterricht nebeneinander benutzt werden.
Die letzte Zahl bezeichnet das Jahr dieses Druckes.

© Ernst Klett Sprachen GmbH, Rotebühlstraße 77, 70178 Stuttgart, 2006.
Alle Rechte vorbehalten.

Internetadresse: www.klett.de / www.lektueren.com

Das Werk und seine Teile sind urheberrechtlich geschützt. Jede Nutzung in anderen als den gesetzlich zugelassenen Fällen bedarf der vorherigen schriftlichen Einwilligung des Verlags. Hinweis zu § 52 a UrhG: Weder das Werk noch seine Teile dürfen ohne eine solche Einwilligung eingescannt und in ein Netzwerk eingestellt werden. Dies gilt auch für Intranets von Schulen und sonstigen Bildungseinrichtungen. Fotomechanische oder andere Wiedergabeverfahren nur mit Genehmigung des Verlags.

Redaktion: Inge Schäfer
Umschlaggestaltung: Elmar Feuerbach
Zeichnungen: Christian Gutendorf, Bad Wurzach
Druck: AZ Druck und Datentechnik GmbH, Kempten/Allgäu

Printed in Germany
ISBN 978-3-12-519702-2

Contents

Introduction	6
1 Geography	8
1 The continent of Europe	8
2 The British Isles	10
Great Britain: natural resources and industries – old and new	10
Agriculture	12
Living conditions	14
3 The United States of America	16
Physical features	16
The forces of nature	18
The USA – a country of superlatives	20
4 The weather forecast	22
Holiday weather	22
5 Looking at the night sky	24
Light and darkness	24
2 History	28
Some important periods and events – from prehistoric times to the present day	28
1 Historic events in Britain	30
Hastings	30
The Gunpowder Plot	34
The Industrial Revolution	34
2 Historic events in America	36
New beginnings – in a 'New World'	36
How the colonies won their independence	36
Opening up the West	36
Slavery in the States	38
3 The Commonwealth: some facts and figures	40
English – a world language	40
3 Conflicts	44
1 Racism and discrimination	44
2 Terrorism – and the war on terror	48
3 Crime	50
4 The media	54
1 The British press	54
2 Television	56
3 Radio	58
4 Cinema	58
5 The Internet	60
5 Politics	64
1 Parliament and the monarchy in Britain	64
General elections	64
Devolution	66
Does Britain still need the monarchy? – Two opinions	66

2 The American political system.	68
The President.	68
Congress	68
The Supreme Court	68
The system of checks and balances	70
3 Europe – and the European Union	72

6 World problems
1 Growth.	76
2 The results of growth	78
3 Think a moment.	78
4 What can be done?	80

7 Education
1 The school system in Britain	84
State schools.	84
Private schools.	84
School work and examinations	84
On the school notice-board.	88
2 Different words in American and British English.	88
3 School in Germany	90

8 Relationships and problems
1 Members of the family.	94
2 Taken from the Problem Page	96
3 Can you do without it?	96
4 Trouble at home	98

9 Young people's interests.
1 The generation gap – does it still exist?	104
2 Don't just stand there – join your local leisure centre	108

10 The world of work.
1 Situations vacant.	112
2 Finding a job.	114
3 A talk with the school careers teacher.	116
4 A letter of application	118

11 Technology
1 Teenagers' views on modern technology	122
2 Two interviews for "Teen Scene"	124
3 The impact of electricity on our lives	126

12 Lifestyle
1 Are you OK?	130
2 Do you really need it?	130
3 Women at work – and at home	132
4 Housing	134
5 I believe	134
6 Travelling.	136
By road.	136
By rail: At the station	136

By bike	138
By air	138
7 Holidays	140
8 Do you like reading?	142

13 Festivities and public holidays ... 146
    1 Celebrations – in Britain and in Germany ... 146
    2 More holidays and special days ... 148
    3 American celebrations ... 150

Tips and skills ... 154
    1 Writing letters ... 154
        1. Introducing yourself ... 154
        2. A letter to a good friend ... 154
        3. Useful phrases for an informal letter ... 155
        4. Asking for information ... 156
        5. Joining a society or a club ... 156
        6. Useful phrases for a formal letter ... 157
    2 Saying what you think ... 158
        1. Expressing an opinion ... 158
        2. Agreeing/disagreeing ... 158
        3. Introducing a different argument ... 158
    3 False friends ... 159
        1. Different meanings ... 159
        2. Different spellings in British English ... 161
    4 Singular and plural words ... 162
        1. True and false pairs ... 162
        2. Other plural nouns which are singular in German ... 162
        3. No plural in English – plural in German ... 163
        4. Plural noun with a singular verb ... 163
        5. Singular noun with a plural verb ... 163
    5 Describing what people are like ... 164
        1. Describing what people look like ... 164
        2. Describing character and qualities ... 164
        3. Describing how people feel ... 165
    6 Spelling and pronunciation ... 165
        1. Some words that are pronounced the same but spelt differently ... 165
        2. Same spelling, different pronunciation ... 167
    7 'Make' or 'do'? ... 167
    8 Useful expressions with common verbs ... 169
    9 Problem words in German ... 173
    10 One word in German, two or more in English ... 175
    11 One word in English, two or more in German ... 182

Key to the exercises ... 185

Irregular verbs ... 189

Index ... 191

Introduction

Words, words, words

When you learn a foreign language, you have to learn a lot of words. But of the many, many words in the English language (over half a million in all!), you really only need to know quite a small number. For every theme or subject, you will find there are 'key words' that help you to express what you want to say (and to understand what you hear and read). *Key Words in Context* contains this useful basic vocabulary.

But learning words can be so boring. And, as every student knows, there are always words that are difficult to remember! However, learning words is easier if you learn them in a *context* – together with other words and phrases that 'belong' to the same theme. *Key Words in Context* is divided into thirteen chapters, each with its own theme. The texts and dialogues have been specially written to include the vocabulary you will need to know for each subject. Topics have been chosen which the various German states recommend for the 'Mittelstufe'. The *key words* have been highlighted in blue (e.g. p. 8: **continent**, **Europe**).

How to work with Key Words in Context

- When you read the texts on the left-hand page, you will find you already know a number of the *key words*. You will probably understand most of the others from the context. The German translation of each highlighted word (or phrase) is given on the right-hand page, as it fits the context. Related words are also sometimes given, many of which you will probably know.
  e.g. p. 15:   **noise** → noisy

- In some cases, words with the same meaning (synonyms) or opposites (antonyms) also appear.
  e.g. p. 13:   **to join s.th. (to s.th.)** = to connect s.th. (to s.th.)
  e.g. p. 15:   **ugly** ↔ beautiful

- Some words may be pronounced differently from what you would expect. To help you in these cases, the phonetics are given in brackets.
  e.g. p. 9:   **continent** [ˈkɒntɪnənt]

Introduction

- Verbs with a star (*) in front of them are irregular. The forms are listed separately (see pages 189–190).
  e.g. p. 11:   **to *be divided into s.th.**

- Each chapter is complete in itself. So you needn't work through the book from beginning to end. Pick out the themes you need – when you need them.

- Don't try to learn too many words at once! 'Little and often' is more effective. Make sure you have the book with you at those times of the day when nothing is happening (when you're waiting for a bus, for example, or sitting on the train).

- The more often you read a text or dialogue, the quicker you will learn the new vocabulary – and the more confidently you will be able to use it!

- At the end of each chapter there are some exercises so that you can check what you have learnt. The key to these exercises is on pages 185–188.

Skills and tips

This part of the book is to help you with other aspects of using vocabulary. It is arranged according to 'problem spots' rather than themes. It shows you, for example, how to write letters in English (and what phrases to use) – and how to express your opinion. There is also a list of 'false friends' (words that look similar in English and German, but have different meanings). And you can also look up how to use those 'tricky' words that appear only in the singular or only in the plural. You will find a list of words that help to describe people – and feelings, too. And there is a section on words that sound the same but are spelt differently. You will also find a list of words that have several meanings, and a section that shows you how common verbs can be used in phrases and idioms.

This chapter will help you especially with your preparation for exams.

Geography

1 Geography

1 The continent of Europe

Europe is the world's second smallest continent. Most of its countries lie on the mainland of the continent. But over a third of its land is made up of islands and peninsulas, so a large number of Europeans live near the sea.

Geography

continent ['kɒntɪnənt]	Kontinent
Europe ['jʊərəp]	Europa
world	Welt
country	Land
mainland ['meɪnlænd]	Festland
to *be made up of s.th.	bestehen aus etwas
island ['aɪlənd]	Insel
peninsula [pə'nɪnsjʊlə]	Halbinsel
European [ˌjʊərə'piːən] *(noun/adj.)*	Europäer(in), europäisch
sea	Meer

country	the people	adjective
Great Britain* (1)	the British/Britons	British
Ireland* (2)	the Irish	Irish
Norway (3)	the Norwegians [nɔː'wiːdʒnz]	Norwegian
Sweden* (4)	the Swedes	Swedish
Denmark* (5)	the Danes	Danish
Finland* (6)	the Finns	Finnish
the Netherlands* (7)	the Dutch	Dutch
Belgium* (8) ['beldʒəm]	the Belgians	Belgian
Luxembourg* (9) ['lʌksəmbɜːg]	the Luxembourgers	Luxembourgian
France* (10)	the French	French
Germany* (11)	the Germans	German
Switzerland (12)	the Swiss	Swiss
Spain* (13)	the Spanish/Spaniards	Spanish
Portugal* (14) ['pɔːtʃʊgl]	the Portuguese [ˌpɔːtʃu'giːz]	Portuguese
Italy* (15)	the Italians	Italian
Greece* (16)	the Greeks	Greek
Turkey (17) ['tɜːkɪ]	the Turks	Turkish
Poland* (18)	the Poles	Polish
the Czech [tʃek] Republic* (19)	the Czechs	Czech
Slovakia* (20) [sləʊ'vækɪə]	the Slovaks ['sləʊvæks]	Slovakian
Hungary* (21) ['hʌŋgərɪ]	the Hungarians [hʌŋ'geərɪənz]	Hungarian
Bosnia-Herzegovina (22) [ˌbɒznɪəˌhɜːzə'gɒvɪnə]	the Bosnians	Bosnian
Croatia (23) [krəʊ'eɪʃə]	the Croats ['krəʊæts]	Croatian
Serbia ['sɜːbɪə] and Montenegro (24) [ˌmɒntɪ'niːgrəʊ]	the Serbs	Serbian
	the Montenegrins	Montenegrin
Malta ['mɔːltə] (25)	the Maltese [ˌ-'-]	Maltese
Ukraine (26) [juː'kreɪn]	the Ukrainians	Ukrainian
Iceland (27)	the Icelanders	Icelandic
Austria* (28) ['ɒstrɪə]	the Austrians	Austrian
Cyprus* ['saɪprəs] (29)	the Cypriots ['sɪprɪəts]	Cypriot

Romania (30) [rʊ'meɪnɪə], Bulgaria (31) [bʌl'geərɪə], Russia (32) ['rʌʃə], Latvia* (33) ['lætvɪə], Lithuania* (34) [ˌlɪθjʊ'eɪnɪə], Estonia* (35), Moldavia (36) [mɒl'deɪvɪə], Byelorussia (37) [ˌbjeləʊ'rʌʃə], Slovenia* (38) [sləʊ'viːnɪə], Macedonia (39) *und* Albania (40), *bilden das Wort für die Bevölkerung und das Adjektiv so wie* Austria, *d. h.* -ns, -n.

* Members of the EU

Geography

2 The British Isles

The British Isles are made up of two large islands, **Britain** and Ireland – and a number of small islands around their **coasts**. Britain itself **is divided into** three parts: England, Scotland and Wales. Together, their official name is Great Britain.

The United Kingdom (often called the UK) includes Great Britain and **Northern Ireland**. **The Republic of Ireland**, which lies on the **southern** side of the **border**, is not part of the UK.

The North Sea lies on the **eastern** side of the British Isles; the Atlantic Ocean is on the **western** side. Britain **is separated from** the mainland of Europe by **the English Channel**. Since 1994, however, when the **Channel Tunnel** was opened, it has become more closely **linked** to the Continent.

Great Britain: natural resources and industries – old and new

England is the oldest **industrialized country** in the world. In the 18th century, when the **Industrial Revolution** began, machines were now able to do work that used to be done **by hand**. **Coal** was needed for the engines that drove the new **machinery**. So the Midlands and the North of England, where there is a lot of coal, soon **developed** into important **industrial areas**.

Manchester became the centre of the **cotton** industry, while Bradford and Leeds were famous for the **wool trade**. The **raw materials** were mainly **imported from abroad**. Special **factories produced** the finished **textiles**, which could then be **exported**.

> – Why do birds fly south in the winter?
> – Because it's too far to walk.

Geography

the British Isles [aɪlz]	die Britischen Inseln
Britain	Britannien
coast	Küste
to *be divided [dɪˈvaɪdɪd] **into s.th.**	geteilt sein in etwas
the United [juːˈnaɪtɪd] **Kingdom**	das Vereinigte Königreich
northern → north, North	nördlich Norden, Nord-
southern → south, South	südlich Süden, Süd-
eastern → east, East	östlich Osten, Ost-
western → west, West	westlich Westen, West-

Wenn north, south, east, west *Teil eines Eigennamens sind, werden sie groß geschrieben.*

Northern Ireland [ˈaɪələnd]	Nordirland
the Republic of Ireland	die Republik Irland
border	Grenze
to *be separated [ˈsepəreɪtɪd] **from s.th.**	getrennt sein von etw.
the English Channel	der Ärmelkanal
the Channel Tunnel	der Eurotunnel
to link s.th. (to s.th.)	etw. (mit etw.) verbinden
natural resources [rɪˈsɔːsɪz]	Bodenschätze
industry	Industrie
industrialized country	Industrieland
the Industrial Revolution	die Industrielle Revolution
by hand	mit der Hand, von Hand
coal	Kohle
machinery [məˈʃiːnərɪ] ⚠ *(singular only)*	Maschinen
to develop [dɪˈveləp]	sich entwickeln
→ to develop s.th.	etw. entwickeln
→ development	Entwicklung
industrial	Industrie-, industriell
area [ˈeərɪə]	Gebiet, Region
cotton [ˈkɒtn]	Baumwolle
wool [wʊl]	Wolle
trade	Handel, Gewerbe
→ to trade	handeln, Handel treiben
raw material [məˈtɪərɪəl]	Rohstoff
to import [-ˈ-] **s.th.**	etw. importieren/einführen
→ import [ˈ--]	Import, Einfuhr
from abroad [əˈbrɔːd]	aus dem Ausland
→ to *be abroad	im Ausland sein
→ to *go abroad	ins Ausland gehen
factory	Fabrik
to produce s.th. → product [ˈ--]	etw. herstellen Produkt
textiles [ˈtekstaɪlz]	Textilien
to export [-ˈ-] **s.th.**	etw. exportieren/ausführen
→ export [ˈ--]	Export, Ausfuhr

Geography

Liverpool became Europe's greatest Atlantic seaport, with seven miles of docks at the mouth of the Mersey. Between 1860 and 1900 over 5 million people emigrated to America from Liverpool Docks. Manchester, also a vast urban area, only a short distance from Liverpool, became an important inland port when it was joined to the sea by the Manchester Ship Canal, which was constructed at the end of the 19th century.

The development of the iron industry began in the 18th century. Coal was needed for the mass production of iron. So, naturally, the iron and steel industry grew especially in areas where there was also coal-mining.

Britain's traditional industries include heavy engineering, shipbuilding and the chemical industry (especially in the North), the manufacturing of textiles, the car industry (especially in the Midlands), and the fishing industry (especially on the East coast). Some of these industries have declined now, and many pits, shipyards and works have had to close. Many cities have new industrial estates, where new companies – in modern industries such as plastics and electronics – have set up business. The demand for coal has declined; natural gas and North Sea oil became more important in the 1980s, when the building and operation of oil rigs, pipelines and refineries brought many new jobs. In present-day Britain, the tourist industry and many different service industries also play an important role.

Agriculture

The eastern part of England has very fertile soil, which makes good farmland. Wheat is one of the main crops. In southern England, there is a lot of dairy farming. Kent, in the South-East, is called the 'Garden of England', because of all the fruit and vegetables that are grown there.

Recently, since summers – even in Britain! – have tended to be warmer, winegrowing has started to become popular in the South. English white wines can taste surprisingly good.

Geography

seaport	Seehafen
docks	Hafenanlagen
mouth	Mündung
urban ['ɜːbən] ↔ rural	städtisch, Stadt- ländlich
inland ['ɪnlənd] **port**	Binnenhafen
to join s.th. (to s.th.)	etw. (mit etw.) verbinden
= to connect s.th. (to s.th.)	
canal [kə'næl]	Kanal
iron ['aɪən]	Eisen
mass [mæs] **production**	Massenproduktion
steel	Stahl
coal-mining → coal mine	Kohlenbergbau Kohlenbergwerk
heavy engineering [ˌendʒɪ'nɪərɪŋ]	Schwerindustrie
shipbuilding	Schiffbau
chemical ['kemɪkl]	chemisch, Chemie-
manufacturing [ˌmænjʊ'fæktʃərɪŋ]	Herstellung, Fabrikation
to decline [dɪ'klaɪn]	in Verfall geraten, nachlassen
pit	Zeche
shipyard ['ʃɪpjɑːd]	(Schiffs-)Werft
works △ *(plural only)*	Fabrik, Betrieb, Werk
industrial estate	Industriegebiet, Gewerbegebiet
company ['kʌmpəni]	(Handels-)Gesellschaft, Firma
plastic	Kunststoff
electronics	Elektronik
to *set up business ['bɪznɪs]	sich niederlassen
→ business	Geschäft, Betrieb
demand [dɪ'mɑːnd] **(for s.th.)**	Nachfrage (nach etw.)
natural gas	Erdgas
operation → to operate s.th.	Bedienung etw. bedienen
oil rig	(Öl-)Bohrinsel
pipeline	(Rohr-)Leitung
refinery [rɪ'faɪnəri]	Raffinerie
service industry	Dienstleistungsbetrieb
agriculture ['ægrɪkʌltʃə]	Landwirtschaft
fertile ['fɜːtaɪl] ↔ infertile	fruchtbar unfruchtbar
soil	Erde, Boden
farmland ['fɑːmlænd]	Ackerland
wheat [wiːt]	Weizen
crop → to bring in the crops	Feldfrucht die Ernte einbringen
dairy ['deəri] **farming**	Milchwirtschaft
fruit [fruːt]	Obst
vegetables ['vedʒtəblz]	Gemüse
winegrowing	Weinbau

13

Geography

The **moors** that are so typical of the North of England, Scotland and Wales, are ideal for **sheep** farming.

Visitors to England are often fascinated by the **hedges** that divide the farmland into **meadows** and **fields**. Many of these hedges were **planted** in the eighteenth century, when big landowners divided their land into compact **farms**. But although many of the hedges are still there, British farms today are usually large – larger than farms in Germany, and often with more modern **equipment**.

Living conditions

Over 30% of Great Britain's **population** live in the South-East of England, many of them in London, which has been the **capital** for nearly 1,000 years. Central London is not an ideal place to live. The **cost of living** is high, the streets are **crowded**, and **noise** is a problem. Most people who work in **the City of London** are **commuters**: they live in quiet **residential areas** in the **suburbs** and travel to work by **public transport**.

Many of Britain's **inner cities** became **uglier** and **shabbier** when traditional industries declined. There is still a lot of **poverty** in some urban areas. But many of the old **buildings** have been **pulled down**, and new **housing estates** have now replaced a lot of the **slums**.

Living out **in the country**, where the **air** is fresh and clean, has become more and more popular – at least for people who can **afford** it. In Britain, not many of the people who live in **rural districts** actually **work on the land**. For those who do, life is often much harder than most people imagine.

Many Scottish people work in the **seafood industry**, for which Scotland is traditionally famous. But North Sea oil and gas have brought big changes – and more **wealth** – to the **inhabitants** of many towns and **villages** on the coast of Scotland and the Shetland Islands. Many thousands of jobs have been created in Scotland by the oil industry, which will probably continue to be of great importance to the **local economy** for many years.

Geography

moor(s)	(Hoch-)Moor, Heidelandschaft
sheep ⚠ (*plural:* sheep)	Schaf
hedge	Hecke
meadow ['medəʊ]	Wiese
field	Feld, Acker
to plant [plɑːnt] **s.th.** → (a) plant	etw. pflanzen Pflanze
farm	Bauernhof
equipment [ɪ'kwɪpmənt] ⚠ (*singular only*)	Ausstattung, Ausrüstung
living conditions	Lebensbedingungen
population [ˌpɒpjʊ'leɪʃn]	Bevölkerung
capital	Hauptstadt
cost of living → to *cost s.th.	Lebenshaltungskosten etw. kosten
crowded → (a) crowd	überfüllt Menschenmenge
noise → noisy	Lärm laut
the City of London	das Banken- und Börsenviertel Londons
→ city	Großstadt
commuter [kə'mjuːtə]	Pendler(in)
→ to commute	pendeln
residential area [ˌrezɪ'denʃl 'eərɪə]	(vornehmes) Wohngebiet
suburb ['sʌbɜːb]	Vorort
public transport	öffentliche Verkehrsmittel
inner city	Innenstadt
ugly ['ʌglɪ] ↔ beautiful	hässlich schön
shabby ['ʃæbɪ]	schäbig, heruntergekommen
poverty ['pɒvətɪ] ↔ wealth	Armut Wohlstand, Reichtum
building	Gebäude, Haus
to pull s.th. down	etwas niederreißen
housing estate ['haʊzɪŋ ɪˌsteɪt]	Wohnsiedlung
slum [slʌm]	Elendsviertel
in the country	auf dem Land
air	Luft
to afford [ə'fɔːd] **s.th.**	sich etwas leisten
rural ['rʊərəl] ↔ urban	ländlich städtisch
district ['--]	Bezirk, Gegend
to work on the land	in der Landwirtschaft arbeiten
seafood industry	Fischerei- und Fischverarbeitungsindustrie
wealth [welθ] ↔ poverty	Wohlstand, Reichtum
inhabitant [ɪn'hæbɪtənt]	Einwohner(in)
village ['vɪlɪdʒ]	Dorf
local ['ləʊkl]	örtlich, hiesig
economy [ɪ'kɒnəmɪ]	Wirtschaft

15

Geography

3 The United States of America

Physical features

The USA is an **enormous** country. The first thing about America that amazes visitors is, in fact, its **size**. The **distance** across the USA from coast to coast is three thousand **miles**; from the Canadian border in the north to the Gulf of Mexico in the south, it is twelve hundred miles. The country has an **area** of 9.3 million **square kilometres** (to compare: the whole of Germany and France together have less than 1 million).

Geographically, the USA has three dominant features: the two long **mountain ranges** on each side of the country (the Appalachians in the east and the Rocky Mountains in the west), and the **wide valley** between them, with its **huge prairie** which rises to the Great **Plains**, and with its large **rivers** which **flow** into the great Mississippi.

Visitors are always impressed by the beauty of the **landscape**. The **scenery** in the west is especially dramatic, with its many types of landscape and **climate**. California has a long **coastline**, **rocky** in places, with miles of **sandy beaches** and lovely **bays**. Further **inland**, there is the **mountainous** region of the Sierra Nevada (the **summit** of Mount Whitney is 4,418 metres **above sea-level**). Not far away is the **wilderness** of endless **desert** that **surrounds** Death Valley, the **lowest** point in the USA (86 metres below sea-level). The **ground** here is very dry and **stony**. There are also **vast National Parks** with beautiful **forests**, rivers and **streams**; and there are miles of **wooded countryside**.

Geography

physical ['fɪzɪkl]	physikalisch, landschaftlich, geophysisch
feature ['fi:tʃə]	Merkmal, Besonderheit
enormous [ɪ'nɔ:məs]	riesig
size	Größe
distance ['dɪstəns]	Entfernung, Ferne
→ distant	(weit) entfernt
mile	Meile
area ['eərɪə]	*hier:* Fläche
square kilometre [ˌskweə kɪ'lɒmɪtə]	Quadratkilometer
mountain range [ˌ--'-]	Bergkette
wide ↔ narrow	breit, weit eng, schmal
valley	Tal
huge [hju:dʒ]	gewaltig, riesig
prairie ['preərɪ]	Prärie (Grasebene)
plain	Ebene
river	Fluss, Strom
to flow [fləʊ]	fließen
landscape	Landschaft
scenery ['si:nərɪ]	Szenerie, Landschaft
climate ['klaɪmɪt]	Klima
coastline	Küstenlinie
rocky → rock	felsig Fels, großer Stein
sandy → sand	sandig Sand
beach	Strand
bay	Bucht
inland ['ɪnlænd]	im Landesinneren
mountainous ['maʊntɪnəs] ↔ flat	gebirgig eben, flach
summit	Gipfel
above/below sea-level	über/unter dem Meeresspiegel
wilderness ['wɪldənɪs] → wild [aɪ]	Wildnis wild
desert ['dezət]	Wüste
to surround [sə'raʊnd] s.th.	etw. umgeben
low ↔ high	niedrig, tief hoch
ground	Boden
stony → stone	steinig Stein
vast [vɑ:st]	sehr groß und weitläufig
National Park	Nationalpark
forest	(großer) Wald
stream [stri:m]	Bach
wooded ['wʊdɪd] → wood	bewaldet (kleiner) Wald
countryside	Land(schaft)

Geography

Up in the **hills**, **dams** have been built to create **reservoirs**, which **supply** water for the cities and for the fields and gardens of southern California.

When the American **glaciers melted** about 5,000 years ago, the Great **Lakes** were formed. Some of the **wildest** countryside on the North American continent is to be found in this area – although there are also large cities, like Chicago and Detroit, on the **shores** of the lakes. Between two of the lakes, the Niagara Falls, America's most spectacular **waterfall**, forms a natural border between the USA and Canada.

The states of Kansas, Iowa and Nebraska, in the **heart** of the USA, are largely **flat**, with huge **expanses** of farmland. The great **open spaces** of the Midwest and the South are ideal for **cattle ranches**. Florida, in the southeast, is also flat. With its **mild** climate, it is famous for the **seaside resorts** along its coastline – and for the Everglades, a wilderness of **swampland** near Miami.

The forces of nature

Disasters caused by the forces of nature are not uncommon in the USA. There are a number of **active volcanoes** near the West Coast; sometimes serious **eruptions** occur. The area around San Francisco is often **affected** by **earthquakes**.

Hurricanes sometimes create chaos in coastal areas, especially in the south and east, while **tornadoes** are **whirlwinds** that cause **damage** especially in inland areas. In the winter months, there are often **blizzards** that **sweep** down the country from the north.

Geography

hill → hilly
dam
reservoir ['rezəvwɑː]
to supply [sə'plaɪ] **s.th.**
 → (a) supply

glacier ['glæsjə]
to melt ↔ **to *freeze**
lake
wild [aɪ] → **wilderness** ['wɪldənɪs]
shore [ʃɔː]
waterfall

heart [hɑːt]
flat ↔ **mountainous, hilly**
expanse [ɪk'spæns]
open spaces
cattle ranch [rɑːntʃ]
mild [maɪld]
seaside resort [rɪ'zɔːt]
swampland ['swɒmplænd]

the forces of nature
 → to force s.o. to do s.th.
disaster [dɪ'zɑːstə]
active ↔ **inactive**
volcano [vɒl'keɪnəʊ]
eruption [ɪ'rʌpʃn] → **to erupt**
to affect s.o./s.th.
earthquake ['ɜːθkweɪk]

hurricane ['hʌrɪkən]
tornado [tɔː'neɪdəʊ]
whirlwind ['wɜːlwɪnd]
damage ['dæmɪdʒ]
 → to damage s.th.
blizzard ['blɪzəd]
to *sweep

Hügel hügelig
Damm
Reservoir, Talsperre
hier: etw. liefern
  Vorrat

Gletscher
schmelzen gefrieren
(der) See
wild Wildnis
Ufer, Strand
Wasserfall

Herz, Mitte
flach gebirgig, hügelig
hier: weiter Raum, Fläche
weites, offenes Land
Viehfarm
mild
Seebad, Ferienort am Meer
Sumpfgebiet

die Naturgewalten
  jdn. zwingen etw. zu tun
Katastrophe
aktiv, tätig inaktiv
Vulkan
Ausbruch ausbrechen
jdn./etw. betreffen
Erdbeben

tropischer Wirbelsturm
Tornado, Wirbelsturm
Wirbelwind
Schaden
  etwas beschädigen
heftiger Schneesturm
fegen

Geography

The USA – a country of superlatives

Here are just a few of the world records held by the United States. It has …

- the most **extensive cave** system in the world: under the ground at the Mammoth Cave National Park in Kentucky. So far, over 300 miles of underground **passageways** have been **discovered** and **mapped**. Mammoth Cave itself has five different **levels**. The lowest level is 110 metres below the **surface**.

- the world's highest mountain (**measured** from its **base** under the sea): Mauna Kea in Hawaii, which is 10,023 metres high (4,205 metres of this **height** is above sea-level).

- the largest **freshwater** lake in the world: Lake Superior, with a total area of 31,800 square miles.

- the largest **gorge** in the world: the Grand **Canyon** in Arizona. It **stretches** over a distance of 217 miles, is between 4 and 13 miles wide, and 1,615 metres **deep**.

- the highest **cliffs**: near Umilehi Point in Hawaii. They stand 1,005 metres above the sea.

- the world's greatest **tides**: in the Bay of Fundy between the USA and Canada. The difference between **high** and **low tide** can be over 16 metres.

- the most enormous tree in the world: 'General Sherman', a giant sequoia tree in the Sequoia National Park, California. This tree would give enough **wood** to produce 5,000,000,000 matches.

- the world's largest **flowering plant**: a giant Chinese wisteria at Sierra Madre, California. When **in flower**, it is covered in one and a half million **blossoms**.

- the **steepest** streets in the world: in San Francisco, with **gradients** up to 31.5%. In parts, the **slopes** are so extreme that cars have to park with their front wheels turned inwards.

Geography

extensive [ɪkˈstensɪv]	ausgedehnt, umfangreich
→ to extend	sich ausdehnen
cave [keɪv]	Höhle
passageway [ˈpæsɪdʒˌweɪ]	Gang
to discover s.th.	etw. entdecken
→ discovery	Entdeckung
to map s.th.	etw. kartographisch darstellen
→ map	Landkarte
level	Ebene, Schicht, Etage
surface [ˈsɜːfɪs]	Oberfläche
to measure [ˈmeʒə] **s.th.**	etw. messen
→ measurement	Maß
base	Basis, Fuß
height [haɪt]	Höhe
→ high	hoch
freshwater ↔ saltwater	Süßwasser Salzwasser
gorge [gɔːdʒ]	Schlucht
canyon [ˈkænjən]	Schlucht
to stretch [stretʃ] **(over s.th.)**	sich (über etw.) erstrecken
deep → depth	tief Tiefe
cliff	Klippe, Felsen
tide [taɪd]	Gezeiten, Ebbe und Flut
high tide	Flut
low tide	Ebbe
wood [wʊd]	*hier:* Holz
flowering → to flower	blühend blühen
plant → to plant s.th.	Pflanze etw. pflanzen
to *be in flower = to flower	in Blüte stehen, blühen
→ flower	Blume
blossom [ˈblɒsəm]	(einzelne) Blüte
steep	steil
gradient [ˈgreɪdjənt]	Steigung
slope	Hang, Neigung

Geography

4 The weather forecast

TV weatherman:

And now for tomorrow's weather. London and the South-East will have **a bright start to the day**, with plenty of sunshine. But it will become **cloudy** later, with **outbreaks of rain** or **drizzle** in some areas.

The South-West and the Channel Islands will have an **unsettled** day. There will be **sea mist** in many coastal areas in the morning, and there may be some **heavy rain** with **high winds** later in the day.

In the Midlands, Wales, Northern Ireland and the North of England, it will be mainly dry. It will be rather **dull** at first, and there may be **patches of fog** in some places. But there will be brighter weather, with some **sunny spells**, in most districts during the afternoon.

Most of Scotland will have another cool day, with **a strong breeze**, especially along the East coast. There may be a few **scattered showers** in the West.

Temperatures in most parts will be similar to today's. Around 8 to 10 **degrees centigrade** – milder in the South-West.

The **outlook** for the next few days: Colder weather will **spread across the country** from the North-East, and temperatures may fall **below freezing point** in some areas. There may even be **the odd fall of snow** or **sleet** on the Scottish hills, with danger of icy roads.

Holiday weather

Harry: Great to see you, Joe! How was Spain?
Joe: Fantastic, Harry. Except for the weather.
Harry: Oh?
Joe: It was good the first day or two. **Not a cloud in the sky**. Really hot. Then one evening we had a terrible **storm**. You know – **thunder** and **lightning** – and it **poured**! After an hour or so, the streets were all **flooded**, so we couldn't leave our hotel. A tree outside the hotel was blown down in the **gale**, so the road was blocked. But we were lucky. The hotel opposite ours **was struck by lightning**!
– Well, the weather never really **cleared up** properly after that. It wasn't warm enough to go swimming. And the sea was too **rough** anyway – the **waves** were enormous.

Geography

weather forecast ['fɔːkɑːst]	Wettervorhersage
weatherman	Meteorologe, ‚Wetterfrosch'
a bright start to the day	freundliches Wetter in der Frühe
cloudy ↔ sunny	wolkig, bewölkt sonnig
outbreaks of rain	Regenperioden
drizzle ['drɪzl]	Nieselregen
unsettled [ˌʌn'setld]	unbeständig
sea mist	feiner Nebel vom Meer
heavy rain	starker Regen
high wind	starker Wind
dull ↔ bright	trüb, bewölkt heiter, freundlich
patches ['pætʃɪz] **of fog** → foggy	Nebelfelder neblig
sunny spells	sonnige Abschnitte
a strong breeze [briːz]	eine starke Brise
scattered showers	vereinzelte Schauer
temperature ['temprətʃə]	Temperatur
degree (centigrade)	Grad (Celsius)
the outlook	die Aussichten
to *spread across the country	sich über das Land ausbreiten
below/above freezing point	unter/über Null
→ to *freeze	(ge)frieren
the odd fall of snow	einzelne Schneefälle
sleet	Schneeregen
not a cloud in the sky	keine Wolke am Himmel
storm	*hier:* Gewitter
thunder	Donner
lightning	Blitz
to pour [pɔː]	gießen
flooded ['flʌdɪd]	überflutet
→ flood	Überschwemmung
gale [geɪl]	starker Wind, Sturm
to *be struck by lightning	vom Blitz getroffen werden
to clear up	sich aufklären, sich aufhellen
rough [rʌf] ↔ calm [kɑːm]	rau, stürmisch ruhig
wave	Welle

Did you hear about the boy who came to school with only one glove on? Well, the teacher asked him why. And he said, "The weather forecast said it might be warm, but on the other hand it might get quite cool."

Geography

Harry: Bad luck! – We had great weather here. A real **heatwave**. It got so **muggy** at times, you could only sit outside if you were **in the shade**. There hasn't been **a wet day** for weeks – we've had a real **drought**.
Joe: Until today. Look at it – **what a downpour**! It's starting to **hail** now, too. See the **hailstones**?
Harry: And the **rainbow**! That's the English climate for you. Full of surprises. Just like Spain!

5 Looking at the sky at night

During the day, before **the sun has set**, it is easy to imagine that **our Earth** is the centre of the **universe**. But **at night**, when it **gets dark** and **the moon rises**, the **sight** of the millions of **stars** and **planets** can make us feel very small.

Does life **exist** anywhere else in the universe? We know there can be no other intelligent life in our own **solar system**. But could there be life on any planets of other suns in **outer space**, perhaps in other **galaxies**? These planets are so far away, of course, that nobody could ever make the journey there. The distances to stars in **the Milky Way** are so enormous that they have to be measured in light years. (A light year is the distance that light travels in one year – at a speed of about 660 million miles an hour!)

> – What did the man from outer space say to the petrol pump?
> – Take your finger out of your ear when I'm talking to you.

Light and darkness

As everyone knows, the changing position of the **globe** as it moves round the sun causes the changing **seasons**. In the winter, it is dark **all day** and **all night** at **the North Pole**; but in the summer, the sun never **sinks** below the **horizon** at all. When **autumn** comes to the northern **hemisphere**, it is **spring** in the countries south of the **equator**.

So what must seasons be like on Pluto, the most **distant** planet in our solar system? Pluto takes nearly 250 years to go round the sun!

Geography

heatwave	Hitzewelle
muggy ['mʌgɪ]	schwül
in the shade	im Schatten
a wet day ↔ a fine day	ein Regentag ein schöner Tag
drought [draʊt]	Trockenperiode, Dürre
What a downpour! ['daʊnpɔː]	Was für ein Wolkenbruch!
to hail [heɪl] → hail	hageln Hagel
hailstone	Hagelkorn
rainbow ['reɪnbəʊ]	Regenbogen

during the day	am Tag
the sun *sets	die Sonne geht unter
our Earth	unsere Erde
→ earth	Erdboden, Erde
universe ['juːnɪvɜːs]	Universum
at night	nachts, in der Nacht
to *get dark ↔ to get light	dunkel werden hell werden
the moon *rises	der Mond geht auf
sight → to *see	Anblick sehen
star	Stern
planet ['plænɪt]	Planet

to exist	existieren, bestehen
solar ['səʊlə] **system**	Sonnensystem
outer ['aʊtə] **space**	der Weltraum, das Weltall
galaxy	Galaxie
the Milky Way	die Milchstraße

globe	Globus, Erdkugel, Erde
→ global ['--]	global, weltweit
season ['siːzn]	Jahreszeit
all day	den ganzen Tag
all night	die ganze Nacht
the North Pole	der Nordpol
to *sink	untergehen, sinken
horizon [hə'raɪzn]	Horizont
autumn ['ɔːtəm]	Herbst
hemisphere ['hemɪˌsfɪə]	Halbkugel
spring	Frühling
equator [ɪ'kweɪtə]	Äquator

distant	(weit) entfernt
→ distance	Entfernung, Ferne

Exercises

a) Find the words that belong together. Then choose the correct German translation from the list below.

1. natural **resources** — _Bodenschätze_ — resources ✔
2. industrialized country — Industrieland — industry ✓
3. raw material — Rohstoffe — transport ✓
4. the English Channel — Ärmelkanal — farming ✓
5. inner city — Innenstadt — Way ✓
6. housing estate — Wohnsiedlung — country ✓
7. inland port — Binnenhafen — estate ✓
8. service industry — Dienstleistung(sb.) — Channel ✓
9. the Channel Tunnel — Eurotunnel — city ✓
10. dairy farming — Milchwirtschaft — material ✓
11. public transport — öff. Verkehrsm. — port
12. the Milky Way — Milchstraße — Tunnel ✓

*der Ärmelkanal ✓   Bodenschätze ✔   Binnenhafen ✓
Dienstleistungsbetrieb ✓   der Eurotunnel ✓   Industrieland ✓
Innenstadt ✓   die Milchstraße ✓   Milchwirtschaft ✓
öffentliche Verkehrsmittel ✓   Rohstoff ✓   Wohnsiedlung ✓*

b) Put in the opposites of these words and expressions:

1. rural: ↔ urban
2. wealth: ↔ poverty
3. narrow: ↔ wide
4. below sea-level: ↔ above sea-level
5. to melt: ↔ _____
6. hilly: ↔ flat
7. a fine day: ↔ _____
8. saltwater: ↔ _____

Exercises 1

c) Which of the three is the odd one out?

1. ☐ island ☐ peninsula ☒ border
2. ☐ ugly ☒ crowded ☐ shabby
3. ☐ low ☐ huge ☒ vast
4. ☐ earth ☒ mist ☐ soil
5. ☐ wood ☐ forest ☒ meadow
6. ☐ rain ☐ drizzle ☐ gale
7. ☐ galaxy ☐ hemisphere ☒ solar system
8. ☒ damage ☐ tornado ☐ earthquake
9. ☐ inhabitants ☒ production ☐ population
10. ☐ gas ☐ oil ☒ steel

d) Think of the English equivalents of these German words, then find the right places for them in the grid below. To help you, some of the letters have already been put in.

Ausbruch ✓
Eisen ✓
Feldfrucht ✓
Firma ✓
Fläche ✓
Gemüse ✓
Hafenanlagen
Hauptstadt ✓
Küste ✓
Landkarte ✓
tropischer Wirbelsturm ✓
Wüste ✓

If you put the letters in the blue squares into the right order, you'll find the expression for
land protected by the state because of its natural beauty:

__National__ __Park__ (2 words)

History

Some important periods and events – from prehistoric times to the present day

12,000 BC	The end of the Ice Age in Northern Europe
800–500 BC	The Iron Age: the Celts come to Britain
55 BC	The Romans first arrive in Britain
5th–9th century AD	The Angles and Saxons, then the Vikings, invade Britain
1066	The Norman Conquest
11th–13th century	The Crusades: Christian armies from Europe go to the Holy Land
1215	King John signs Magna Carta
1265	The first Parliament (a meeting of knights, barons and townspeople) comes together in England
14th century	A plague, known as the Black Death, sweeps through Europe and kills half the population
15th century	The end of the Middle Ages
1492	Christopher Columbus discovers America
16th century	The Tudor Age: Henry VIII founds the Church of England; England becomes a sea power; for the next 300 years the British Navy is the strongest in the world
1689	The Bill of Rights is passed: no English monarch may rule without Parliament
1775	The American War of Independence begins
1789	The French Revolution
ca. 1750–1850	The Industrial Revolution
1861–1865	The American Civil War
1837–1901	The age of Queen Victoria: a time of many reforms, inventions and great material progress
1914–1918	The First World War
1939-1945	The Second World War
1946–1990	The Cold War years: a period of great tension between the West and the Soviet Bloc
1990	The reunification of Germany
2001	11th September ('Nine eleven'): terrorists attack the USA
	The USA begins a war on terror

History 2

period [ˈpɪərɪəd]	Zeitalter, Periode
event [-ˈ-]	Ereignis
prehistoric [ˌpriːhɪˈstɒrɪk]	vorgeschichtlich
to the present day	bis zum heutigen Tag
BC (= **b**efore **C**hrist)	vor Christus
Ice Age	Eiszeit
→ Stone Age, Bronze [brɒnz] Age	Steinzeit, Bronzezeit
Iron [ˈaɪən] **Age**	Eisenzeit
the Celts [kelts]	die Kelten
the Romans	die Römer
century [ˈsentʃərɪ]	Jahrhundert
AD (= **a**nno **D**omini)	nach Christus
the Angles [ˈæŋglz] **and Saxons**	die Angeln und Sachsen
the Vikings [ˈvaɪkɪŋz]	die Wikinger
to invade [-ˈ-] **(a country)**	(in ein Land) einmarschieren
→ invasion	Invasion, Eindringen
the Norman Conquest [ˈkɒŋkwest]	die normannische Eroberung
the Crusades [kruːˈseɪdz]	die Kreuzzüge
army [ˈɑːmɪ]	Armee
king	König
to sign s.th.	etwas unterzeichnen
Parliament [ˈpɑːləmənt]	Parlament
knight [naɪt]	Ritter
baron [ˈbærən] → baroness	Baron Baronin
plague [pleɪg]	Pest
to kill s.o.	jdn. töten
the Middle Ages	das Mittelalter
to discover s.th. → discovery	etwas entdecken Entdeckung
to found s.th.	etwas gründen
the Church of England	die anglikanische Kirche
sea power	Seemacht
navy [ˈneɪvɪ]	(Kriegs-)Marine
monarch [ˈmɒnək] → monarchy	Monarch(in) Monarchie
to rule → ruler	regieren, herrschen Herrscher(in)
the War of Independence	der Unabhängigkeitskrieg
revolution [ˌrevəˈluːʃn]	Revolution
the Industrial Revolution	die Industrielle Revolution
the (American) Civil [ˈsɪvl] **War**	der (US) Bürgerkrieg
queen	Königin
invention [-ˈ--] → to invent s.th.	Erfindung etwas erfinden
material [məˈtɪərɪəl] → material	materiell Stoff
progress ⚠ *(singular only)*	Fortschritt(e)
the First/Second World War	der Erste/Zweite Weltkrieg
the Cold War	der Kalte Krieg
reunification [ˌ----ˈ--]	Wiedervereinigung
terrorist	Terrorist(in)
to attack s.o./s.th.	jdn./etwas angreifen
↔ to defend s.o./s.th.	jdn./etwas verteidigen
war on terror	Kampf gegen den Terror

1 Historic events in Britain

Hastings

1066 is one of the most important **dates** in Britain's history. It was the year when England was invaded for the last time.

When the King of England, Edward the Confessor, **died** in the spring of 1066, he left no son to **succeed** him. Harold, an English **nobleman**, was chosen by the English as his **successor**. But two other men also had a **claim** to the **throne**. One was the King of Norway. The other was the **Duke** of Normandy. As Harold would not give up his **kingdom**, Duke William and the Normans decided to attack. The King of Norway also made plans to **fight** for the English throne, so Harold was **threatened** by two **enemies** at the same time.

The Normans made preparations to **conquer** England. They built 800 ships and filled them with **stores**, with **weapons**, and with horses. They also loaded the ships with parts of wooden **forts**, which they planned to put together after the **invasion**.

In September, while William was waiting for the right wind to take his ships across the Channel, the King of Norway **landed** with his men in the North of England. Harold's army **marched** north to **defend** the country against the **invaders**. They **defeated** the Norwegians at the **Battle** of Stamford Bridge. But the battle was hard, and many **soldiers lost their lives**.

Harold and his men were resting at York when news reached them that William of Normandy had landed on the Sussex coast.

After a ten-day march, Harold and his Saxon army arrived **exhausted** at Hastings, where the Norman soldiers had **camped**.

Next morning, on October 14th, the Normans attacked. Their soldiers were **armed** mainly with **bows** and **arrows**. The Saxons fought mainly with **battle-axes**, although **swords** and **shields** were used by both sides. The battle was long and **bloody**, and many men were killed or **wounded**.

History

historic	historisch
date	Datum, Zeitpunkt, Jahreszahl
to die → death [deθ]	sterben Tod
to succeed [sək'siːd] **s.o.**	jdm. nachfolgen
nobleman → noblewoman	Adliger Adlige
successor	Nachfolger(in)
to *have a claim to s.th.	Anspruch auf etwas haben
→ to claim s.th.	etwas beanspruchen
throne [θrəʊn]	Thron
duke → duchess ['dʌtʃɪs]	Herzog Herzogin
kingdom	Königreich
to *fight (for s.th.)	(um etwas) kämpfen
to threaten ['θretn] **s.o.** → threat	jdn. bedrohen Bedrohung
enemy	Feind(in)
to conquer ['kɒŋkə] **s.th.**	etwas erobern
store	Vorrat
weapon ['wepən]	Waffe
fort	Fort, Festung
invasion [ɪn'veɪʒn]	Invasion
to land	landen
to march [mɑːtʃ]	marschieren
to defend [dɪ'fend] **s.o./s.th.**	jdn./etwas verteidigen
invader [ɪn'veɪdə]	Eindringling
to defeat [dɪ'fiːt] **s.o.** → defeat	jdn. besiegen Niederlage
battle	Schlacht
soldier ['səʊldʒə]	Soldat(in)
to *lose [luːz] **one's life**	ums Leben kommen
exhausted [ɪg'zɔːstɪd]	erschöpft
to camp	*hier:* das Lager aufstellen
to *be armed → armour [ɑːmə]	bewaffnet sein Rüstung
bow [bəʊ]	Bogen
arrow	Pfeil
battle-axe → axe	Streitaxt Beil
sword [sɔːd]	Schwert
shield [ʃiːld]	Schild
bloody ['blʌdɪ] → blood	blutig Blut
to wound [wuːnd] **s.o.**	jdn. verwunden

31

History

At first, the Saxons had taken up position on a hill and were able to fight back the Normans as they attacked. But then the Normans **retreated**. Seeing this, the Saxons rushed down from their hill and ran after them. The Normans, however, began fighting again, and the Saxons, who had lost their **advantage**, were now attacked from both sides. After that, the battle was soon over. Luck was on the Normans' side: Harold was killed – **shot** in the eye by an arrow. When the Saxons saw that their **leader** was **dead** and the battle **lost**, they **gave up**. Many of the soldiers **fled**, leaving their king dead on the **battlefield**.

So William had **won the day**. He marched with his men to London, where he was **crowned** King in Westminster Abbey on Christmas Day 1066.

But the **victory** at Hastings was only the beginning of William's conquest. For a long time the Saxon **people feared** and hated the Normans. Over the next four years, **revolts** broke out all over the country. But they were not organized, so William was able **to put them down** and **restore** the **peace**. He gave the Saxon noblemen's **estates** to Norman barons, and he **established** his **power** by building hundreds of **castles** and forts all over England. (The most famous of these is the Tower of London.) William **treated** the people fairly when they **obeyed** him. But he could also be very **cruel**. In the North, he **punished** the people's **rebellion brutally** – simply by **destroying** everything. His men **burned** the crops, **slaughtered** the cattle, **set fire to** the houses and farms.

By 1070 the brutal work was finished, and nearly all of England was **under** Norman **control**. The English **ruling class** was **wiped out**, and the country was ruled by a **powerful** French-speaking **aristocracy**.

Teacher: What does Hastings 1066 mean to you?
Pupil: William the Conqueror's telephone number, sir.

History

to retreat — sich zurückziehen
advantage ↔ disadvantage — Vorteil   Nachteil
to *shoot (s.o.) — (jdn. er)schießen, jdn. treffen
leader — Anführer(in), Führer(in)
  → to *lead (s.o.)   (jdn.) führen
dead ↔ alive — tot   lebendig, am Leben
to *lose s.th. — etwas verlieren
to *give (s.th.) up — (etwas) aufgeben
to *flee — fliehen
battlefield — Schlachtfeld

to *win the day — den Kampf gewinnen
to **crown** [kraʊn] s.o. (king/queen) — jdn. (zum König/zur Königin) krönen
  → crown   Krone

victory ['vɪktəri] ↔ defeat — Sieg   Niederlage
people — *hier:* Volk
to **fear** [fɪə] s.o./s.th. → fear — jnd./etwas fürchten   Furcht
revolt [rɪ'vəʊlt] — Aufstand, Aufruhr
to *put down a revolt — einen Aufstand niederschlagen
to **restore** [-'-] s.th. — etwas wiederherstellen
peace → peaceful — Frieden   friedlich
estate [ɪ'steɪt] — Landgut
to **establish** [ɪ'stæblɪʃ] s.th. — etwas aufbauen, etwas festigen
power — Macht
castle ['kɑːsl] — Burg
to **treat** s.o. (well/badly/...) — jdn. (gut/schlecht/...) behandeln
  → treatment   Behandlung
to **obey** [ə'beɪ] (s.o.) — (jdm.) gehorchen
  ↔ to disobey (s.o.)   (jdm.) nicht gehorchen
cruel [krʊəl] ↔ kind — grausam   gütig, freundlich
to **punish** ['pʌnɪʃ] s.o./s.th. — jdn./etwas bestrafen
  → punishment   Strafe
rebellion [rɪ'beljən] — Rebellion, Aufstand
  → to rebel [-'-] (against s.o./s.th.)   (gegen jdn./etwas) rebellieren
brutal ['bruːtl] — brutal, grausam
to **destroy** [dɪ'strɔɪ] s.th. — etwas zerstören
  → destruction   Zerstörung
to *burn s.th. — etwas verbrennen
to **slaughter** ['slɔːtə] an animal — ein Tier schlachten
to *set fire to s.th. — etwas in Brand setzen

to *be under (s.o.'s) control — unter (jds.) Kontrolle sein
ruling class — Oberschicht
to **wipe** [waɪp] s.th. out — etwas völlig vernichten
powerful — mächtig
aristocracy [ˌærɪ'stɒkrəsi] — Adel, Elite

History

The Gunpowder Plot

When James I came to the throne in 1603, England was officially a Protestant country. In those days, religion was the most important thing in many people's lives. At first, James was tolerant of the Catholics in England, but this made Parliament angry, so laws against Catholics were made stricter again. In frustration, a group of Catholic fanatics made a plan to blow up the king and the Houses of Parliament on November 5th, 1605. But the plot was discovered, and Guy Fawkes, one of the leaders, was arrested and thrown into prison. Later he was tortured, and then brought to trial. He was condemned to death and executed for high treason. Four of the plotters were killed when resisting arrest, another died in prison, and the rest – like Fawkes himself – were all tried and hanged.
(See 'Festivities and public holidays' p. 146 for details of 'Guy Fawkes Night' in England today.)

The Industrial Revolution

Up until the middle of the 18th century, a lot of work – such as spinning and weaving – was done at home. Then, great changes took place, and people's lives and methods of working were never the same again. Machines that were powered by water – and later driven by steam – were invented. These inventions meant that cloth and other goods could be produced much more quickly. Many workers were needed to run these big machines, so poor people moved from the country into the towns, where they could be near the new factories.

Life for the workers, who lived in overcrowded houses, was often grim and miserable. The factory owners found it cheaper to employ women and children. Before the Factory Acts of the 1840s became law, even little children of nine or younger worked 12 hours a day – or sometimes longer – in the factories or down in the coal mines. Accidents often happened, because there were no laws to make sure the machines were safe.

History

gunpowder → gun	Schießpulver Gewehr, Pistole
plot	Verschwörung
to *come to the throne [θrəʊn]	den Thron besteigen
Protestant ['---] (adj./noun)	protestantisch; Protestant(in)
in those days	damals
religion [rɪ'lɪdʒən] → religious	Religion religiös
tolerant ['tɒlərənt] (of s.o.)	tolerant (jdm. gegenüber)
→ to tolerate s.o./s.th.	jdn./etwas dulden
Catholic ['kæθlɪk] (adj./noun)	katholisch; Katholik(in)
law	Gesetz
fanatic [fə'nætɪk] → fanatical	Fanatiker(in) fanatisch
to *blow s.th./s.o. up	etwas/jdn. in die Luft sprengen
the Houses of Parliament	*Tagungsort des brit. Parlaments*
to arrest [ə'rest] s.o.	jdn. verhaften
to *throw s.o. into prison	jdn. ins Gefängnis werfen
to torture ['tɔːtʃə] s.o. → torture	jdn. foltern Folter
to *bring s.o. to trial ['traɪəl]	jdn. vor Gericht bringen
to condemn [kən'dem] s.o. to death	jdn. zum Tode verurteilen
to execute ['---] s.o.	jdn. hinrichten
→ execution [ˌ--'--]	Hinrichtung
high treason ['triːzn]	Hochverrat
plotter	Verschwörer(in)
to resist (s.th.)	Widerstand (gegen etwas) leisten
to try s.o. → trial	jdn. vor Gericht stellen Prozess
to hang s.o.	jdn. erhängen
to *spin (s.th.)	(etwas) spinnen
to *weave (s.th.)	(etwas) weben
change → to change	Veränderung sich verändern
to *take place	stattfinden
method ['meθəd]	Methode
machine [mə'ʃiːn]	Maschine, Gerät
to power s.th./to *drive s.th.	etwas antreiben
steam	Dampf
to invent s.th.	etwas erfinden
invention	Erfindung
cloth	Stoff, Tuch
goods ⚠ (plural only)	Waren, Güter
to produce s.th. → product ['--]	etwas herstellen Produkt
to *run a machine	eine Maschine bedienen
factory	Fabrik
overcrowded → crowd	überfüllt (Menschen-)Menge
grim	trostlos, grimmig
miserable	elend, unglücklich
owner → to own s.th.	Besitzer(in) etwas besitzen
to employ s.o.	jdn. beschäftigen, jdn. einstellen
coal mine	Kohlenbergwerk

35

History

The smoke from the factory chimneys made the towns dirty. The water in the rivers was also often badly polluted, and diseases spread quickly, so many people died young.

In time, the steam engine was also used to drive locomotives, and at last after a lot of argument in Parliament – George Stephenson was allowed to build a railway line between Stockton and Darlington in the North of England. This line, the first public railway line, was opened in 1825. The first train on it, pulled by Stephenson's engine, *Locomotion*, only travelled at 19 kilometres an hour! But a new age had begun, and twenty years later people were travelling in trains all over the country.
(See 'Geography' p. 10 for the rise of industries in the 18th century.)

2 Historic events in America

New beginnings – in a 'New World'

Virginia, the first British colony in America, was founded in 1607. Thirteen years later, the 'Pilgrims', who sailed over on the 'Mayflower', settled further north and established their own democratic community. Many of them were Puritan refugees who had left Britain in search of religious freedom. Countless settlers in the years that followed were immigrants escaping from religious persecution in their home countries. Others – like many of the Irish who emigrated in the 19th century – were driven from home by famine.

How the colonies won their independence

By the middle of the 18th century, there were 13 British colonies on the East coast. Many of the colonists were angry because they were not represented in the British Parliament in London. When the British government decided on new taxes for the colonists, the colonists resisted. The War of Independence began. Britain and America were at war until 1783. But the Declaration of Independence was signed before that: on July 4th 1776, representatives of the 13 States signed this historic document.

Opening up the West

After Independence, people began to move westward. More and more immigrants were arriving in the East, so it was natural to want to explore the unknown territory further inland. People were prepared to suffer hardship at first, in the hope of building a better life. In the 1830s and 1840s, thousands of people were on the move, and the frontier (wherever civilization came to an end and the wilderness began) was pushed further and further to the West.

History

smoke	Rauch
chimney	Schornstein, Kamin
to pollute s.th.	etwas verschutzen
→ pollution	Umweltverschmutzung
disease [dɪˈziːz]	Krankheit, Seuche
to *spread	sich verbreiten
steam engine [ˈendʒɪn]	Dampfmaschine
locomotive [--ˈ--] → locomotion	Lokomotive Fortbewegung
railway line	Eisenbahnlinie
engine *(of a train)*	Lokomotive
to travel	fahren, reisen
colony [ˈ---]	Kolonie
pilgrim	Pilger(in)
to settle	sich niederlassen, sich ansiedeln
community [kəˈmjuːnətɪ]	Gemeinschaft
refugee [ˌrefjʊˈdʒiː]	Flüchtling
in search [sɜːtʃ] of s.th.	auf der Suche nach etwas
freedom	Freiheit
settler → settlement	Siedler(in) Siedlung
immigrant [ˈɪmɪgrənt]	Einwanderer, Einwanderin
persecution [ˌpɜːsɪˈkjuːʃn]	Verfolgung
→ to persecute [ˈpɜːsɪkjuːt] s.o.	jdn. verfolgen
to emigrate	auswandern
famine [ˈfæmɪn]	Hungersnot
independence	Unabhängigkeit
colonist [ˈ---]	Siedler(in) (einer Kolonie)
to represent [ˌ--ˈ-] s.o.	jdn. vertreten
government	Regierung
tax	Steuer
to *be at war	Krieg (gegeneinander) führen
the Declaration of Independence	die Unabhängigkeitserklärung
representative [ˌreprɪˈzentətɪv]	Vertreter(in)
document [ˈ---]	Dokument, Urkunde
to open s.th. up	etwas erschließen
to explore s.th.	etwas erforschen
territory [ˈterɪtrɪ]	Territorium, Gebiet, Land
to suffer [ˈsʌfə] (s.th.) → suffering	(etwas er)leiden Leid
hardship	schwere Not
to *be on the move	in Bewegung sein, unterwegs sein
frontier	Grenze zwischen Zivilisation und Wildnis
civilization [ˌsɪvɪlaɪˈzeɪʃn]	Zivilisation, erschlossenes Gebiet
→ civilized	zivilisiert
wilderness [ˈwɪldənəs]	Wildnis
→ wild [waɪld]	wild

37

History

The **pioneers** travelled west in **wagon trains**. On their way along the **trail**, they often had to fight Indians, who were trying to **protect** their **hunting grounds** from the white invaders. Some of these **native** American **tribes** were **fierce** and **warlike**, others were more **peaceful**. Many **treaties** were **made** with the Indians – but were **broken** again as soon as the whites decided they needed the Indians' land. The Indians' greatest victory – at the Battle of the Little Bighorn in 1876 – was called a **massacre** by the whites. Fourteen years later, at Wounded Knee, American soldiers killed 300 Sioux men, women and children, although they wished to **surrender**. Either it was an act of **revenge**, or a terrible mistake.

Most of the Indians were **driven** from their **tribal lands** and **forced** to move to **reservations** – often thousands of miles from their home. Many Indians died on the way. For those who **survived** the journey, the new life was hard.

The **Native Americans** officially became US **citizens** in 1928. But they have not forgotten their history, their **customs**, their **heroes** and the **ancient traditions** of their **ancestors**.

Slavery **in the States**

The first black **slaves** were brought on ships from Africa in the early 17th century. Two hundred years later, the **cotton plantations** in the Southern states of America depended on slavery. But by the 1830s, slavery had disappeared in the Northern states, where people were firmly against it. The North and South could not **come to an agreement**, and in 1860 the Southern states left the **Union**. Abraham Lincoln was President at that time. In order to keep all the states of the Union together, he led the North in the Civil War against the **rebellious** South. The North won the war in 1865, and slavery in all the States was **abolished**. Lincoln was **assassinated** five days after the end of the war.

History 2

pioneer [ˌpaɪəˈnɪə]	Pionier(in)
wagon [ˈwægən] **train**	Zug von Planwagen
trail	Spur, Weg
to protect s.o./s.th. (from s.th.)	jdn./etwas (vor etwas) (be)schützen
hunting ground	Jagdgebiet
→ to hunt (s.o./s.th.)	(jdn./etwas) jagen
native [ˈneɪtɪv] *(adj./noun)*	einheimisch; Eingeborene(r)
tribe [traɪb]	Stamm
fierce [fɪəs]	wild, grimmig
warlike	kriegerisch
peaceful	friedlich
to *make/*break a treaty	einen Vertrag schließen/brechen
massacre [ˈmæsəkə]	Massaker
to surrender	sich ergeben, kapitulieren
→ surrender	Kapitulation
revenge [rɪˈvendʒ]	Rache
to *drive s.o. from a place	jdn. von einem Ort vertreiben
tribal [ˈtraɪbl] **land**	Stammesland
to force s.o. to *do s.th.	jdn. zwingen, etwas zu tun
reservation [ˌrezəˈveɪʃn]	Reservat
to survive (s.th.)	(etwas) überleben
Native American	amerikanische(r) Ureinwohner(in), Indianer(in)
citizen [ˈsɪtɪzn]	(Staats-)Bürger(in)
custom [ˈkʌstəm]	Sitte
hero → heroine	Held Heldin
ancient [ˈeɪnʃənt]	uralt
tradition [-ˈ--]	Tradition
ancestor	Vorfahre/Vorfahrin
slavery [ˈsleɪvəri]	Sklaverei
slave [sleɪv]	Sklave/Sklavin
cotton plantation [-ˈ--]	Baumwollplantage
to *come to an agreement	sich einig werden
→ to agree (to s.th.)	(einer Sache) zustimmen
Union [ˈjuːnjən]	Verband, Union (der Vereinigten Staaten)
rebellious [rɪˈbeljəs]	aufständisch, widerstrebend
to abolish [əˈbɒlɪʃ] **s.th.**	etwas abschaffen
→ abolition [ˌ--ˈ--]	Abschaffung
to assassinate [əˈsæsɪneɪt] **s.o.**	jdn. (aus politischen Gründen) ermorden, ein Attentat auf jdn. verüben
→ assassination	Attentat

39

History

3 The Commonwealth: some facts and figures

- The British Commonwealth of Nations came into being in 1926. It consists of 53 states, of many different races and cultures.
- All Commonwealth countries once belonged to the British Empire.
- 100 years ago the Empire was at its height. It was the biggest empire the world had ever known. Through it, Britain controlled a large part of the world's trade.
- During the 20th century, more and more of Britain's colonies wanted self-government and became independent of the 'mother country'. But by remaining members of the Commonwealth, they kept their link with Britain.
- Many English-sounding place names (Wellington in New Zealand, for example) in Commonwealth countries are reminders of their colonial past.
- The British monarch is Head of the Commonwealth, and also Head of State in some of the countries.
- In the 1950s, a lot of people from the Commonwealth came to work in Britain. Now, about 8% of Britain's population are non-whites and of Commonwealth origin.

English – a world language

In parts of the world where native speakers of English settled in large numbers – such as North America or Australia – English naturally became the main language. In parts of the Empire where the British lived as rulers but did not settle permanently – such as India – it became an official language.

Today, English is the mother tongue of more than 400 million people, most of them in North America. At least another 400 million people speak it as a second language in countries where it is the official language.

English is learnt by more people worldwide than any other language, and it can be used by about a third of the world's population.

Thanks to the influence of the United States in the world today – and to the use of the Internet – English has become more important than ever before.

History

to *come into being	entstehen
race	Rasse
culture ['kʌltʃə] → cultural	Kultur kulturell
once	(früher) einmal
empire ['empaɪə]	(Welt-)Reich
100 years ago	vor 100 Jahren
to *be at one's height	auf dem Höhepunkt sein
trade	Handel
self-government	Selbstverwaltung, Unabhängigkeit
independent	unabhängig
member	Mitglied
link	Verbindung, Beziehung
colonial [kə'ləʊnjəl]	kolonial
past	Vergangenheit
Head	Oberhaupt
Head of State	Staatsoberhaupt
non-white	Farbige(r)
origin ['ɒrɪdʒɪn] → original [-'---]	Herkunft ursprünglich

> Girl: *I wish we lived hundreds of years ago!*
> Teacher: *Why?*
> Girl: *Then there wouldn't be so much history to learn.*

world language	Weltsprache
native speaker	Muttersprachler(in)
ruler	Herrscher(in)
permanent ['pɜːmənənt]	dauerhaft, ständig
↔ temporary ['tempərərɪ]	vorübergehend, vorläufig
official language	Amtssprache
mother tongue [tʌŋ]	Muttersprache
= native language	
worldwide	weltweit
influence ['ɪnflʊəns]	Einfluss
→ to influence s.o./s.th.	jdn./etwas beeinflussen

Exercises

2

a) Put the right words in the right places. The letters in the coloured squares form a word that is especially important to German history.

Soon after Harold became **(5)** of England in 1066, William **(3)** of Normandy made plans to **(6)** for the English **(1)**, because he also had a **(7)** to it.

When William and his men **(4)** on the Sussex coast, Harold was still in the North of England, where he had to **(2)** the country against the Norwegians. Harold's army was able to **(9)** them at the **(10)** of Stamford Bridge. But after a 10-day march south to Hastings, the Saxon **(12)** were exhausted.

On the morning of October 14th, the Normans **(8)**. After a long, long day on the field, Harold was **(11)** when he was shot in the eye by an arrow. The Saxons had to give up. William and his men marched to London, and two months later, on Christmas Day 1066, William was **(13)** King of England in Westminster Abbey.

42

Exercises

b) Complete the facts, choosing the right words from the box.

> centuries ✔ coal mines colonists community
> employ factories freedom goods hunting
> Industrial machines monarch Parliament pioneers
> powerful queens ✔ refugees reservations rule
> suffer territory trains

1. For many _**centuries**_ English kings and _queens_ were very _____, and could do more or less as they liked. But since 1689, when the Bill of Rights was passed, no English _____ has been allowed to _____ without _____.

2. The new _____ that were invented at the time of the _____ Revolution meant that _____ could be produced more quickly. Lots of women and children worked long hours in the new _____ and even down in the dark _____, because they were cheaper to _____ than men.

3. Many of the _____ who first settled in America were Puritan _____ who had left England because they wanted religious _____ . Although they had to _____ terrible hardship at first, in the end they established their own democratic _____.

4. The _____, Americans who wanted to explore new _____ further inland in the 1830s and 1840s, travelled west in wagon _____. Often there was trouble with Indians, who were trying to protect their _____ grounds. In the end, most of the Indians were driven from their land and forced to live on _____.

43

Conflicts

1 Racism and discrimination

Our world is full of conflicts, especially between people of different races, nationalities and cultures. Unfortunately, we all have a natural tendency to feel suspicious of people whose customs or religion, skin colour, language or accent is different from our own. Hatred, aggression and violence towards foreigners or minority groups in the community are often caused by prejudice – that is, by stereotyped ideas about people or things we do not properly understand.

Wherever there is a mixture of races or a clash of cultures, there is racism and discrimination. History is full of examples.

- When slavery came to an end in the USA in 1865, racial discrimination still turned the blacks into second-class citizens. For many years, the African Americans were still oppressed; in public places like restaurants, parks and buses, they were not allowed to use the same areas as whites, and children had to go to different schools. In 1954, when segregation in schools was abolished, there were many whites who reacted against the Supreme Court's decision.

  But the struggle for equal rights went on. Martin Luther King, the greatest leader of the Civil Rights Movement, inspired African Americans to protest against racial discrimination without using force. He led peaceful demonstrations and protest marches; his aim was tolerance and understanding between black and white.

Conflicts

conflict ['kɒnflɪkt]	Konflikt
racism ['reɪsɪzm] → racist *(adj./noun)*	Rassismus rassistisch; Rassist(in)
discrimination [-,--'--]	Diskriminierung
race	Rasse
culture ['kʌltʃə]	Kultur
suspicious of s.o./s.th.	misstrauisch gegenüber jdm./etwas
→ suspicion	Verdacht, Misstrauen
custom ['kʌstəm] = tradition	Sitte
religion [rɪ'lɪdʒən] → religious	Religion, Glaube religiös
skin colour	Hautfarbe
accent ['æksent]	Akzent
hatred ['heɪtrɪd] → to hate s.o./s.th.	Hass jdn./etwas hassen
aggression [ə'greʃn]	Aggression, Aggressivität
→ aggressive	aggressiv
violence ['vaɪələns]	Gewalt, Gewalttätigkeit
→ violent	gewalttätig
foreigner ['fɒrənə] → foreign	Ausländer(in) fremd
minority [maɪ'nɒrɪtɪ] group	Minderheit
community [kə'mju:nətɪ]	Gemeinschaft, Gemeinde
prejudice ['predʒədɪs]	Vorurteil, Voreingenommenheit
→ prejudiced against s.o./s.th.	voreingenommen gegen jdn./etwas
stereotyped ['stɪərɪətaɪpt]	klischeehaft, stereotyp
clash	Konflikt, Zusammenstoß
→ to clash	zusammenstoßen, aneinder geraten
slavery → slave	Sklaverei Sklave, Sklavin
racial discrimination	Rassendiskriminierung
second-class citizen ['sɪtɪzn]	Bürger(in) zweiter Klasse
to oppress [ə'pres] s.o.	jdn. unterdrücken
→ oppression	Unterdrückung
segregation [,segrɪ'geɪʃn]	(Rassen-)Trennung
to abolish [ə'bɒlɪʃ] s.th.	etwas abschaffen
→ abolition [--,--']	Abschaffung
to react against s.th.	negativ auf etwas reagieren
→ reaction	Reaktion
struggle = battle	(langer) Kampf
equal rights	gleiche Rechte
Civil ['sɪvl] Rights Movement	Bürgerrechtsbewegung
to protest [prə'test] (against s.th.)	(gegen etwas) protestieren
force	Gewalt
→ to force s.o. to do s.th.	jdn. zwingen etwas zu tun
peaceful → peace	friedlich Frieden
demonstration [,demən'streɪʃn]	Demonstration
protest ['prəʊtest] march	Protestmarsch
tolerance ['tɒlərəns]	Toleranz, Duldsamkeit
↔ intolerance	Intoleranz
understanding	Verständnis

3 Conflicts

Opportunities for blacks soon improved, but many problems remained. Even today, although African Americans have full **equality** and are officially **integrated**, large numbers of them live in **ghettos**. Successful blacks, who have **adapted to** the lifestyle of the white community, often feel little **sympathy** for these poorer ones.

- When the British **settled** in Australia, the **Aborigines** (who had been **natives** of Australia for 60,000 years or more) were **treated** much the same as the Indians in North America. Their **way of life** was not **familiar** to the white **immigrants**, who considered them **inferior**, **drove** them **off** their land and put them into **reservations**. They did not get equal rights until 1967. Since then, over half the Aborigine population have moved to towns and cities. Now, at last, the Australian government has **recognized** the Aborigines' right to their own land. There are still many who have not given up their old traditions. But others feel **caught between** the **two cultures** and have no real **sense of identity**.

- In the 1960s and 70s, when **non-whites** from Commonwealth countries began to settle in Britain in growing numbers, many white people were against the idea of a **multi-cultural society**. Although the **Racial Equality Act** is now supposed to prevent unfair treatment and discrimination, people's **negative attitudes** can be hard to change.

  Intolerance towards **ethnic minorities** can take many forms. Sometimes people are **attacked** and **beaten up** in the streets; others are **threatened** or **damage is done** to their homes. Children are sometimes treated **unkindly**, **bullied** at school or **blamed** for things they have not done.

  Tension between different **ethnic groups** (between people of African **origin**, for example, and people from Asia) also causes problems, especially in big cities. People with the same **background** often live in the same areas, and sometimes form **gangs** that **make trouble** by attacking **rival** groups.

  On the other hand, there are many non-whites in Britain, especially in the big cities, who feel completely at home in the white community, and at the same time are **proud of** their own culture. They can enjoy **the best of both worlds**.

Conflicts

equality [ɪˈkwɒlɪtɪ] → equal	Gleichheit gleich
integrated	eingegliedert, integriert
ghetto	Ghetto
to adapt to s.th.	sich an etwas anpassen
sympathy [ˈsɪmpəθɪ]	Mitgefühl, Teilnahme
→ to sympathize (with s.o.)	(mit jdm.) mitfühlen
to settle	*hier:* sich niederlassen
the Aborigines [ˌæbəˈrɪdʒɪnɪz]	*die Ureinwohner Australiens*
native [ˈneɪtɪv]	Eingeborene(r), Ureinwohner(in)
to treat s.o. (well/badly/…)	jdn. (gut/schlecht/…) behandeln
→ treatment	Behandlung
way of life	Lebensstil, Lebensart, Lebensweise
familiar [fəˈmɪljə]	vertraut, bekannt
immigrant [ˈɪmɪgrənt]	Einwanderer, Einwanderin
inferior [ɪnˈfɪərɪə]	minderwertig
→ inferiority [-,--ˈ---]	Minderwertigkeit
to *drive s.o. off s.th.	jdn. von etwas vertreiben
reservation [ˌrezəˈveɪʃn]	Reservat
to recognize [ˈrekəgnaɪz] s.o./s.th.	jdn./etwas (an)erkennen
to *be caught between two cultures	zwischen zwei Kulturen stehen
sense of identity [aɪˈdentɪtɪ]	Identitätsbewusstsein
non-white	Farbige(r)
multi-cultural society	multikulturelle Gesellschaft
Racial Equality Act	Rassengleichheitsgesetz
negative attitude [ˈətɪtjuːd]	negative Haltung/Einstellung
ethnic minority [maɪˈnɒrɪtɪ]	ethnische Minderheit
to attack s.o. ↔ to defend s.o.	jdn. angreifen jdn. verteidigen
to *beat s.o. up	jdn. zusammenschlagen
to threaten [θretn] s.o. → threat	jdn. bedrohen Bedrohung
to *do damage [ˈdæmɪdʒ] to s.th.	etwas beschädigen
unkind ↔ kind	unfreundlich freundlich, nett
to bully [ˈbʊlɪ] s.o. → bully	jdn. tyrannisieren Rüpel
to blame [bleɪm] s.o. (for s.th.)	jdm. die Schuld (an etwas) geben
tension [ˈtenʃn] → tense	Spannung(en) (an)gespannt
ethnic group	ethnische Gruppe
origin [ˈɒrɪdʒɪn] → original [-ˈ---]	Herkunft ursprünglich
background	Hintergrund, *hier:* Herkunft, Verhältnisse
gang	Bande
to *make trouble	Schwierigkeiten machen, Unruhe stiften
rival [ˈraɪvl]	konkurrierend
→ rival	Rivale, Rivalin, Konkurrent(in)
to *be proud of s.o./s.th. → pride	auf jdn./etwas stolz sein Stolz
the best of both worlds	das Beste aus beiden Welten

Conflicts

- In other European countries there is also conflict between people of different origins. In Germany, foreigners have often been victims of prejudice and unfair treatment. There has been cruelty and hostility towards migrants and asylum seekers. Arson attacks on foreigners' homes and on buildings used as temporary homes for refugees have caused tragedy.

  Although most people agree that hatred of foreigners is wrong, there have been bitter quarrels in Europe over immigration laws. The influx of so many people coming from other countries and applying for political asylum has caused fear and resentment.

2 Terrorism – and the war on terror

Terrorism is the use of violence, usually with political or religious motives, by groups of people who feel they cannot achieve their aims in more peaceful ways. The brutal methods terrorists use include murder, kidnapping and bomb attacks. Sometimes planes are hijacked, and people taken as hostages. Suicide bombings can cause terrible explosions in which many people are injured or killed.

In the terrorist attacks on the USA on September 11 2001, when four planes were hijacked, two of which crashed into the twin towers of the World Trade Center in New York City, thousands of people died. The US government saw these attacks as acts of war. The Americans, deeply shocked, felt threatened as never before; for the first time in history, they had been attacked on their own soil. The 'war on terror' began – in an attempt to make America – and the world – a safer place.

Terror has become one of the greatest problems of our 21st century world. But many critics agree that the war on terror can never be won by military might. Relationship building between nations and cultures must take priority.

Conflicts 3

victim	Opfer
cruelty [ˈkrʊəltɪ] → cruel	Grausamkeit grausam
hostility [hɒˈstɪlətɪ]	Feindseligkeit
migrant [ˈmaɪgrənt]	Zuwanderer, Zuwanderin
asylum [əˈsaɪləm] **seeker**	Asylsuchende(r), Asylbewerber(in)
arson [ˈɑːsn] **attack**	Brandanschlag
refugee [ˌrefjʊˈdʒiː]	Flüchtling
tragedy [ˈtrædʒədɪ] → tragic	Tragödie tragisch
hatred [ˈheɪtrɪd] **of foreigners** [ˈfɒrɪnəz]	Fremdenhass, Ausländerfeindlichkeit
quarrel [ˈkwɒrəl]	Streit, Auseinandersetzung
→ to quarrel	(sich) streiten
immigration ↔ **emigration**	Einwanderung Auswanderung
influx [ˈɪnflʌks]	Zustrom
to apply for political asylum	um politisches Asyl bitten
fear [fɪə]	Angst, Furcht
→ to fear s.o./s.th.	sich vor jdm./etwas fürchten
resentment [rɪˈzentmənt]	Ärger, Groll
→ to resent s.th.	etwas übel nehmen
terrorism [ˈ----]	Terrorismus
war on terror	Kampf gegen den Terror
motive [ˈməʊtɪv]	Motiv, Beweggrund
to achieve an aim	ein Ziel erreichen
brutal [ˈbruːtl]	brutal, bestialisch
terrorist *(noun/adj.)*	Terrorist(in); terroristisch, Terror-
murder → to murder s.o.	Mord jdn. ermorden
→ murderer	Mörder(in)
to kidnap s.o. → kidnapping	jdn. entführen Entführung
bomb [bɒm] **attack**	Bombenanschlag
to hijack [ˈhaɪdʒæk] **(a plane)**	(ein Flugzeug) entführen
hostage [ˈhɒstɪdʒ]	Geisel
suicide bombing [ˈsuːɪsaɪd ˌbɒmɪŋ]	Selbstmordattentat
explosion → to explode	Explosion explodieren
to injure [ˈɪndʒə] **s.o.** → injury	jdn. verletzen Verletzung
to kill s.o.	jdn. töten
terrorist attack	Terroranschlag
to crash into s.th.	auf etwas stürzen/aufprallen
an act of war	eine kriegerische Handlung
shocked → shocking	schockiert, entsetzt schockierend
on one's own soil	auf eigenem Boden
attempt → to attempt s.th.	Versuch etwas versuchen
to *make the world a safer place	die Welt sicherer machen
critic → to criticize s.o./s.th.	Kritiker(in) jdn./etwas kritisieren
military [ˈmɪlɪtrɪ] **might**	militärische Stärke
relationship building	der Aufbau von Beziehungen
to *take priority [praɪˈɒrətɪ]	Vorrang haben

Conflicts

3 Crime

Police report rise in violent offences such as murder by hitting and kicking

Cases of armed robbery in London down this year by 25%

Britain puts 2,500 more police officers on the beat

Three boys arrested for plotting to blow up their school

Britain needs more high security jails

Half of all pupils say they have broken the law

In a survey of 11- to 16-year-olds, 49% said they had committed a crime at least once. In fact, almost a quarter of the crimes recorded in Britain are committed by children under 17. The most common offences are theft and handling stolen goods, and burglary. Other crimes include vandalism, carrying a knife or other weapon, and mugging. In extreme cases, children have been found guilty of kidnapping other children, and sometimes even of murder. In 'problem areas' innocent people are often afraid to leave their homes, even in daylight. Many feel that punishments for young offenders should be more severe. Courts can put them under close supervision. In some cases, uncontrollable criminals under 18 can even be sent to prison. Most go to young offender institutions. These offer counselling and vocational training.

76-year-old woman fined for shoplifting

Student, 21, on trial for rape

> After a series of crimes in the Birmingham area, Inspector Smith told newspaper reporters that he is now looking for a man with one eye. If he doesn't find him, he's going to use both eyes.

Conflicts

crime	Verbrechen, Straftat
police △ (+ *plural verb*)	Polizei
to report s.th.	etwas berichten/melden
violent ['vaɪələnt] → violence	gewalttätig Gewalt(tätigkeit)
offence	Straftat, Delikt
to *hit (s.o.)	(jnd.) schlagen
to kick (s.o.)	(jdn.) treten
case	Fall
armed robbery → to rob s.o.	bewaffneter Raub jdn. berauben
police officer	Polizeibeamter, -beamtin
on the beat	auf Streife
to arrest [-'-] s.o. (for s.th.)	jdn. (wegen etwas) verhaften
to plot s.th.	etwas im Geheimen planen
→ plot	Verschwörung
to *blow s.th. up	etwas in die Luft sprengen
high security jail	Hochsicherheitsgefängnis
→ to *go to jail/prison	ins Gefängnis kommen
to fine s.o.	jdn. zu einer Geldstrafe verurteilen
→ fine	Geldstrafe
shoplifting ['-,--]	Ladendiebstahl
on trial ['traɪəl] (for s.th.) → trial	angeklagt (wegen etw.) Prozess
rape	Vergewaltigung
→ to rape s.o. → rapist	jdn. vergewaltigen Vergewaltiger
to *break the law	gegen das Gesetz verstoßen
to commit a crime	ein Verbrechen begehen
theft → thief △ (*pl.* thieves)	Diebstahl Dieb(in)
handling stolen goods	Hehlerei
→ to *steal s.th.	etwas stehlen
burglary → burglar	Einbruch Einbrecher(in)
→ to burgle a house/to *break into a house	in ein Haus einbrechen
vandalism ['---]	Vandalismus, Zerstörungswut
→ vandal → to vandalize s.th.	Rowdy etwas mutwillig zerstören
weapon ['wepn]	Waffe
mugging → to mug s.o.	Straßenraub jdn. überfallen
→ mugger	Straßenräuber(in)
guilty ['gɪltɪ] (of a crime)	(eines Verbrechens) schuldig
innocent ['---]	unschuldig
punishment → to punish s.o.	Strafe jdn. bestrafen
offender	(Straf-)Täter(in), Straffällige(r)
severe [sɪ'vɪə]	hart, streng
court [kɔːt]	Gericht
to *put s.o. under close supervision [ˌsuːpə'vɪʒn]	jdn. unter strenge Überwachung stellen
criminal ['krɪmɪnl] → crime	Verbrecher(in) Verbrechen
prison → prisoner	Gefängnis Gefangene(r)
young offender institution	Jugendstrafanstalt
counselling	psychologische Betreuung, Therapie
vocational training	Berufsausbildung

51

3 Exercises

a) **Which words go together? To find the right expressions, choose from the words on the right. Then find the correct German translation from the list below.**

1. ethnic *minority* — *ethnische Minderheit*
2. equal _____ _____
3. suicide _____ _____
4. asylum _____ _____
5. terrorist _____ _____
6. skin _____ _____
7. multi-cultural _____ _____
8. immigration _____ _____
9. police _____ _____
10. armed _____ _____

colour
attack
officer
society
minority ✔
law
bombing
rights
robbery
seeker

*Asylsuchender   bewaffneter Raub   Einwanderungsgesetz
ethnische Minderheit ✔   gleiche Rechte   Hautfarbe
multikulturelle Gesellschaft   Polizeibeamter   Selbstmordattentat
Terroranschlag*

b) **Choose the best word to complete each sentence.**

1. Feelings of hatred and aggression towards foreigners are often caused by ….
   ❏ violence   ❏ prejudice   ❏ segregation

2. Martin Luther King wanted blacks to fight for their rights without using ….
   ❏ force   ❏ tolerance   ❏ demonstrations

3. The Aborigines are the … people of Australia.
   ❏ immigrant   ❏ native   ❏ inferior

4. A lot of crimes in Britain are … by children under 17.
   ❏ arrested   ❏ reported   ❏ committed

5. Another word for stealing is ….
   ❏ theft   ❏ offence   ❏ mugging

Exercises 3

c) **Complete the table with suitable words.**

English word	German translation	Word from the same family
murder	*Mord*	murderer
crime	Verbrechen	criminal
theft	*Diebstahl*	thief
cruel	Grausam	
to hate s.o./s.th.		
	Bedrohung	

d) **Can you find the hidden words? They all have something to do with crime and the law.**

1. A knife is a kind of **weapon**.

   anpewo
   weapon

2. If you are innocent of a crime, you are not _____.

3. Breaking into a building in order to steal something is called _____.

   o n i s l o x e p

4. Someone under 18 who has broken the law is called a young _____.

   l y t u g i

   n e i f

5. Another word for prison is _____.

   g o n f i s h l i p t

6. Taking something from a store secretly without paying for it is known as _____.

   a n p e w o ✓

   l i j a

7. If you blow something up, you cause an _____.

   g r a y b r u l

   d a n s l i m v a

8. The punishment for a less severe offence is often just a _____.

   f r e d f o n e

9. Offences such as breaking windows or throwing park benches into a pond are called _____.

The media

Every day an enormous stream of information is **communicated** to the **public** by 'the media' – that is, by **newspapers** and **magazines**, **television** and **radio** – and by the Internet. Most people's ideas and attitudes are **influenced** greatly by the media – whether they realize it or not!

1 The British press

Nearly everyone in Britain reads newspapers. People buy their papers from a **newsagent** – or at a **newsstand**. Some households have more than one **daily paper delivered** – and two or three different **Sunday papers**. Most papers are **national papers**, but there are also **local papers** with local **news**. '**Serious' papers** include *The Times, The Daily Telegraph, The Guardian* and *The Independent*. **Popular papers**, which are sometimes called **tabloids** because of their smaller size, have shorter, more **sensational articles**, more **photos** and larger **headlines**. They tend to concentrate more than the 'serious' papers on **topics** such as crime and **scandal**. The **best-sellers** among them are *The Daily Mail* and *The Daily Express, The Mirror, The Sun* – and *The News of the World*, which appears on Sundays. Recently, some of the 'serious' papers have also been **available** in tabloid form, which can make them more **attractive** to people who want a paper to read on the way to and from work. All the big papers are, of course, keen to **attract** new **readers** and to sell as many **copies** as they possibly can!

As well as the usual newspaper **reports, interviews** and articles written by **journalists**, most papers **print letters to the editor**, **crossword puzzles**, **reviews** and so on – and, of course, **advertisements**. They often also **publish** special **supplements** and **colour magazines**.

The British have a huge number of different **weekly** and **monthly** magazines, which cover every interest – from fashion to fishing.

The media 4

the media ['miːdɪə] ⚠ *(plural)* → medium	die Medien Medium
to communicate [-'---] s.th. → communication [-,--'--]	etwas übermitteln/vermitteln Kommunikation
the public → public	die Öffentlichkeit öffentlich
newspaper/paper	Zeitung
magazine [ˌmæɡəˈziːn]	Zeitschrift, Magazin
television	Fernsehen
radio	Radio, Rundfunk
to influence s.o./s.th. → influence	jdn./etwas beeinflussen Einfluss
the press	die Presse
newsagent	Zeitungshändler(in)
newsstand	Zeitungsstand, -kiosk
daily ['deɪlɪ] (paper)	Tageszeitung
to deliver s.th.	etwas liefern/zustellen
Sunday paper	Sonntagszeitung
national paper	überregionale Zeitung
local ['ləʊkl] paper	Lokalzeitung
news ⚠ *(+ singular verb)*	Nachrichten
serious paper	seriöse Zeitung
popular paper	Massenblatt, Boulevardzeitung
tabloid ['tæblɔɪd]	(kleinformatige) Boulevardzeitung
sensational [senˈseɪʃənl]	sensationell
article ['ɑːtɪkl]	Artikel
photo/photograph	Foto, Aufnahme
headline	Schlagzeile
topic → topical	Thema aktuell
scandal ['skændəl]	*hier:* Skandalgeschichten
best-seller	Bestseller
available	erhältlich
attractive	attraktiv
to attract s.o.	jdn. anziehen
reader	Leser(in)
copy	*hier:* Exemplar
report → reporter	Bericht Reporter(in)
interview ['ɪntəvjuː]	Interview
journalist ['dʒɜːnəlɪst] → journalism	Journalist(in) Journalismus
to print s.th.	etwas drucken
letter to the editor → editor	Leserbrief Herausgeber(in)
crossword puzzle ['pʌzl]	Kreuzworträtsel
review [rɪˈvjuː]	Kritik, Besprechung (eines Films usw.)
advertisement [ədˈvɜːtɪsmənt] = advert ['ædvɜːt], ad	Anzeige, Werbung
to publish s.th. → publisher	etwas veröffentlichen Verlag
supplement ['sʌplɪmənt]	*hier:* Beilage
colour magazine	Farbbeilage, Magazin
weekly (magazine)	Wochen-(Zeitschrift)
monthly (magazine)	Monats-(Zeitschrift)

4 The media

2 Television

Some British **viewers'** opinions:

"Well, I **watch TV** sometimes – like everyone else. But I usually try to plan my viewing, and watch the **programmes** I've marked in the **TV guide**. If there's nothing good **on**, I **switch off**. I never **sit in front of the set** all evening. The programmes I like best are old **films**, **TV plays** and **serials** – the more **episodes** the better! Sometimes there's a good **thriller** on a Sunday evening."

"There's a lot of talk about the bad influence of TV – but television isn't just **entertainment**. It can be very **educational**. I watch **current affairs** programmes, like 'Panorama'. And I enjoy **documentaries** and nature programmes. I find the news is **presented** best on **ITV**. But the **BBC** also has very good **newsreaders** and **presenters**."

"We've got a **satellite dish** – we haven't got **digital TV** yet, but we're in no hurry to have that really. There's so much **choice** already! All in all, my parents mostly watch the two main **channels**: BBC1 and ITV1. My brother and I like MTV – but we **zap** a lot between channels if we can't decide what to watch. We all like **comedies**, **cartoons** and **soaps** – even my Dad **turns up the volume** when they're on! We also like **game shows** and some of the **chat shows**. And my Mum likes **variety shows**. She also loves watching **repeats** of her old favourites. Nobody watches **breakfast TV** in our house – no time!"

"I'm not normally a **TV addict**, but I do love watching sport, especially the **live outside broadcasts** from Wimbledon every summer. I'm **glued to the set** during Wimbledon fortnight. All those exciting matches! And the **commentators** are usually very good indeed. Now, if there's one thing I don't enjoy when I'm watching TV, it's the **commercials**. I often **turn the sound off** when they come on – or I **switch over** to a different channel. That's one of the things I like about the programmes on BBC – no **advertising**."

> – *Television will never take the place of newspapers.*
> – *Why not?*
> – *Well, have you ever tried killing a fly with a TV set?*

The media

viewer	(Fernseh-)Zuschauer(in)
to watch TV	fernsehen
programme ['prəʊgræm]	Sendung
TV guide	Fernsehzeitschrift
to *be on	(im Fernsehen) laufen
to switch off ↔ to switch on	ausschalten einschalten
to *sit in front of the (TV) set	vor dem Fernseher sitzen
film *(BE)* = movie *(AE)*	(Spiel-)Film
TV play	Fernsehspiel
serial ['sɪərɪəl]	Fernsehserie
episode ['epɪsəʊd]	*hier:* Folge, Fortsetzung
thriller	Thriller, Krimi
entertainment [ˌ--'--]	Unterhaltung
→ to entertain s.o.	jdn. unterhalten
educational	*hier:* lehrreich, pädagogisch wertvoll
current affairs	Aktuelles, (politische) Tagesthemen
documentary [ˌdɒkjʊ'mentrɪ]	Dokumentarfilm
to present [-'-] s.th.	*hier:* etwas präsentieren
ITV (= Independent Television)	
the BBC (= British Broadcasting Corporation)	*britische Fernsehanstalten*
newsreader	Nachrichtensprecher(in)
presenter	Moderator(in)
satellite ['sætəlaɪt] dish	Satellitenschüssel
digital ['dɪdʒɪtl] TV	Digitalfernsehen
choice → to *choose s.th.	Auswahl etwas (aus)wählen
(TV) channel	Kanal, Sender, Programm
to zap (between channels)	ständig umschalten
comedy	Komödie
cartoon	Zeichentrickfilm
soap (opera)	Seifenoper, rührselige Familienserie
to turn up the volume	die Lautstärke aufdrehen
game show	Fernsehquiz, Quizshow
chat show	Talkshow
variety [və'raɪətɪ] show	Fernsehshow
repeat → to repeat s.th.	Wiederholung etwas wiederholen
breakfast TV	Frühstücksfernsehen
to *be a TV addict ['ædɪkt]	‚fernsehsüchtig' sein
live [laɪv]	Direkt-, Live-
outside broadcast ['brɔːdkɑːst]	nicht im Studio produzierte Sendung
→ to *broadcast s.th. (live)	etwas (live) senden/übertragen
to *be glued [gluːd] to the set	am Fernseher kleben
commentator	Kommentator(in), Fernsehreporter(in)
(TV) commercial [kə'mɜːʃl]	Werbespot
to turn the sound off	den Ton abschalten
to switch over (to ...)	umschalten (zu ...)
advertising ['ædvətaɪzɪŋ]	Werbung

The media

3 Radio

The first **radio stations** began their **transmissions** in the 1920s. In Britain, the BBC at first had a national **monopoly** of the medium. **Commercial radio** at last became legal in 1972, and by the 1990s almost 100 **local radio** stations had **gone on the air**.

Millions of people regularly **listen** to music **on the radio**, and there are still many who enjoy listening to **radio plays**.

4 Cinema

The world's first **movie theater** was built in Pittsburgh, USA, in 1905. In those days there were only **silent films**. During and after the First World War, America became dominant in the **film industry**; Hollywood, with its world-famous **studios**, was its capital. To **produce** a film in the classic Hollywood style, **actors** and **actresses**, **cameramen**, **producers**, writers and **technicians** all work together, led by a film **director**.

When television became more and more popular in the 1950s and 1960s, many cinemas had to close. To attract bigger **audiences**, **filmmakers** began to concentrate more on **science fiction** and **horror films**, with fascinating **trick photography** and other exciting **special effects**. Big **box-office hits** were often films containing very violent, ugly **scenes**. By the 1990s, many people in the USA and in Britain had become worried about the harm done to society by violence on the **screen**. **Film stars** were still often **idolized**. But they were not always the **role models** they had been in the 'golden years' of Hollywood.

At the beginning of the 21st century, the interest in films **based on** stories that are **set** in the world of **fantasy** – such as the *Harry Potter* books and *The Lord of the Rings* – was enormous. New **advances** in **computer technology** had made it possible to produce films of this kind.

Thanks to the invention of **video** and **DVD** recorders, of course, movie fans can also enjoy their favourite cinema hits as often as they like – at home.

The media — 4

radio station — Rundfunkstation, Radiosender
transmission — Übertragung, Sendung
→ to transmit s.th. — etwas senden
monopoly [mə'nɒpəlɪ] — Monopol
commercial [kə'mɜːʃl] **radio** — Privatsender
local ['ləʊkl] **radio** — Lokalradio, Lokalsender
to *go on the air — gesendet werden, (im Radio) zu hören sein

to listen to (s.th. on) the radio — (etwas im) Radio hören
→ listener — Hörer(in)
radio play — Hörspiel

cinema ['sɪnəmə] *(BE)* — Kino *(= Filmkunst und Filmtheater)*
movie theater *(AE)* — Kino *(= Filmtheater)*
→ movie *(AE)* — Film
silent film — Stummfilm
film industry — Filmindustrie
studio — Studio
to produce a film — einen Film produzieren
actor, actress — Schauspieler, Schauspielerin
cameraman → camerawoman — Kameramann   Kamerafrau
producer — Produzent(in)
technician [tek'nɪʃn] — Techniker(in)
director — Regisseur(in)
→ to direct a film — bei einem Film Regie führen

audience ['ɔːdɪəns] — Publikum, Zuschauer
filmmaker — Filmhersteller(in), Filmemacher(in)
science fiction — Sciencefiction
horror film → horrible — Horrorfilm   schrecklich
trick photography [fə'tɒgrəfɪ] — Trickfotografie, Trickaufnahmen
special effects — Spezialeffekte
box-office hit — Kassenschlager
scene [siːn] — Szene
screen — Leinwand, Bildschirm
film star — Filmstar
→ to star in a film — in einem Film eine Hauptrolle spielen

to idolize ['aɪdəlaɪz] s.o. — jdn. vergöttern
→ idol ['aɪdl] — Idol
role model — Vorbild

to *be based on s.th. — auf etwas basieren
to *be set in a place — an einem Ort spielen
fantasy ['---] — Phantasie, Fantasy
advance [əd'vɑːns] — Fortschritt
computer technology [tek'nɒlədʒɪ] — Computertechnik

video — Video
DVD [ˌdiːviːˈdiː] — DVD

59

The media

5 The Internet

Like the first computers, the Internet was developed in the USA. The idea, which was born in the 1960s, was to build up a **network** that could **connect** computer systems together. The first American computer network was used as a **link** between US universities. It was a long time before 'ordinary' owners of **PCs** were able to use the **World Wide Web**.

By the early 1990s, there were about a hundred **websites** that could be **visited on the net**. As more and more **personal computers** came into use, more and more people were able to **log into** the World Wide Web. **Via** the normal telephone network, people now **had access to** huge amounts of information, which they could **download** and **print out** for their own use.

In the meantime, access to the Internet has become **interactive**: millions of **e-mails** are exchanged every day. With the **instant messenger services** which are offered by **online providers**, it is possible for Internet users to type **messages** to each other. Thanks to the latest **web cameras**, people can even see and talk to each other when they **are online**. Many people have a **home page** of their own on the net, which they **update** regularly. There are **chat rooms** at many sites and users can make useful **contributions** to topical discussions – or just chat with one another – online. To **save charges**, however, many people prefer to write longer contributions or e-mails **offline** before sending them. For those without a computer of their own there are Internet cafés where a computer with an online **connection** can be **hired**.

If you have a credit card, you can book an airline flight, organize your next holiday or buy almost anything online without leaving your desk.

Some people are so fascinated by all these online possibilities that they spend several hours a day **surfing the net**. Nowadays it is indeed difficult to imagine a world without the Internet.

The media

network
to connect s.th. (to s.th. else)
→ to connect with s.th.

link
→ to link s.th. to s.th. else
PC [ˌpiːˈsiː] (= personal computer)
the World Wide Web

website
to visit a (web)site on the net
→ the net   → ⚠ on the net
personal computer
to log into the (World Wide) Web
→ to log into a website
via [ˈvaɪə]
to *have access [ˈækses] **to s.th.**
to download [ˌdaʊnˈləʊd] **s.th.**
to print s.th. out
→ a print-out

interactive [ˌɪntərˈæktɪv]
e-mail
instant messenger service
→ instant [ˈ--]
→ messenger [ˈmesɪndʒə]
online provider [ˌɒnlaɪn prəˈvaɪdə]
message [ˈmesɪdʒ]
web camera
to *be online [ˌ-ˈ-]
→ to *go online ↔ to go offline
home page
to update [-ˈ-] **s.th.**
chat room
→ to chat
→ chat
contribution [ˌkɒntrɪˈbjuːʃn]
to save charges
offline
connection
to hire s.th.

to surf [sɜːf] **the net**

Netz(werk)
etwas (mit etwas anderem) verbinden
  eine Verbindung mit etwas herstellen
Verbindung, Glied (in einer Kette)
  etwas mit etwas anderem verbinden
PC (= „Personalcomputer")
das Internet, das „weltweite Netz"

Webseite
eine Seite im Internet aufrufen
  das Internet   im Internet
PC
sich ins Internet einloggen
  sich in eine Webseite einloggen
über, mit Hilfe von
Zugang zu etwas haben
etwas herunterladen
etwas ausdrucken
  ein Ausdruck

interaktiv
E-Mail
Dienst für den Online-Chat
  sofortige(r/s)
  Bote, Botin
Anbieter von Online-Diensten
Nachricht, Botschaft
Webkamera
(im Netz) eingeloggt sein
  sich einloggen   sich ausloggen
Homepage, „Begrüßungsseite"
etwas auf den neusten Stand bringen
Chatraum
  sich unterhalten, plaudern
  Unterhaltung, Schwätzchen
Beitrag
Gebühren sparen
nicht am Netz angeschlossen
Verbindung
etwas mieten

im Internet surfen

61

Exercises

4

a) Write the English equivalents of these German words in the grid below. To help you find the right place, one letter of each word is given.

> Bildschirm   Kanal (Programm)   Kritik (eines Films)
> Moderator   pädagogisch wertvoll   Publikum   Regisseur
> Schlagzeile   Sendung   Unterhaltung   veröffentlichen
> Werbespot   Zeitungshändler

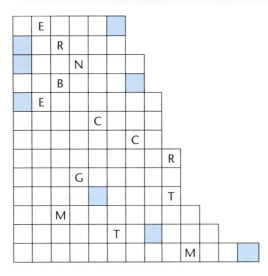

If you put the letters in the blue squares into the right order, you'll find the expression for something that a lot of people like watching on TV:

_____ _____ (2 words)

b) Find the pairs of words that go together. Then translate the expressions into German.

> current✔   popular   soap   movie   opera   theater   hit
> role   satellite   crossword   paper   dish   model
> box-office   affairs✔   puzzle

<u>current affairs: Aktuelles, (politische) Tagesthemen</u>

_____

62

Exercises 4

_____
_____
_____
_____
_____
_____

c) Rick is just starting up his PC when his brother Ken comes into his room. Complete their conversation. To help you, the first letter of each word you need is given.

Ken: Are you using the computer, Rick?

Rick: I'm just going *o*_____. I want to see if I have any new

*e*_____. Why?

Ken: I want to *l*_____ into a special *w*_____ to

help me with my geography homework: Loch Ness and the

Highlands. Our teacher wants us to *d*_____ a map and

*p*_____ it out.

Rick: Well, let's do that first. I'll start up my *o*_____

*p*_____. Have you got the address?

Ken: Yes, it's multimap.com. Can you let me type it in?

Rick: Do you know how to *c*_____ with the *n*_____?

Ken: Of course I do! We *v*_____ a lot of websites at school.

Rick: Do you *s*_____ the net at school all the time, then?

Ken: Of course not. But our teachers say we should have *a*_____

to the net at home, too. Ah! Here's the page I need. But it's busy.

Rick: Never mind. Try again later before I go *o*_____.

Ken: OK, but don't spend too long at any of those *c*_____

*r*_____! I've got to start doing my homework soon.

63

Politics

1 Parliament and the monarchy in Britain

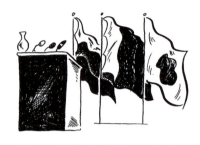

Britain is not a republic like Germany or the USA. It is a constitutional monarchy. This means that the political power of the King or Queen is limited. He or she has no official right to support or disagree with any particular policy. All political decisions are made by Parliament and the Government.

The British Parliament consists of the House of Commons and the House of Lords. They both meet in the Houses of Parliament in London.

Some of the members of the House of Lords are bishops or judges; some have inherited their seat. Others (now a larger number than in the past) are made life peers by the monarch. The House of Lords cannot make laws itself; it cannot reject laws that have been passed by the House of Commons. But before a bill can become an Act of Parliament, it must be accepted by the Lords, who can also make their own suggestions.

The House of Commons makes laws, and decides how to spend the taxpayers' money. It is made up of two 'sides': the Members of Parliament belonging to the party in power, and those belonging to the Opposition.

General elections

There are over 650 constituencies in Britain. In a general election, the voters elect one candidate in each of these constituencies. This is decided by majority vote: the person that most people in a constituency have voted for becomes a Member of Parliament. The party with the most MPs has the right to form a government, and the party leader becomes Prime Minister. He or she chooses the ministers to be in charge of different government departments. The party or parties that have lost the election now form the Opposition.

Politics

politics ['pɒlɪtɪks] → political	Politik politisch
Parliament ['pɑːləmənt]	(das) Parlament
monarchy ['mɒnəkɪ]	Monarchie
republic [rɪ'pʌblɪk]	Republik
constitutional [ˌkɒnstɪ'tjuːʃənl]	verfassungsmäßig, konstitutionell
power → in power	Macht an der Macht
limited → limit	begrenzt Grenze
official	offiziell, amtlich
right	Recht
to support s.o./s.th.	jdn./etwas unterstützen
→ supporter	Anhänger(in), Befürworter(in)
to disagree (with s.th.)	nicht einverstanden sein (mit etwas)
policy	(eine bestimmte) Politik, „Linie"
decision [dɪ'sɪʒn] → to decide s.th.	Entscheidung etwas entscheiden
government ['gʌvənmənt]	Regierung
the House of Commons	das Unterhaus
the House of Lords	das Oberhaus
member	Mitglied
bishop ['bɪʃəp]	Bischof/Bischöfin
judge [dʒʌdʒ]	Richter(in)
to inherit [ɪn'herɪt] s.th.	etwas erben
seat	Sitz
life peer [pɪə]	Mitglied des Oberhauses auf Lebenszeit
monarch ['mɒnək]	Monarch(in)
to *make a law	ein Gesetz entwerfen
to reject [rɪ'dʒekt] a law	ein Gesetz verwerfen
to pass a law	ein Gesetz verabschieden
bill	Gesetzesvorlage
Act of Parliament	vom Parlament verabschiedetes Gesetz
to accept s.th.	etwas annehmen/akzeptieren
taxpayer	Steuerzahler(in)
Member of Parliament (MP)	Parlamentsabgeordnete(r)
(political) party	Partei
the Opposition [ˌɒpə'zɪʃn]	die Opposition
general election [ɪ'lekʃn]	Parlamentswahlen
constituency [kən'stɪtjuənsɪ]	Wahlkreis
voter → vote	Wähler(in) Stimme
to elect [ɪ'lekt] s.o.	jdn. wählen
candidate ['kændɪdət]	Kandidat(in)
majority [mə'dʒɒrɪtɪ] vote	Mehrheitswahl
to vote for/against s.o.	für/gegen jdn. stimmen
to form a government	eine Regierung bilden
leader	*hier:* Vorsitzende(r)
prime minister [ˌpraɪm 'mɪnɪstə]	Premierminister(in)
minister	Minister(in)
to *be in charge of s.th.	verantwortlich für etwas sein
government department	Ministerium

Politics

Devolution

Although Northern Ireland, Scotland and Wales belong to the UK, they each have their own **regional assembly**, which gives them the power to make some of their own laws.

Political parties

For many years, the two leading parties in Britain have been the **Conservative Party** and the **Labour Party**. Because of the **voting system**, smaller parties, such as the **Liberal Democrats**, have never **come to power**. They would naturally welcome a change to **proportional representation**, the system used in Germany, as it might give them the chance to form part of a **coalition**. But the **two-party system** is one of Britain's firmest **traditions**.

Does Britain still need the monarchy? – Two opinions

I am a taxpayer. And I don't see why the **state** should use my **taxes** in order to pay the millions of pounds a year that are needed to **keep** the monarchy **going**.

In a **democracy**, all **representatives** of the **people** should be elected. Monarchs, **dukes**, **princes** and **princesses** have their place in history books – or in **fairy tales** – but not in a modern **society**.

How can the **public** feel any respect for the **Royal Family**, anyway? Every day the papers are full of the latest **scandal** about the House of Windsor. In my opinion, the days of the monarchy are numbered. I certainly hope so.

Y. Keeper-King, Oxford

The monarchy is the one political **institution** that everyone can **identify with**. All true **patriots** want to keep the monarchy. The Royal Family have many **duties**, and they **serve** our nation well.

Politicians are often **corrupt**, but the Royal Family are above **party politics**. They stand for all that is best in this country.

Officially, we are **ruled** by our monarch. If we **abolished** the monarchy, who would represent the country as its **Head of State**? Who would do the Royal Family's work for **charities** and other important organizations? Now we are '**subjects**'; then we would be '**citizens**'. And all our colourful **ceremonies** – like the state opening of Parliament – would disappear for ever. How sad!

Roy L. Fan, Manchester

Politics

devolution [ˌdiːvəˈluːʃn]	Dezentralisierung
regional assembly	Landesversammlung
the Conservative (Tory) Party	
the Labour [ˈleɪbə] Party	*politische Parteien in GB*
the Liberal [ˈlɪbərəl] Democrats	
voting system	Wahlsystem
to *come to power	an die Macht kommen
proportional representation	Verhältniswahl
coalition [ˌkəʊəˈlɪʃn]	Koalition
two-party system	Zweiparteiensystem
tradition [trəˈdɪʃn] → traditional	Tradition traditionell
state	Staat
tax	Steuer
to *keep s.th. going	etwas aufrecht erhalten
democracy [dɪˈmɒkrəsɪ]	Demokratie
→ democratic [--ˈ--]	demokratisch
representative → to represent s.o.	Vertreter(in) jdn. vertreten
the people ⚠ *(singular)*	das Volk
duke [djuːk] → duchess [ˈdʌtʃɪs]	Herzog Herzogin
prince, princess	Prinz, Prinzessin
fairy [ˈfeərɪ] tale → fairy	Märchen Fee
society [səˈsaɪətɪ] → social [ˈsəʊʃl]	Gesellschaft gesellschaftlich
the public → public	die Öffentlichkeit öffentlich
the Royal Family	die königliche Familie
scandal [ˈskændl]	*hier:* Skandalgeschichten
institution [ˌɪnstɪˈtjuːʃn]	Einrichtung, Institution
to identify [aɪˈdentɪfaɪ] with s.o./s.th.	sich mit jdm./etwas identifizieren
patriot [ˈpætrɪət] → patriotic	Patriot(in) patriotisch
duty [ˈdjuːtɪ] → to *do one's duty	Pflicht, Aufgabe seine Pflicht tun
to serve s.o./s.th. → service	jdm./einer Sache dienen Dienst
politician [ˌpɒlɪˈtɪʃn] → politics	Politiker(in) Politik
corrupt [kəˈrʌpt]	bestechlich, korrupt
party politics	Parteipolitik
to rule (s.o.) → ruler	(jdn.) regieren Herrscher(in)
to abolish [əˈbɒlɪʃ] s.th.	etwas abschaffen
Head of State	Staatsoberhaupt
charity [ˈtʃærətɪ]	Wohltätigkeitsverein
subject [ˈsʌbʒɪkt]	*hier:* Untertan(in)
citizen [ˈsɪtɪzn]	(Staats-)Bürger(in)
ceremony [ˈserɪmənɪ]	Zeremonie, Feierlichkeit

Politics

2 The American political system

The American Government has three branches: the President, Congress and the Supreme Court.

The President

The President of the USA is the Head of State, and is elected by the people. Before this, he or she has to be nominated by delegates of his or her party. The President stays in office for four years, and may be re-elected for one more term of four years.

A presidential election is a major event in the USA. The candidates who run for office have a very busy time – making speeches and leading the election campaign.

The President is the political leader of the country and is also its chief representative. In this way the President combines the functions of the monarch and the Prime Minister in Britain. This makes the American President a very influential figure. The President's family, known as the 'First Family', are also very much in the public eye.

Congress

While the President represents the executive branch (the Administration), Congress is the legislative branch of the American government: its job is to make laws.

Congress consists of two houses: the House of Representatives and the Senate. Each of the 50 American states has two senators in the Senate, however big or small the state is. The number of representatives in the House of Representatives depends on the population of each state.

The Supreme Court

The Supreme Court is the highest court in the USA. It watches over the American Constitution, and decides if a law or a decision of a lower court is unconstitutional.

Politics 5

branch [brɑːntʃ]	Zweig
president ['---]	Präsident(in)
Congress ['kɒŋgres]	der Kongress *(das amerikanische Parlament)*
the Supreme Court [suˌpriːm 'kɔːt]	der Oberste Gerichtshof der USA
to nominate s.o.	jdn. ernennen
delegate	bevollmächtigte(r) Vertreter(in), Delegierte(r)
in office	im Amt
to re-elect s.o.	jdn. wieder wählen
term	*hier:* Amtszeit
event [-'-]	Ereignis
to *run for office	für ein Amt kandidieren
to *make a speech	eine Rede halten
election campaign [kæm'peɪn]	Wahlkampf, Wahlkampagne
function ['fʌŋkʃn]	Aufgabe, Funktion
influential [ˌɪnflʊ'enʃl]	einflussreich
→ influence ['---]	Einfluss
the First Family	die Präsidentenfamilie (USA)
in the public eye	im Blickpunkt der Öffentlichkeit
executive [ɪg'zekjʊtɪv] branch	Exekutive
Administration [ədˌmɪnɪ'streɪʃn] *(AE)* = Government *(BE)*	*hier:* Regierung
legislative ['ledʒɪslətɪv] branch	Legislative
the House of Representatives	das Repräsentantenhaus
the Senate ['senɪt]	der Senat *(Oberhaus des amerikanischen Parlaments)*
state	(Bundes-)Staat
senator ['senətə]	Senator(in)
population [ˌpɒpjʊ'leɪʃn]	*hier:* Einwohnerzahl
unconstitutional	verfassungswidrig

69

Politics

***The** system of checks and balances*

While the British Prime Minister (like the German **Chancellor**) is the leader of the government and also a Member of Parliament, the three branches in America are clearly **separated**. A British prime minister could not **govern** if his or her party didn't **have the majority** in Parliament. But American presidents have often been faced with a majority of the other party in Congress. The two major parties are the **Democrats** and the **Republicans**.

How the branches check on each other:

- The President can **veto** laws passed by Congress.
  But Congress can **overrule** the President's veto if there is a two-thirds majority **in favour of** the law.

- The President **appoints** judges to the Supreme Court.
  But the Court has the power to decide whether Presidential Acts are constitutional or not.

- The Senate must **confirm** the judges chosen by the president for the Supreme Court.
  On the other hand, the Supreme Court can **declare** laws passed by Congress as unconstitutional.

Washington is the seat of the American **Federal** Government. Each state also has a separate **constitution**, a state senate, and its own **governor** and **courts of justice**.

Politics

system of checks and balances	System der Gewaltenteilung und gegenseitigen Gewaltenkontrolle
chancellor ['tʃɑːnsələ]	Kanzler(in)
to separate s.th. ['sepəreɪt]	etwas trennen
→ separate ['seprət]	getrennt
to govern → government	regieren Regierung
to *have the majority [mə'dʒɒrɪtɪ]	die Mehrheit haben
the Democrats ['deməkræts] the Republicans [rɪ'pʌblɪkənz]	*die zwei wichtigsten Parteien der USA*
to veto ['viːtəʊ] s.th. → veto	Veto gegen etwas einlegen Veto
to overrule [ˌ--'-] s.th./s.o.	etwas ablehnen/jdn. überstimmen
to *be in favour ['feɪvə] of s.th.	für etwas sein
to appoint [ə'pɔɪnt] s.o.	jdn ernennen
to confirm [kən'fɜːm] s.o./s.th.	jdn./etwas bestätigen
to declare s.th. as (unconstitutional/…)	etwas für (verfassungswidrig/…) erklären
federal	Bundes-
constitution	Verfassung
governor ['gʌvənə]	Gouverneur(in)
court of justice ['dʒʌstɪs]	Gerichtshof
→ justice	Gerechtigkeit

"In the name of democracy, welcome! Up to now we've had a one-party system."

Politics

3 Europe – and the European Union

The origins of the European Community (EC) date back to the 1950s, when the idea of economic cooperation between European countries was first developed. At first, the Common Market, as it was then often called, had six member states. Britain did not join until 1973.

Twenty years later, a single market was introduced, which ended border controls. A plan for full economic and monetary union led to the introduction of a single currency, the Euro, in 1999. In 2002, Euro notes and coins came into circulation. Some EU countries, including the UK and Denmark, chose not – or not yet – to replace their own national currencies. In 2004 the EU suddenly became much bigger when ten new countries, most of them in eastern areas of Europe, joined. Plans for a European constitution were begun.

Here are some opinions:

"Free trade within Europe is fine, but I'm against political union. There are so many different countries in Europe. You can't expect them all to want the same policies just because they're linked together by the EU! It's important for individual countries to be able to hold a referendum on really big issues before they're decided on."

"Mobility for students and teachers within Europe is a big advantage. In the past, British qualifications, diplomas and so on, were often not recognized in other European countries – and vice versa. Now there are better opportunities for people who want to move around."

"It's a good thing for Europe to be united, especially in foreign policy. We need to make Europe stronger, stand together and defend our European values."

"The European Commission has too much power already. There seem to be a lot of silly rules and regulations! Too much conformity is a bad thing. I think regional diversity and individuality are vital to people's feelings of identity and national pride."

Politics 5

the European Union ['juːnjən] (EU)	die Europäische Union (EU)
origin ['ɒrɪdʒɪn]	Ursprung, Herkunft
the European Community (EC)	die Europäische Gemeinschaft (EG)
economic cooperation [kəʊˌɒpəˈreɪʃn]	wirtschaftliche Zusammenarbeit
the Common Market	der Gemeinsame Markt
member state	Mitgliedsland
to join (an organization/...)	(einer Organisation/...) beitreten
single market	europäischer Binnenmarkt
border control	Grenzkontrolle
economic and monetary ['mʌnɪtrɪ] union ['juːnjən]	Wirtschafts- und Währungsunion
single currency ['kʌrənsɪ]	einheitliche Währung
Euro ['jʊərəʊ]	Euro
(bank) note	Geldschein
coin	Münze
to *come into circulation	in Umlauf kommen
to replace s.th.	etwas ersetzen
free trade	Freihandel
political union	politische Vereinigung/Union
to link s.th. (together)	etwas verbinden/aneinander koppeln
referendum [ˌrefəˈrendəm]	Referendum, Volksentscheid
issue ['ɪʃuː]	Angelegenheit, Thema, Frage
mobility → mobile ['məʊbaɪl]	Beweglichkeit, Mobilität mobil
advantage ↔ disadvantage	Vorteil Nachteil
qualifications [ˌkwɒlɪfɪˈkeɪʃnz]	*hier:* Zeugnisse
diploma [dɪˈpləʊmə]	Diplom
to recognize s.o./s.th.	*hier:* jdn./etwas anerkennen
vice versa [ˌvaɪsɪˈvɜːsə]	umgekehrt
opportunity [ˌɒpəˈtjuːnɪtɪ]	Gelegenheit, Chance, Möglichkeit
united	vereinigt
foreign ['fɒrɪn] policy	Außenpolitik
values ['væljuːz]	Werte
the European Commission	die Europäische Kommission
rules and regulations	Regeln und Bestimmungen
conformity	Konformismus
diversity [daɪˈvɜːsətɪ]	Vielfalt
individuality [ˌɪndɪˌvɪdʒʊˈælɪtɪ]	Individualität
to *be vital ['vaɪtl] to s.o./s.th	lebenswichtig für jdn./etwas sein
identity [aɪˈdentətɪ]	Identität
national pride	Nationalstolz

Exercises

a) Choose the right word to complete each sentence.

1. Britain, unlike Germany, is a constitutional ….
   - ☐ republic   ☐ power   ☐ monarchy
2. British Members of Parliament (MPs) meet in the House of ….
   - ☐ Representatives   ☐ Commons   ☐ Lords
3. In a general election, voters elect one candidate in each ….
   - ☐ constituency   ☐ state   ☐ party
4. The three branches of the American Government are the President, Congress and ….
   - ☐ the Senate   ☐ the Supreme Court   ☐ the Administration
5. An American President is not allowed to stay … longer than eight years.
   - ☐ in office   ☐ in the public eye   ☐ influential
6. The two major political parties in the USA are the Democrats and the ….
   - ☐ Liberals   ☐ Conservatives   ☐ Republicans

b) What's the word in English?

1. *Steuerzahler:* _____
2. *Ministerium:* _____
3. *Außenpolitik:* _____
4. *Wahlsystem:* _____
5. *Parteipolitik:* _____
6. *Wahlkampf:* _____
7. *Kanzler:* _____
8. *Mehrheit:* _____

Exercises 5

c) **Which of the three is the odd one out?**

- ☐ currency   ☐ note   ☐ coin
- ☐ rules   ☐ values   ☐ regulations
- ☐ individuality   ☐ diversity   ☐ mobility
- ☐ president   ☐ duke   ☐ prince
- ☐ citizen   ☐ voter   ☐ subject

d) **Choose the right preposition.**

1. Who are you going to vote _____?
2. I disagree _____ this new policy.
3. Will the Liberal Democrats ever come _____ power?
4. When did George W. Bush first run _____ office?
5. There is a majority in favour _____ this new law.
6. Who is _____ charge of this department?
7. I don't think the monarchy is an institution everyone can identify _____.
8. The Supreme Court can declare laws _____ unconstitutional.

as
for
for
in
of
to
with
with

e) **Complete the table with suitable words.**

English word	German translation	Word from the same family
	jdm. dienen	
advantage		
	Politiker	
to govern		
	etwas unterstützen	

World problems

1 Growth

The biggest problem that the world faces today is the problem of growth.

- World population is growing fast, and more and more people are starving. In the 40 years between 1960 and 2000, the population of the earth doubled – from 3 billion to 6 billion. By the middle of this century it is expected to reach an incredible 9 billion.

- Industrial production is also growing. This has led to a rise in the material standard of living – but it has also resulted in pollution of the environment.

- Pollution is growing, too. The earth's atmosphere, for example, contains more and more carbon dioxide and other gases as the years go by. This is mainly because of the burning of fossil fuels and the destruction of forests.

- Cities are growing, the use of fertilizers and pesticides is growing; nuclear wastes (the by-products of nuclear power production) and other waste products are building up; traffic is increasing, more and more energy is being consumed, and more and more natural resources are being used up.

World problems

the world	die Welt
growth → to *grow	Wachstum wachsen
population	Bevölkerung
to starve	(ver)hungern
→ starvation [-'--]	Verhungern, Hungertod
the earth	die Erde
to double ['dʌbl]	sich verdoppeln
billion	Milliarde
incredible	unglaublich
industrial [ɪn'dʌstrɪəl] **production**	Industrieproduktion
→ industry ['---]	Industrie
rise ↔ **decline**	Anstieg Rückgang, Verschlechterung
material [mə'tɪərɪəl] → material	materiell Stoff
standard of living	Lebensstandard
to result in s.th. → result	zu etwas führen Folge, Ergebnis
pollution	(Umwelt-)Verschmutzung
→ to pollute s.th.	etwas verschmutzen
environment [ɪn'vaɪrənmənt]	Umwelt
atmosphere ['--,-]	Atmosphäre
carbon dioxide ['kɑ:bəndaɪ'ɒksaɪd]	Kohlendioxid
gas [gæs]	Gas
to *burn (s.th.)	(etwas ver)brennen
fossil fuel [,fɒsl 'fju:əl]	fossiler Brennstoff
destruction → to destroy s.th.	Zerstörung etwas zerstören
forest	(großer) Wald
fertilizer ['fɜ:tɪlaɪzə]	Dünger, Düngemittel
→ fertile ['fɜ:taɪl]	fruchtbar
pesticide ['pestɪsaɪd]	Pestizid, Schädlingsbekämpfungsmittel
nuclear ['nju:klɪə]	Kern-, Atom-, nuklear
waste	*hier:* Müll, Abfall, Nebenprodukt
by-product ['baɪ,prɒdʌkt]	Nebenprodukt
nuclear power	Atomkraft, Kernenergie
waste product	Abfallstoff, Abfallprodukt
to *build up	*hier:* sich ansammeln
traffic	Verkehr
to increase [-'-]	zunehmen, stärker werden
→ increase ['--]	Zunahme, Steigerung
energy ['enədʒɪ]	Energie
to consume [kən'sju:m] **s.th.**	etwas verbrauchen
→ consumer	Verbraucher(in)
natural resources [rɪ'sɔ:sɪz]	Bodenschätze, Naturschätze
to use s.th. up	etwas aufbrauchen

World problems

2 The results of growth

Traditionally, the idea of growth has been welcomed. In rich countries, **economic growth** is mostly seen – at least by politicians – as a sign of **progress**. In poor parts of the world, a large family promises parents economic **security** and hope for the **future**.

But there are **limits** to the earth's **capacity** for growth. For example, in order to **survive**, a growing population needs larger and larger **supplies** of fresh water, food, **raw materials** and fossil fuels. At the same time, the earth has to **absorb** more and more waste and pollution. Unfortunately, the **sources** of materials and energy cannot **last** forever – and the earth cannot go on absorbing all our waste products without showing signs of **damage**. The 'holes' in the **ozone layer**, for example, seem to be **caused**, at least in part, by our waste products. There is also the problem of the '**greenhouse effect**', which is likely to cause **global warming.** A global **climate change** would have **long-term effects** that are very difficult to **predict**.

It seems certain that if growth is allowed to continue, the situation on our **planet** will **get out of control**: **eventually** there will be water and food **shortages** in more and more countries, energy and materials that cannot be **replaced** will **run out**; because of pollution and shortages, **diseases** will **spread** more easily, and there will be a dramatic **decline** in our **health**.

3 Think a moment …

There are now over 800 million motor **vehicles** in the world. They consume one third of the world's total oil production. But about three quarters of these vehicles are in the West. **Worldwide**, only a very small percentage of people own a car. In fact, hundreds of millions of people live in **poor housing** – or are **homeless** – and have no chance of owning washing-machines, televisions or cars anyway. (75% of the world population have never even made a phone call!)

Exhaust fumes are already helping to cause **acid rain** and to **harm** the complex **ecosystems** of our planet Earth. So what will happen when the standard of living in **developing countries** improves – and everyone everywhere wants a car?

B. Green, Shipton-under-Wychwood

World problems 6

economic growth	Wirtschaftswachstum
progress △ *(singular only)*	Fortschritt(e)
security → secure	Sicherheit sicher
future ↔ past	Zukunft Vergangenheit
limit → to limit s.th.	Grenze etwas begrenzen
capacity [kəˈpæsəti]	Kapazität, Aufnahmefähigkeit
to survive (s.th.)	(etwas) überleben
supply [səˈplaɪ]	Vorrat, Versorgung
→ to supply s.o. with s.th.	jdn. mit etw. versorgen
raw material [məˈtɪərɪəl]	Rohstoff
to absorb [əbˈzɔːb] s.th.	etwas aufnehmen/aufsaugen
source [sɔːs]	Quelle
to last	*hier:* (aus)reichen, halten
→ long-lasting	dauerhaft
damage [ˈdæmɪdʒ] △ *(singular only)*	Schaden
→ to damage s.th.	etwas beschädigen
ozone [ˈəʊzəʊn] layer	Ozonschicht
to cause s.th. → cause	etwas verursachen Ursache
greenhouse effect	Treibhauseffekt
global [ˈgləʊbl] → globe	global, weltweit Erdkugel
global warming	Erwärmung der Erdatmosphäre
climate [ˈklaɪmɪt] change	Klimaveränderung
long-term effect	Langzeitwirkung
to predict [-ˈ-] s.th. → prediction	etw. voraussagen Voraussage
planet [ˈplænɪt]	Planet
to *get out of control	außer Kontrolle geraten
eventually [ɪˈventʃʊəli] = in the end	schließlich, nach einer gewissen Zeit
shortage [ˈʃɔːtɪdʒ]	Knappheit, Mangel
to replace [rɪˈpleɪs] s.th.	etwas ersetzen
to *run out	*hier:* ausgehen, zu Ende gehen
disease [dɪˈziːz]	Krankheit, Seuche
to *spread [spred]	sich ausbreiten
decline [dɪˈklaɪn]	Rückgang, Verschlechterung
↔ rise	Anstieg
health → healthy	Gesundheit gesund
vehicle [ˈvɪəkl]	Fahrzeug
worldwide [ˌ-ˈ-] *(adj. & adv.)*	weltweit
poor	*hier:* schlecht
housing [ˈhaʊzɪŋ] △ *(singular only)*	Unterkunft, Wohnungen
homeless	obdachlos, heimatlos
→ homelessness	Obdachlosigkeit
exhaust [ɪgˈzɔːst] fumes	Abgase
acid rain [ˌæsɪd ˈreɪn]	saurer Regen
to harm s.th./s.o.	etwas schädigen, jdn. verletzen
→ harmful ↔ harmless	schädlich harmlos
ecosystem [ˈiːkəʊˌsɪstəm]	Ökosystem
→ ecology [iːˈkɒlədʒi]	Ökologie
developing country	Entwicklungsland

World problems

4 What can be done?

Here are some of the things you can do to help **save** our planet:

- Use your car as little as you can, and **share** it whenever possible. You can also **save petrol** by driving more slowly.

- Always **sort your rubbish** before you **throw it away**: Buy drinks in **returnable bottles** whenever you can. But if there is no **deposit** on your bottles, don't just throw them in the **dustbin**. Take them to a **bottle bank**. Your local **recycling** centre also accepts old cans and newspapers. **Re-use** paper, **plastic bags**, etc., as much as you can.

- Buy local food (to **cut down on** pollution caused by **transporting** food around the world), and eat less meat (so more land is free for forests – and for **wildlife**). You can also **protect** the environment (and your health!) by eating **organic food** whenever possible.

- **Support** plans for **alternative technology** (e.g. the use of **solar energy** to **heat** water; **water power** or **wind power** to **generate electricity**).

- Develop your own **environment-friendly lifestyle**. (**Avoid wasting** energy – for example, by switching off lights, turning down the heating, etc.; choose hobbies – or holidays – that are energy-saving and do not require too much **equipment**.)

- Support an organization that helps people in developing countries (e.g. improving education and **birth control**, helping to fight against **poverty** and **famine**, and against **AIDS** and other problems). There are also **charities** that help to protect animals and plants that are in danger of **becoming extinct**. Every **donation** is useful.

Act now! **It's up to you**!
Make an effort before WE become the world's next **endangered species**!

"We made it! We made it! We're on the Endangered Species list!"

World problems

to save s.o./s.th. (from s.th.)	*hier:* jdn./etwas (vor etwas) retten
to share s.th.	etwas (mit anderen) teilen
to save petrol	Benzin sparen
to sort (one's) rubbish	(seinen) Müll sortieren
to *throw s.th. away ↔ to *keep s.th.	etwas wegwerfen etwas behalten
returnable bottle	Pfandflasche
deposit [dɪˈpɒzɪt]	Pfand
dustbin *(BE)* = garbage can *(AE)*	Mülleimer, Mülltonne
bottle bank	Altglascontainer
recycling	Wiederverwertung, Recycling
→ to recycle s.th.	etwas wieder verwerten
to re-use s.th.	etwas wieder verwenden
plastic bag	Plastiktüte
to *cut down on s.th.	etwas reduzieren
to transport [-ˈ-] s.th.	etwas transportieren
→ transport [ˈ--]	Transport
wildlife [ˈwaɪldlaɪf]	Tierwelt (Tiere in freier Wildbahn)
to protect s.o./s.th. (from s.th.)	jdn./etwas (vor etwas) schützen
organic [ɔːˈgænɪk] food	Öko-Lebensmittel, Biokost
to support s.o./s.th.	jdn./etwas unterstützen
→ support	Unterstützung
alternative technology [-ˈ---]	alternative Technologie
solar [ˈsəʊlə] energy	Sonnenenergie
to heat s.th.	etwas erhitzen/(auf)heizen
→ heat → heating	Hitze Heizung
water power	Wasserkraft
wind power	Windenergie
to generate s.th. = to produce s.th.	etwas erzeugen
electricity [ˌ--ˈ---] → electric [-ˈ--]	Strom elektrisch
environment-friendly	umweltfreundlich
lifestyle	Lebensstil
to avoid s.th.	etwas vermeiden
to waste s.th. ↔ to save s.th.	etwas verschwenden etwas sparen
equipment [ɪˈkwɪpmənt]	Ausrüstung
→ to equip s.o./s.th. (with s.th.)	jdn./etwas (mit etwas) ausrüsten
birth control	Geburtenkontrolle
poverty [ˈpɒvəti] → poor	Armut arm
famine [ˈfæmɪn]	Hungersnot
AIDS	AIDS
charity [ˈtʃærəti]	Wohltätigkeitsverein
to *become extinct = to die out	aussterben
donation [dəʊˈneɪʃn]	Spende
→ to donate s.th.	etwas spenden
it's up to you	es liegt an dir, es hängt von dir ab
to *make an effort [ˈefət]	sich anstrengen, sich bemühen
endangered species [ˈspiːʃiːz]	(vom Aussterben) bedrohte Art
→ to endanger s.o./s.th.	jdn./etwas gefährden

Exercises

a) Read the clues below, then write the answers in the grid. The letters in the blue squares give the name of a gas found in the earth's atmosphere.

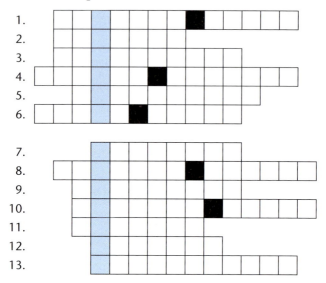

1. You can't have … production without waste products.
2. Cars and other vehicles that are moving on the roads.
3. Putting … on the ground helps plants to grow better.
4. The 'greenhouse effect' is expected to cause ….
5. The number of people living in a place are its ….
6. If the … is damaged, the sun becomes more harmful to our skin.
7. If people have too little food and water, … can spread more easily.
8. If average temperatures get noticeably higher (or lower), there will be a ….
9. Industrial waste can result in … of the atmoshere.
10. A car that runs on petrol produces ….
11. A thousand million.
12. Food shortages eventually lead to a … in people's health.
13. Everyone should try to develop an …-friendly lifestyle!

Exercises 6

b) **Find the expressions that mean the same as the German words below. (Always choose two words – one from each 'cloud'.)**

> organic economic plastic
> bottle returnable✔ water
> long-term waste developing

> bottle✔ effect country
> growth bank power
> bag food product

1. *Pfandflasche:*   *returnable bottle* _____
2. *Altglascontainer:* _____
3. *Wirtschaftswachstum:* _____
4. *Wasserkraft:* _____
5. *Abfallstoff:* _____
6. *Langzeitwirkung:* _____
7. *Biokost:* _____
8. *Plastiktüte:* _____
9. *Entwicklungsland:* _____

c) **Find the opposites (↔) – or words that mean the same (synonyms, =).**

1. to produce s.th.   = _____
   (e.g. electricity)

2. to die out   = _____
   (e.g. a species of animal)

3. to keep s.th.   ↔ _____
   (e.g. an old magazine)

4. to save s.th.   ↔ _____
   (e.g. energy)

5. a decline   ↔ a _____
   (e.g. in the standard of living)

83

Education

1 The school system in Britain

State schools

In Britain, children first **go to school** when they are five. They usually go to **primary school** until they are eleven. After that they go to **secondary school**. There are a few state **grammar schools**, but most **pupils attend comprehensive schools**. The first-year classes at these schools are of **mixed ability**, but after that they are usually divided into different groups for **lessons** in **academic subjects**.

A large number of comprehensives in Britain today are '**independent specialist schools**'. These schools **put emphasis on** certain 'special subjects' (like **sports** or **IT**, for example), and about 10 per cent of the pupils there are chosen because that is the subject they are especially **good at**.

Private schools

Private schools are **fee-paying** schools; they are not **run by the state**. Many of them are **boarding schools**. Among them are the famous **public schools**, such as Eton, Harrow and Rugby, which have very old traditions and usually have a high **academic standard**. Many of these private schools are boys' or girls' schools, but some are **co-educational** (**mixed schools**).

Although fees keep going up, private schools have become more and more popular in Britain; more than 7 per cent of all pupils now go to one of these schools.

School work and examinations

Although most schools expect their pupils to do homework every evening, some **head teachers** believe that all work should be done at school, and that evenings should be free. At one school in England, pupils' **grades** in exams improved by 20% after they had stopped doing homework.

Most schools **set exams** at the end of every school year, to **test** pupils' ability. School **reports** come out at the end of each **term**, or at least twice a year. At the age of 15 or 16, pupils **take** their **GCSEs** (**General Certificate of Secondary Education**); GCSE **results** depend on **course work** as well as **written examinations**.

Education 7

education [ˌedjʊˈkeɪʃn]	Erziehung(swesen), Bildung(swesen)
→ to educate s.o.	jdn. erziehen/ausbilden
state school	staatliche Schule
to *go to school	in die Schule gehen
primary [ˈpraɪmərɪ] school	Grundschule
secondary [ˈsekəndrɪ] school	weiter führende Schule
grammar school	etwa: Gymnasium
pupil [ˈpjuːpl]	Schüler(in)
to attend a school	eine Schule besuchen
→ to attend school	die Schule besuchen
comprehensive [ˌkɒmprɪˈhensɪv] school	Gesamtschule
(mixed) ability	(unterschiedliche) Begabung/Fähigkeiten
lesson	(Unterrichts-)Stunde
academic [ˌækəˈdemɪk] subject	natur- oder geisteswissenschaftliches Schulfach
independent specialist school	auf bestimmte Fächer spezialisierte staatliche Schule
to *put emphasis [ˈemfəsɪs] on s.th.	Gewicht/Wert auf etwas legen
sports	Sport(arten)
IT (= Information Technology)	Informatik
to *be good/bad/… at s.th.	gut/schlecht/… in etwas sein
private [ˈpraɪvət] school	Privatschule
to *pay a fee [fiː]	hier: Schulgeld bezahlen
to *be run by the state	staatlich geführt werden
boarding [ˈbɔːdɪŋ] school	Internat
public [ˈpʌblɪk] school	Privatschule (von hohem Rang)
academic standard	schulisches Niveau
co-educational [ˌkəʊedjʊˈkeɪʃənl] (school)	(Schule) für Mädchen und Jungen
mixed school	gemischte Schule
examination	Prüfung, Examen
head teacher	Schulleiter(in), Rektor(in)
grade	(Prüfungs-)Note
to *set an exam	hier: eine Prüfung abhalten
to test s.th. → test	etwas. überprüfen Test
(school) report	Zeugnis
term	Trimester (in GB wird das Schuljahr in drei Trimester geteilt)
to *take an exam	eine Prüfung schreiben/machen
General Certificate [səˈtɪfɪkət] of Secondary Education (GCSE)	Prüfung, die etwa dem Realschul-/Hauptschulabschluss entspricht
result [rɪˈzʌlt]	Ergebnis
course work	schriftliche Leistung innerhalb eines Schuljahres
written exam(ination)	schriftliche Prüfung

7 Education

At some schools, certain GCSE subjects are **compulsory**. Depending on the school, compulsory subjects on the **curriculum** may be English, one **foreign language**, **General Science** and **Maths**. Pupils take courses that are **appropriate** to their ability.

Optional subjects on the **timetable** may include **Art**, **Biology**, **Business Studies**, **Chemistry**, **Physics**, **Geography** and **History**, Information Technology, **Music**, **Physical Education**, **Religious Studies**, and a second foreign language.

After GCSE, most people **leave school** and go on to **college** or start an **apprenticeship**. Some decide to look for a job without a **training course**.

But it is possible to stay on at school for two more years, in the **sixth form**, to prepare for **A-Level** exams. This can also be done at **sixth form college**. If you want to **go to university**, you usually need good grades in at least two A-Level subjects as **qualifications**. A-Levels include **practical exams** (in science subjects, for example) and **oral exams** (in languages). If you do not **pass** a subject at A-Level, you can **re-sit** the exams in the subject you **failed**. It is usual to **choose** A-Level subjects which are sensible combinations (not, for example, English, Maths and Geography but perhaps Maths, Physics and Chemistry) and which will be useful in your later **career**. For example, if you want to **study** French and German at university, good exam results in these subjects will be expected when you **apply for a place**.

First student: *How were your exam questions?*
Second student: *They were easy! But I had trouble with the answers.*

Dad: *Do you need any help with your homework, son?*
Boy: *No thanks, Dad. I can get it wrong without your help.*

Pupil: *Should someone be punished for something they haven't done?*
Teacher: *No, of course not!*
Pupil: *Good – I haven't done my homework.*

Education 7

compulsory [kəmˈpʌlsəri]	obligatorisch, Pflicht-
curriculum [kəˈrɪkjələm]	Lehrplan
foreign language [ˌfɒrɪn ˈlæŋgwɪdʒ]	Fremdsprache
General Science [ˈsaɪəns]	Naturwissenschaften (Kombination aus Biologie, Chemie und Physik)
Maths [mæθs] (= Mathematics)	Mathe(matik)
appropriate [əˈprəʊpriət] (to s.th.)	(einer Sache) angemessen
optional [ˈɒpʃənl]	fakultativ, Wahl-
timetable	*hier:* Stundenplan
Art	Kunst
Biology [baɪˈɒlədʒi]	Biologie
Business [ˈbɪznɪs] Studies	Wirtschaftskunde
Chemistry [ˈkemɪstri]	Chemie
Physics [ˈfɪzɪks]	Physik
Geography [dʒɪˈɒgrəfi]	Erdkunde
History	Geschichte
Music [ˈmjuːzɪk]	Musik
Physical Education (PE)	Sport (als Schulfach)
Religious [rɪˈlɪdʒəs] Studies	Religion (als Schulfach)
to *leave school	die Schule verlassen, von der Schule abgehen
college	Fachschule, Berufsschule
apprenticeship [əˈprentɪʃɪp] → apprentice	Lehre Lehrling, Auszubildende(r)
training course	Lehre, Berufsausbildung
sixth form	Oberstufe (die letzten 2 Schuljahre)
A-Level (= Advanced Level)	*etwa:* Abitur
sixth form college	*Schule, die Oberstufenschüler auf „A-Level" vorbereitet*
to *go to university	studieren
qualifications [ˌkwɒlɪfɪˈkeɪʃnz]	*hier:* Schulabschluss(zeugnis), Voraussetzung
practical exam	praktische Prüfung
oral [ˈɔːrəl] exam	mündliche Prüfung
to pass (an exam)	(eine Prüfung) bestehen
to *sit/re-sit an exam	eine Prüfung machen/wiederholen
to fail (an exam)	(in einer Prüfung) durchfallen
to *choose s.th. → choice	etwas wählen Wahl
career [kəˈrɪə]	Laufbahn, Beruf, Karriere
to study a subject	ein Fach studieren
to apply [əˈplaɪ] for a place → application [ˌæplɪˈkeɪʃn]	sich um einen (Studien-)Platz bewerben Bewerbung

87

7 Education

On the school notice-board

Friday, 4.45 p.m.:
Choir practice (with **orchestra**!) in the **Assembly Hall**.

Who left their PE **kit** (new!) on the **sports ground** after **Games** last Wednesday? Please collect from the **staffroom**!

Why not **join** the Photo **Club**? **Meetings**: In the new **library** during the **lunch break** on Tuesdays.

Rules
- No smoking in school or in the school **grounds**.
- Leave your bicycles only in the **bicycle shed** behind the **playground**.
- Food may only be eaten in the **cafeteria**, never in the **classrooms** or **corridors**.
- The **science laboratories**, the computer room and the **gym** are **out of bounds** except when a **member of staff** is **present**.
- Remember to bring a **doctor's certificate** if you are **absent** for more than 5 days.
  – The **Headmaster** –

2 Different words in American and British English

in American English	in British English
elementary [--'---] school	primary school
high school	secondary school
grade	class
campus ['kæmpəs]	grounds
student	pupil
diploma [dɪ'pləʊmə]	certificate
to graduate (from high school)	to leave school (with A-Level qualifications)
vacation	holidays
recess [-'-]	break
principal ['---]	head (teacher)
janitor	**caretaker**
public school	state school
grade	grade (in exams)
	mark (in tests, for school work)
notebook	**exercise book**
period ['pɪərɪəd]	lesson
schedule ['skedʒuːl]	timetable

Education 7

notice-board	Schwarzes Brett, Anschlagbrett
choir ['kwaɪə] **practice**	Chorprobe
orchestra ['ɔːkɪstrə]	Orchester
assembly hall	Aula
kit	Ausrüstung, „Zeug"
sports ground	Sportplatz
Games	(Mannschafts-)Spiele (als Schulfach)
staffroom → **staff** [stɑːf]	Lehrerzimmer Lehrpersonal
to join a club	*hier:* einer AG beitreten
meeting	Treffen, Versammlung
library ['laɪbrərɪ]	Bibliothek
lunch break [breɪk]	Mittagspause
rule → **school rules**	Regel, Vorschrift Schulordnung
grounds ⚠ *(plural only)*	Gelände
bicycle shed	Fahrradschuppen, Fahrradunterstand
playground	Schulhof
cafeteria [ˌkæfə'tɪərɪə]	Cafeteria
classroom	Klassenzimmer
corridor ['kɒrɪdɔː]	Gang
science laboratory [lə'bɒrətrɪ]	Labor (für Naturwissenschaften)
⚠ **gym** [dʒɪm]	⚠ Turnhalle
(= **gym**nasium [dʒɪm'neɪzjəm])	
⚠ **grammar school**	⚠ Gymnasium
out of bounds	nicht zu betreten
member of staff	Lehrkraft
to *be present ['preznt]	anwesend sein
doctor's certificate [sə'tɪfɪkət]	ärztliches Attest
to *be absent ['æbsənt]	fehlen, abwesend sein
headmaster → **headmistress** (*also:* head, head teacher)	Schuldirektor Schuldirektorin
janitor ['dʒænɪtə] *(AE)*/ **caretaker** *(BE)*	Hausmeister(in)
mark	(Schul-)Note
notebook *(AE)*/**exercise book** *(BE)*	Heft

Mum: *Come on, John! You'll be late for school.*
Tom: *I don't want to go to school. The teachers don't like me, the children don't like me. Nobody likes me.*
Mum *But you have to go, John.*
Tom: *Why should I?*
Mum: *You know quite well! Firstly, you're 46 years old, and secondly, you're the headmaster.*

Education

3 School in Germany

Nick Burton spent six months at a school in Germany. When he got back home, he told his friends about the system in Germany …

"It's hard to explain in English about school life in Germany. This is because a lot of German traditions and institutions have no real **equivalent** in Britain.

There wasn't a comprehensive school where I stayed, but three different types of school. I went to a 'Realschule' – that's a secondary school where pupils leave at 16. There was no **school uniform**! Instead of **revising** for school exams every summer like we do, German pupils **work for class tests** all through the year. So you can't be **lazy** for long! Marks in these tests seemed very important, especially near the end of the school year, when most people **worked out** their **average** marks even before the reports came out! In Germany the best mark is 1 (like **Grade A** with us), and the worst is 6 (that's a **fail**). Some parents pay for their children to have **private lessons** in subjects they are bad at. They don't get **special help** at school like we do. In my class, two people **stayed down** because of bad marks.

Schools in Germany have rules of course, like we do, and you are **punished** if you break them. If you **behave** badly or don't **hand work in**, you may **get detention**, or you may be given **extra work**. If you **cheat** in tests – or **copy** from your neighbour – really **strict** teachers won't **mark your paper**, but will give you a 6 automatically! Sometimes a person's name is put down in the **register** – that's a bit like an **order mark**. If you get too many order marks, you may get detention, or you may even be **suspended**. In really extreme cases, pupils can be **expelled**, like they can with us.

One afternoon it was very hot, and my friend and I **skipped** PE and went swimming instead. Sometimes lessons are **cancelled** when the weather is really hot. Once or twice a year most classes go on an **excursion**, and sometimes there's a **day out**. And, like with us, there are **exchange** visits between schools in different countries.

People at the **school I was at** get a **school leaving certificate** at the end of the 10th year. It's a bit like our GCSEs, but you don't have to **do written exams** in all parts of Germany. I had another friend who was at the grammar school (she was a **form captain**). They take their **school leaving exams** two years later. These are like A-Levels, except that you have to take courses in more subjects – they can't **drop** as many as we can. They just have more lessons in their **main subjects**."

Education 7

equivalent [ɪˈkwɪvələnt]	Entsprechung
school uniform [ˈjuːnɪfɔːm]	Schuluniform
to revise [rɪˈvaɪz] **(for an exam)**	sich durch Wiederholen des Stoffes (auf eine Prüfung) vorbereiten
→ revision [rɪˈvɪʒn]	Wiederholung
to work (for a test)	(für eine Arbeit) lernen
class test	Klassenarbeit
lazy	faul
to work s.th. out	etwas ausrechnen
average [ˈævrɪdʒ] *(noun/adjetive)*	Durchschnitt, durchschnittlich
→ on average	im Durchschnitt
Grade A	Note 1
fail [feɪl]	Note 6 (durchgefallen)
private lessons	Nachhilfe
special help	Förderunterricht
to stay down	sitzen bleiben
to punish s.o./s,th. → **punishment**	jdn./etwas bestrafen Strafe
to behave [bɪˈheɪv] **(well/badly)**	sich (gut/schlecht) betragen
→ behaviour [bɪˈheɪvjə]	Betragen, Verhalten
to hand work in	eine Arbeit/Hausaufgaben abgeben
to *get detention	nachsitzen müssen
→ detention	Arrest; Haft
extra work	eine Strafarbeit
to cheat	schummeln, mogeln
to copy (from s.o.)	(von jdm.) abschreiben
strict	streng
to mark a paper	eine Arbeit korrigieren
register [ˈredʒɪstə]	Klassenbuch; Namenliste
order mark	*etwa:* Eintrag ins Klassenbuch
to *be suspended [səˈspendɪd]	zeitweilig vom Unterricht ausgeschlossen werden
to *be expelled	von der Schule „fliegen"
to skip a lesson	eine Unterrichtsstunde schwänzen
to *be cancelled	ausfallen, gestrichen werden
excursion [ɪkˈskɜːʃn]	Exkursion, Ausflug (mit Bus oder Bahn)
day out	Ausflug, Wandertag
exchange [ɪksˈtʃeɪndʒ]	Austausch
to *be at a school	an einer Schule sein
school leaving certificate [səˈtɪfɪkət]	Schulabschlusszeugnis
to *do written exams	schriftliche Prüfungen machen
form captain [ˈkæptɪn]	Klassensprecher(in)
school leaving exams	Abschlussprüfung
to drop a subject	ein Fach abwählen
main subject	Hauptfach; *auch:* Neigungsfach

Exercises 7

a) Can you find the words?

1. British children start _primary_ school at the age of five. *mapirry*
2. Most secondary schools are _____ schools. *pheveremsicon*
3. Pupils at _____ school only y at home in the holidays. *grinabod*
4. GCSE stands for _____ Certificate of Secondary Education. *ragelen*
5. Course work is important, as well as written _____. *maxes*
6. Most people _____ school after GCSE. *avele*
7. But pupils that stay on at school for two more years can prepare for _____. *eveall*
8. You need good _____ in the subjects of your choice if you want to apply for a place at university. *sluters*

b) Give the American English equivalents of these British English expressions.

1. class: _____
2. exercise book: _____
3. lesson: _____
4. pupil: _____
5. secondary school: _____
6. head teacher: _____
7. holidays: _____
8. timetable: _____

Exercises 7

c) Find the words that go together with these nouns. Then write down the correct German translation for each expression.

> academic doctor's foreign grammar
> Information lunch main oral ✔ Physical
> sixth sports

1. _oral_ examination: **mündliche Prüfung**
2. _____ break: _____
3. _____ standard: _____
4. _____ ground: _____
5. _____ form: _____
6. _____ school: _____
7. _____ language: _____
8. _____ subject: _____
9. _____ Technology: _____
10. _____ certificate: _____
11. _____ Education: _____

d) Which is the odd one out?

1. ❏ mixed school   ❏ co-educational school   ❏ public school
2. ❏ to be cancelled ❏ to be absent   ❏ to be present
3. ❏ day out   ❏ exchange   ❏ excursion
4. ❏ Physics   ❏ Chemistry   ❏ History
5. ❏ training course ❏ college   ❏ university
6. ❏ library   ❏ playground   ❏ science laboratory
7. ❏ to revise   ❏ to cheat   ❏ to copy
8. ❏ grade   ❏ rule   ❏ mark

Relationships and problems

1 Members of the family

Linda: There's a party at Alex's house on Saturday. Are you going?

Sue: I can't! It's my parents' silver **wedding**, and they want all the family to be there. We've got so many **relations**! My **grandparents** are coming, and all my **aunts** and **uncles**. Even my **great-grandmother** will be there! She's coming with her daughter – that's my **great-aunt**! She's my **godmother**, too.

Linda: And any younger members of the family?

Sue: Oh yes, it won't be just the older **generation**! My **cousins** Mark and Jenny are coming. You know – the **twins**. They're fifteen now. My baby **nephew** Ben will be the youngest!

Linda: You never told me you had a nephew!

Sue: Yes, my **half-sister** Lucy's son. Lucy is ten years older than me. She **got married** last year, don't you remember?

Linda: Oh yes! Doesn't her **husband** come from Denmark?

Sue: No, Sweden! She **got to know** him at university. – So now I've got a Swedish **brother-in-law**!

Linda: I didn't know Lucy was your half-sister.

Sue: Yes, my father was **married** before. Lucy is his **daughter** from his first **marriage**. My mother is his second **wife**. So she's my real mother – and Lucy's **stepmother**.

Linda: It all sounds very complicated! But it must be nice to have all those **relatives**. My mother and father haven't got any **brothers and sisters** – and I'm an **only child**, too.

Relationships and problems 8

relationship	Beziehung, Verhältnis
member of the family	Familienmitglied
wedding	Hochzeit
relation	Verwandte(r)
→ to *be related to s.o.	mit jdm. verwandt sein
grandparents	Großeltern
→ grandmother/grandma	Großmutter/Oma
→ grandfather/grandpa	Großvater/Opa
aunt [ɑːnt]	Tante
uncle [ˈʌŋkl]	Onkel
great-grandmother	Urgroßmutter
→ great-grandfather	Urgroßvater
great-aunt → great-uncle	Großtante Großonkel
godmother → godfather	Patentante Patenonkel
generation [ˌdʒenəˈreɪʃn]	Generation
cousin [ˈkʌzn]	Cousin, Cousine
twins	Zwillinge
nephew [ˈnefjuː]	Neffe
→ niece [niːs]	Nichte
half-sister → half-brother	Halbschwester Halbbruder
to *get married	heiraten
husband [ˈhʌzbənd]	Ehemann
to *get to *know s.o.	jdn. kennen lernen
brother-in-law	Schwager
→ sister-in-law	Schwägerin
→ mother-in-law	Schwiegermutter;
→ father-in-law	Schwiegervater
married	verheiratet
daughter → son	Tochter Sohn
marriage [ˈmærɪdʒ]	Ehe
wife	Ehefrau
stepmother → stepfather	Stiefmutter Stiefvater
→ stepsister → stepbrother	Stiefschwester Stiefbruder
relative [ˈ---] = relation	Verwandte(r)
brothers and sisters	Geschwister
an only child	ein Einzelkind

95

8 Relationships and problems

2 Taken from the Problem Page

Dear Debbie,

Please help me! I haven't got a **boyfriend**, but I'm **crazy about** a boy who lives in our road. I **met** him at a party – and it was **love at first sight**! I'd like to ask him for a **date**, but I'm too **shy**. I don't think he's **going out** with anyone else. I'd be **heart-broken** – and **jealous** – if he was! How can I make him **fall in love with** me? What's your **advice**?

Kim (15)

Dear Debbie,

What can I do about my mother? My parents are **divorced**, so I'm part of a **one-parent family**. Now my mother has started a new relationship, and she wants her new partner to **move in with** us! He is **separated**, but he's got two children – and they're **awful**!! I've tried to talk to my mother, but she says **it's none of my business**.

Unhappy (16)

Dear Debbie,

My best friend thinks she's **pregnant**, but she's too scared to tell her mum. She **daren't** say anything to her boyfriend – she's sure he would **chuck** her if he knew. I've told her she ought to see a doctor, but she feels too **embarrassed**. What can I do to help her? I don't want her to **ruin her life**.

Worried (16)

3 Can you do without it?

Addiction can take many forms. The **alcoholic** is addicted to alcohol, the **drug addict** can't stop **taking drugs**. But there are other **substances** that seem less **harmful**, such as the **nicotine** in **cigarettes**, or even the **caffeine** in coffee, which can cause problems if they are **taken to excess**.

Marian: My mother always told me not to **smoke**, but I wanted to **try it out** – like my friends! It started as a kind of **rebellion** against **authority**, but then I found I couldn't stop. I'm glad I've **given it up** now! These days I always look for the **non-smoking areas** in restaurants, and I must say, I feel much **healthier** altogether.

Relationships and problems

boyfriend → girlfriend	fester Freund feste Freundin
to *be crazy about s.o./s.th.	verrückt nach jdm./etwas sein
to *meet s.o.	*hier:* jdn. kennen lernen
love at first sight	Liebe auf den ersten Blick
date → to date s.o. *(AE)*	Rendezvous mit jdm. (aus)gehen
shy	schüchtern
to *go out with s.o. *(BE)*	mit jdm. (aus)gehen
heart-broken [ˈhɑːtˌbrəʊkn]	untröstlich
→ to *break s.o.'s heart	jdm. das Herz brechen
jealous [ˈdʒeləs]	eifersüchtig
to *fall in love (with s.o.)	sich (in jdn.) verlieben
advice ⚠ *(singular only)*	Rat
→ to advise s.o. to do s.th.	jdm. raten etwas zu tun
divorced [dɪˈvɔːst] → divorce	geschieden Scheidung
one-parent family	Familie mit einem allein erziehenden Elternteil
to move in with s.o.	zu jdm. ziehen
separated [ˈsepəreɪtɪd]	getrennt
→ separation [ˌ--ˈ--]	Trennung
awful [ˈɔːfl]	schrecklich
it's none of my business [ˈbɪznɪs]	es geht mich nichts an
pregnant [ˈpregnənt]	schwanger
→ pregnancy	Schwangerschaft
I daren't [deənt] **do s.th.**	ich wage es nicht, etwas zu tun
to chuck s.o. *(informal)*	Schluss mit jdm. machen
embarrassed	verlegen, beschämt
to ruin one's life	sein Leben ruinieren
to *do without s.th.	ohne etwas auskommen
addiction [əˈdɪkʃn]	Sucht
alcoholic [ˌ--ˈ---]	Alkoholiker(in)
→ alcoholism [ˈælkəhɒlɪzm]	Alkoholismus
drug addict [ˈædɪkt]	Drogensüchtige(r)
to *take drugs	Drogen nehmen
substance [ˈsʌbstəns]	Stoff
harmful ↔ harmless	schädlich harmlos
nicotine [ˈnɪkətiːn]	Nikotin
cigarette [ˌsɪgəˈret]	Zigarette
caffeine [ˈkæfiːn]	Koffein
to *take s.th. to excess [ɪkˈses]	etwas im Übermaß zu sich nehmen
to smoke	rauchen
to try s.th. out	etwas ausprobieren
rebellion [rɪˈbeljən]	Aufstand, Rebellion
→ to rebel [-ˈ-] (against s.th.)	(gegen etwas) rebellieren
authority [ɔːˈθɒrətɪ]	*hier:* Autorität
to *give s.th. up	etwas aufgeben, mit etwas aufhören
non-smoking area [ˈeərɪə]	Nichtraucherzone, rauchfreie Zone
healthy [ˈhelθɪ] → health	gesund Gesundheit

8 Relationships and problems

John: I usually only smoke at parties. I've never taken drugs. But when I was about thirteen, I tried **glue-sniffing** with a friend. Then his mother **caught** us and **told us off**! Luckily my parents never **got to know about** it. I've only been **drunk** once, but that was enough, I had such a terrible **hangover**. It was **embarrassing**, too, as I was staying at a friend's house, and I **was sick** all over the carpet!

Sally: How awful! The only thing I've ever been addicted to is **spending money**. Mostly on clothes! I used to think I'd be more **popular** if I followed the latest **trends**. Of course, everyone wants to feel **accepted**. But now I think it's a bit **childish** if everyone always tries to **keep up with** everyone else.

Mike: You're right, it's **ridiculous**! After all, real friends accept you for your **personality** and your **values**, not for your **appearance**. Whenever I start to feel **uncomfortable** or **inferior** because of what I'm wearing (or *not* wearing!), I try to **ignore** the feeling – and stop **worrying**!

Jessica: It's not so easy, though. If people start being **unkind** and **tease** you about your clothes, you automatically feel **awkward** and **unattractive**. Nobody likes being **laughed at**.

4 Trouble at home

Here are some of the things that so often cause trouble, unhappiness – and **arguments** – in the family …

Sam: I can't **talk things over** properly with my parents. When something **goes wrong**, they're never **prepared** to have a **discussion** about it. They always think they're right and I'm wrong. They never even *try* to see things from *my* **point of view**. Then they **blame** me if I **blow up**! Maybe I'm a bit **rude** to them sometimes. But I don't **apologize**. Why should I?

Relationships and problems 8

glue-sniffing ['gluːˌsnɪfɪŋ]	(Klebstoff-)Schnüffeln
to *catch s.o. (doing s.th.)	jdn. (bei etwas) erwischen/ertappen
to *tell s.o. off (for doing s.th.)	jdn. (wegen etwas) ausschimpfen/ schelten
to *get to *know about s.th.	etwas herausfinden, etwas mitbekommen
drunk	betrunken
hangover ['-,--]	Kater
embarrassing	peinlich
to *be sick	sich übergeben
to *spend money (on s.th.)	Geld (für etwas) ausgeben
popular ['pɒpjʊlə]	beliebt
→ popularity [ˌ--'---]	Beliebtheit
trend	Mode, Trend
accepted	anerkannt, akzeptiert
childish	kindisch
to *keep up with s.o.	mit jdm. mithalten
ridiculous [rɪ'dɪkjʊləs]	lächerlich
personality [ˌ--'---]	Persönlichkeit
values ['væljuːz]	Werte
appearance	Aussehen, Äußeres
uncomfortable [ʌn'kʌmfətəbl]	unbehaglich
inferior [ɪn'fɪərɪə]	unterlegen, minderwertig
↔ superior [suː'pɪərɪə]	überlegen, hervorragend
to ignore s.o./s.th.	jdn./etwas nicht beachten
to worry (about s.th.)	sich Sorgen (wegen etwas) machen
unkind [-'-] ↔ kind	gemein liebenswürdig
to tease [tiːz] s.o. (about s.th.)	jdn. (wegen etwas) aufziehen
awkward ['ɔːkwəd]	*hier:* verlegen
unattractive ↔ attractive	unattraktiv, hässlich attraktiv
to laugh at s.o.	jdn. auslachen
trouble	Ärger, Schwierigkeiten
argument ['ɑːgjʊmənt]	Auseinandersetzung
→ to argue	sich streiten
to talk things over with s.o.	die Dinge mit jdm. besprechen
to *go wrong	schief laufen
to *be prepared to do s.th.	bereit sein, etwas zu tun
discussion [dɪ'skʌʃn]	Diskussion, Streitgespräch
→ to discuss s.th.	etwas besprechen
point of view [vjuː]	Standpunkt, Sicht
⚠ from my point of view	aus meiner Sicht
to blame [bleɪm] s.o. (for s.th.)	jdm. die Schuld (an etwas) geben
to *blow up	explodieren, in die Luft gehen
rude [ruːd] ↔ polite	unhöflich höflich
to apologize [ə'pɒlədʒaɪz] (to s.o. for s.th.) = to say sorry (to s.o. for s.th.)	sich (bei jdm. für etw.) entschuldigen

99

8 Relationships and problems

Judy: My mother always criticizes me a lot. I hate that. She always complains about everything. One day she doesn't approve of my hairstyle, and the next day it's my behaviour at home, or my social life. Then she accuses me of being selfish and irresponsible – or not making an effort at school. Sometimes things get so bad I feel like leaving home altogether and living my own life as an independent adult. Then at least I could do as I please.

Robin: I sometimes feel depressed or bad-tempered when I get up. My father gets impatient then. He can't stand bad moods! I suppose it's natural for parents to get annoyed, too, sometimes. After all, they bring you up and do what they think best. But I think they should respect you more – and treat you more like a grown-up.

Liz: I normally get on well with my parents. They're very fond of me, and they aren't strict at all. If anything goes wrong, they're really sympathetic. They give me enough pocket money, too, and lots of privileges. But I sometimes feel I can't live up to their expectations. This puts me under pressure quite a bit. I sometimes even think it would be easier if they didn't care about me so much!

Paul: My mum worries all the time, especially if I'm out late at night. She says she's responsible for me and all that. But I think it's important for people my age to learn to look after themselves. Parents ought to trust their children more, instead of always expecting the worst!

"Blow out the candles and make a wish: we've already made ours."

Relationships and problems

to criticize ['krɪtɪsaɪz] s.o./s.th. → criticism	jdn./etwas kritisieren Kritik
to hate s.o./s.th. → hatred ['heɪtrɪd]	jdn./etwas hassen Hass
to complain about s.th./s.o.	sich über etwas/jdn. beschweren/ beklagen
to approve of s.th.	etwas gutheißen/billigen
hairstyle	Frisur
behaviour [bɪ'heɪvjə] → to behave (well/badly/…)	Verhalten sich (gut/schlecht/…) benehmen
social ['səʊʃl] life	Freizeitgestaltung mit Freunden
to accuse s.o. of doing s.th.	jdn. beschuldigen, etwas zu tun/ etwas getan zu haben
selfish	selbstsüchtig, egoistisch
irresponsible [ˌɪrɪ'spɒnsəbl]	verantwortungslos
to *make an effort ['efət]	sich bemühen, sich anstrengen
to *feel like doing s.th.	(gute) Lust haben, etwas zu tun
to *leave home	von zu Hause weggehen, ausziehen
to live your own life	sein eigenes Leben führen
independent	unabhängig, selbständig
adult ['ædʌlt] (noun/adj.) = grown-up	Erwachsene(r), erwachsen
to *do as you please	tun, was einem gefällt/passt
depressed	deprimiert, niedergeschlagen
to *be bad-tempered	schlechte Laune haben
impatient [ɪm'peɪʃnt] ↔ patient	ungeduldig geduldig
I can't stand s.th./s.o.	ich kann etwas/jdn. nicht ausstehen
mood [muːd] → moody	Laune launisch
to *get annoyed	sich ärgern, sich aufregen
to *bring s.o. up	jdn. großziehen/aufziehen
to *do what you think best	tun, was man für das Beste hält
to respect s.o. → respect	jdn. respektieren Respekt
to treat s.o. (well/badly/…)	jdn. (gut/schlecht/…) behandeln
grown-up ['--] (noun/adj.) = adult ['--]	Erwachsene(r), erwachsen
to *get on well with s.o.	sich gut mit jdm. verstehen
to *be fond of s.o./s.th.	jdn./etwas mögen/gern haben
strict	streng
sympathetic [ˌsɪmpə'θetɪk] → sympathy ['---]	verständnisvoll, mitfühlend Mitleid, Mitgefühl
pocket money	Taschengeld
privilege ['prɪvɪlɪdʒ]	Sonderrecht, Privileg
to live up to s.o.'s expectations [ˌekspek'teɪʃnz]	jds. Erwartungen gerecht werden
to *put s.o. under pressure ['preʃə]	jdn. unter Druck setzen
to care about s.o.	hier: sich um jdn. sorgen, jdn. lieben
to *be responsible [rɪ'spɒnsɪbl] (for s.o./s.th.)	verantwortlich (für jdn./etwas) sein
to look after oneself	selbst auf sich aufpassen
to trust s.o. → trust	jdm. vertrauen Vertrauen

101

8 Exercises

a) Who is it?

1. Your mother's brother is your _____.
2. Your father's mother is your _____.
3. Your brother's daughter is your _____.
4. Your sister's husband is your _____.
5. Your mother's parents are your _____.
6. If your mother marries again, her husband will be your _____.
7. Someone without any brothers and sisters is an _____.
8. The woman a man marries is his _____.

b) Which word goes with which expression?

1. Smoking? Why don't you give it _____?
2. I can't do _____ my cup of tea!
3. I'm crazy _____ this girl I've met!
4. It was love _____ first sight.
5. What do you spend your money _____?
6. My parents blame me _____ everything!
7. I'm very fond _____ my grandpa.
8. We're old enough to look _____ ourselves!
9. Dad doesn't approve _____ my new boyfriend.
10. Guess who Kim's going out _____!
11. She's fallen in love _____ your brother.
12. I can't live up _____ Mum's expectations.
13. You ought to talk things _____ with Dad.
14. I hate it when people laugh _____ me.

about
after
at
at
for
on
of
of
over
to
up
with
with
without

Exercises

c) Translate the adjectives in the box below, then put them in the correct place in the grid. To help you, one letter is given for each adjective.

> *betrunken egoistisch eifersüchtig gemein geschieden getrennt lächerlich niedergeschlagen schädlich schwanger selbständig ungeduldig verantwortungslos verlegen*

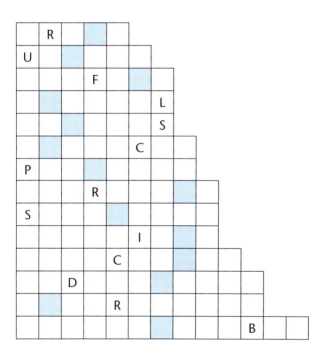

If you put the letters in the blue squares into the right order, you'll find another expression from this chapter. It describes a certain part of a public place (e.g. a café or restaurant):

_ _ _ - _ _ _ _ _ _ _ _ _ _ _

Young people's interests

1 The generation gap – does it still exist?

Last week we asked for your comments on the generation gap and said that we would publish the best 'father/son' and 'mother/daughter' letters in our next issue. Here are our choices:

FATHER'S VIEW:

There have always been differences between the generations, and I expect there always will be! My son says I don't understand him. My father didn't understand me, either! He had done very different things in his spare time 'when he was a boy' – but his interests and hobbies held no attraction for me: collecting stamps, cycling, hiking through the countryside, even dancing!

My generation's ideas of leisure activities were things like hitch-hiking to Turkey and back, journeys to Spain or touring around North Africa in our summer holidays (student hostels, of course: camping was something for the boy scouts of my father's generation). We went to parties and discos. I went bowling every Friday night with a few friends. During the summer we went on trips to open-air concerts or pop festivals. We got to know other young people that way. We also did a lot more sport at school than today's kids! A lot of them these days hardly get any exercise at all!

SON'S OPINION:

When my father talks about sport he means team games like soccer, rugby, cricket, hockey and, of course, athletics. My generation thinks more of individual pursuits like windsurfing, skateboarding and hang-gliding. One or two of the people I know are even into extreme sports like white-water rafting or bungee jumping. They get their thrills from the risks involved. The more energetic of Dad's friends would have joined tennis or squash clubs in his day!

Young people's interests 9

generation [ˌdʒenəˈreɪʃn] gap	Generationskonflikt
→ gap	Lücke
spare time	Freizeit
interest	Interesse
→ to *be interested in s.th.	sich für etwas interessieren
attraction [əˈtrækʃn]	Anziehungskraft, Attraktion
collecting stamps	Briefmarkensammeln
cycling → to cycle	Radfahren Rad fahren
hiking [ˈhaɪkɪŋ] → to hike	Wandern wandern
countryside	Landschaft
dancing → to dance	Tanzen tanzen
leisure [ˈleʒə] activity	Freizeitaktivität
hitch-hiking → to hitch-hike	Trampen per Anhalter fahren
journey	Reise
to tour [tʊə] around (a country)	(in einem Land) herumreisen
camping	Zelten
boy scout [skaʊt] → girl guide	Pfadfinder Pfadfinderin
bowling [əʊ] → bowling alley	Bowling, Kegeln Kegelbahn
trip	Ausflug, Reise
open-air concert	Freiluftkonzert
pop festival	Popmusik-Fest
to *get to know s.o.	jdn. kennen lernen
exercise	*hier:* Bewegung
team game	Mannschaftsspiel
soccer [ˈsɒkə] (Association football)	Fußball
rugby [ʌ]	Rugby
cricket [ˈkrɪkɪt]	Kricket
athletics [æθˈletɪks]	Leichtathletik
pursuit [pəˈsjuːt]	Beschäftigung, Aktivität
windsurfing	Windsurfen
skateboarding	Skateboardfahren
hang-gliding	Drachenfliegen
to *be into s.th.	auf etwas „stehen", an etwas (als Hobby) sehr interessiert sein
extreme sports	Extremsport(arten)
white-water rafting	Wildwasserflößen/-rafting
bungee [ˈbʌndʒɪ] jumping	Bungeespringen
thrill	Nervenkitzel
risk → to risk s.th.	Risiko etwas riskieren
energetic [ˌenəˈdʒetɪk]	aktiv, energiegeladen
to join a club	Mitglied eines Clubs werden
squash [skwɒʃ]	Squash

9 Young people's interests

MOTHER …

When I was younger I loved the **theatre**, and **took part** in a lot of **amateur productions** and **performances** of sometimes quite avant-garde **plays**. Some of these were **performed** with the help of the school **orchestra** on the school **stage**. And of course they were for an **audience** of parents or friends who did not criticize our **acting**. As for music, we thought we were really '**with it**' when we were young!

When I was a girl, I was not much good at **outdoor sports**, but I loved dancing. I wanted to take **ballet** lessons, too, but my parents decided that I should learn something more 'useful'. So I **enrolled** in a **judo course** at the local sports club. I enjoyed it, but I never got as far as **gaining** my **black belt**. Courses in **self-defence** for young women were **all the rage** when I was a girl, and they still are, I suppose. Nowadays they call this sort of thing **martial arts**, but it doesn't seem very artistic to me! I still wish I'd taken ballet lessons.

… AND DAUGHTER

I sometimes go to the theatre with Mum and Dad, but I prefer going to the **cinema**. Today's teenagers seem to be a bit more **musical** than their parents. I've been having piano lessons for five years now, which I really enjoy. At the moment I'm **practising** quite a difficult **piece** by Schubert. I also play the guitar. I'm even in the school rock band. Not so many people of my parents' generation seem to **play an instrument** or **make their own music** nowadays. I listen to music on my MP3 player all the time – except at school, of course!

Sports and games? Well, we play hockey at school, but, to be honest, I'm not much into team games. Last winter I went on a school trip to Austria to do winter sports. We did a bit of **skiing** and **snowboarding** but I wasn't very good at it! I think I'll **stick to** summer outdoor sports like swimming and **surfing.** I did a lot of that on holiday in Cornwall last summer. One of my friends at school is a member of a **diving** club in our town. I'm not so keen on diving, but I did a bit of **snorkelling** when we were in Greece last summer..

Apart from that, there are plenty of indoor activities for girls (and boys!) at school or at our local **leisure centre**. Quite a few of my friends are into **line dancing** or **tap dancing**, and even some of the mothers go!

Young people's interests 9

theatre [ˈθɪətə]	Theater
to *take part (in s.th.)	(an etwas) teilnehmen
amateur [ˈæmətə]	Amateur(in); Amateur-, Hobby-
production	Inszenierung
→ to produce a play	ein Stück inszenieren
performance	Aufführung
play	(Theater-)Stück
to perform s.th.	etwas aufführen
orchestra [ˈɔːkɪstrə]	Orchester
stage	Bühne
audience [ˈɔːdɪəns]	Publikum, Zuschauer
acting	Schauspielerei; *hier:* schauspielerische Leistung
→ to act	*hier:* in einem Stück spielen
to *be 'with it' *(slang)*	voll im Trend sein
outdoor sports ↔ indoor sports	Freiluftsport(arten) Hallensport
ballet [ˈbæleɪ]	Ballet
to enrol [ɪnˈrəʊl]	sich einschreiben lassen
judo [ˈdʒuːdəʊ]	Judo
course	Kurs
to gain s.th.	etwas erreichen/erhalten/gewinnen
black belt	schwarzer Gürtel (Auszeichnung)
self-defence	Selbstverteidigung
→ to defend o.s.	sich verteidigen
all the rage	sehr beliebt, „total in"
martial [ˈmɑːʃl] arts	Kampfsportarten
cinema [ˈsɪnəmə]	Kino
musical [ˈmjuːzɪkl]	musikalisch
to practise (s.th.) → practice	(etwas) üben Übung, Training
piece (of music)	(Musik-)Stück
to play an instrument [ˈ---]	ein Instrument spielen
to *make music	Musik machen
→ musician [mjuːˈzɪʃn]	Musiker(in)
skiing → to ski	Skifahren Ski fahren
snowboarding → snowboard	Snowboarding Snowboard
to *stick to s.th.	bei etwas bleiben
surfing → sufboard	Surfen, Wellenreiten Surfbrett
diving	Tauchen; Kunstspringen
→ to dive	tauchen; einen Kopfsprung machen
snorkelling → snorkel	Schnorcheln Schnorchel
leisure [ˈleʒə] centre	Freizeitzentrum
line dancing	Line-Tanz(en)
tap dancing	Stepptanz

Young people's interests

2 Don't just stand there – join your local leisure centre!

Are you an active sportsman or sportswoman?

Would you just like to get fit and stay fit?

Or are you more interested in meeting old friends or making new ones?

Why not join your local leisure centre? Our leisure centre is more than just a swimming pool, a couple of squash courts and a gym for working out.

We offer a wide range of indoor and outdoor games and sports: from badminton, basketball, boxing, football, judo, tennis, volleyball to mountaineering and rock-climbing. Or what about learning to sail?

Our athletics teams regularly take part in competitions. And our athletes have won many individual prizes. Perhaps you are interested in American games? We can even offer beginners' courses in American football and baseball.

Our experienced coaches and instructors will show you how to get the most out of your kind of sport. We also organize visits to sports facilities which we do not have here for members who want to go ice-skating at the local ice-rink, or who are interested in skiing or doing water sports like scuba-diving, sailing, rowing and canoeing. But we believe that amateur sport should be more than a challenge, it should be fun. Our teams play to win, but they play fair. If we lose a match or do badly in a tournament, we blame ourselves, not the referee or the umpire.

But it's not all sport. Our leisure centre organizes other activities: theatre or cinema visits, and bridge or whist parties for people who enjoy playing cards; painting and drawing courses for all age groups; keep fit sessions for everybody.

Young people's interests 9

sportsman, sportswoman	Sportler(in)
to *meet friends	sich mit Freunden treffen
to *make friends	Freundschaften schließen
gym [dʒɪm]	Turnhalle; *hier:* Fitnessraum/-studio
to work out	(an Geräten) trainieren
mountaineering [--'--]	Bergsteigen
rock-climbing	Klettern
to *learn to do s.th.	lernen, etwas zu tun
to sail → sailing	segeln Segeln
team	Mannschaft
competition	Wettbewerb
→ to compete (in s.th.)	teilnehmen (an etwas)
athlete ['æθliːt]	Leichtathlet(in)
prize [praɪz]	Preis *(Gewinn)*
experienced → experience	erfahren Erfahrung; Erlebnis
coach	Coach, Trainer(in)
→ to coach s.o.	jdn trainieren
instructor	Lehrer(in)
facilities [-'---]	Einrichtungen
ice-skating	Eislaufen, Schlittschuhlaufen
ice-rink	Eisbahn, Schlittschuhbahn
water sports	Wassersport(arten)
scuba-diving ['skuːbəˌdaɪvɪŋ]	Sporttauchen
rowing ['rəʊɪŋ] → to row	Rudern rudern
canoeing [kə'nuːɪŋ]	Kanufahren
challenge	Herausforderung
to *be fun	Spaß machen
to *win	gewinnen
to play fair	fair spielen
to *lose (s.th.)	(etwas) verlieren
match	Spiel, Match
tournament	Turnier
referee [ˌrefə'riː] *(football, rugby)*	Schiedsrichter(in)
umpire ['ʌmpaɪə] *(tennis, cricket)*	Schiedsrichter(in)
bridge/whist	Bridge-/Whistspiel *(Kartenspiele)*
to play cards	Karten spielen
to paint (s.th.)	(etwas) malen
to *draw (s.th.)	(etwas) zeichnen
to *keep fit = to stay fit	fit bleiben, sich fit halten
session	Stunde, „Sitzung"

9 Exercises

a) Choose the right word to complete each of the following sentences.

1. "Soccer is my favourite ….
   - ☐ sport ☐ match ☐ play
2. There's a big … on TV tonight: Manchester United versus Arsenal." – "Are you going to watch it?" –
   - ☐ play ☐ match ☐ sport
3. "No. Worst luck! I've got to go to the school … tonight! –
   - ☐ piece ☐ play ☐ game
4. My sister's … in it." –
   - ☐ produced ☐ acting ☐ performed
5. "I'll see you there! I'll be in the …, too! My brother's in it." –
   - ☐ cinema ☐ stage ☐ audience
6. "I didn't know that. I hope it's a good …. Last year's was terrible!"
   - ☐ acting ☐ performance ☐ theatre

b) Put a suitable word into the sentences below. Sometimes we have given the first letter of the word you need.

1. "What do you do in your _s_____ time?" –

2. "That depends. At the weekends we often get our bikes out and go _____." –

3. "We?" – "I _____ some friends outside the Leisure Centre on Sundays if the weather's good.

4. We ride right out of town into the _c_____. Sometimes we ride 30 or 40 kilometres. Why don't you come with us?" –

5. "That sounds a bit too _e_____ for me!" –

6. "A bit of exercise helps you to keep _____ !" –

7. "I get enough exercise walking to school, thanks! What do you do if it's raining?" – "Well, there are plenty of indoor _l_____ activities at the Centre:

8. Swimming, table-tennis, squash, …. You can take _____ in all kinds of group activities. You're not really a sporty type, are you?"

Exercises 9

9. "Well, I prefer indoor games, actually. But last week I

   _____ a club." –

10. "Wow! What sort of club?" – "I like playing _____ so I

    became a member of the bridge club."

c) Phil is writing to his Russian pen-friend Tania about his hobbies and interests, but when Tania tries to read his e-mail, she finds that her computer conversion program has made a 'salad' of some of the words. Can you help her? Write the correct spelling of the words in the box on the right.

Dear Tania,

Thank you for your e-mail. You ask me about my hobbies and interests. Well, we do a lot of sport at school: *bygru* in winter and *selthicat* in summer as well as our national game *tercick*, but I wear glasses, so I'm not very good at that!

_____

_____

_____

I like pop music, of course. Last week I went to an *epno-rai* concert in the park here. It was great! Most of my friends were in the concert. It was near Birmingham, so that meant it was quite a long *renyouj* from here. Do you have a video or DVD player? Or do you go to the *acenim* sometimes? You tell me that you love the outdoor life and that you went *gipnamc* in the holidays. My friends and I are going on a *ript* to the seaside next weekend. I want to learn to *lasi*. The father of a friend of mine is an *ortcrustni* at a leisure centre near Brighton. There's a *ruceso* for beginners there next weekend. It's a big centre, so they have all the *seitaclifi* that we need. I'm not a great swimmer, so this will be a bit of a *legnalech* for me!

_____

_____

_____

_____

_____

_____

_____

_____

_____

I also like painting and *gwinrad*. My art teacher thinks I'm quite good. I sent one of my pictures in to an art *notemiptoic* last month, but I don't expect to win a prize!

_____

_____

Please write again soon!

Phil

111

The world of work

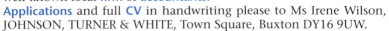

1 Situations vacant

Experienced SECRETARY needed for well-known local **firm** of **accountants**. **Applications** and full **CV** in handwriting please to Ms Irene Wilson, JOHNSON, TURNER & WHITE, Town Square, Buxton DY16 9UW.

SMITH'S BOOKSHOP
has a **vacancy** for an intelligent **shop assistant**. Full **on-the-job training** and good **working conditions**. Phone 01766 830208 and ask for Doug.

NO **SUCCESS** WITH JOB APPLICATONS?
Have you tried your local **JOBCENTRE**? We have all the latest job **offers**. Our **careers service** can help even people with few **qualifications**. Or why not get your qualifications through our **vocational courses**? To find your local office and arrange a personal **interview** with one of our **careers officers**, visit our website at www.jobcentreplus.gov.uk.

WANTED **gardener** and **painter and decorator** for small hotel: Ring (01873) 859 801.

Share in our success.
Are you under 20 and tired of working on an **assembly line**?
We still have two vacancies for **skilled workers** in our newly-opened **factory**. **Previous** experience in **engineering** an **advantage**. Box 2296.

Interested in money?
The Royal Bank of Scotland is looking for young people who would like to **train for** a **career** in **banking**. **Earn good money** while you learn about the world of **finance**. You will find a pleasant atmosphere and friendly **colleagues** at our banks. Ask the **manager** of any RBS **branch** for full details, or visit the careers page on our website:
www.rbs.com/careers.

THIRD-WORLD AID
Our organization needs teachers, **doctors**, **nurses** and **technicians** who want to work in a developing country for at least a year. All **applicants** should be under 30. Ring Jill Adams on (01256) 167097 for details.

The world of work   10

situations vacant ['veɪkənt]	Stellenangebote, freie Stellen,
→ situation	*hier:* Stelle
experienced	erfahren
→ to *have experience	Erfahrung haben
secretary ['sekrətrɪ]	Sekretär(in)
firm	Firma
accountant [əˈkaʊntənt]	Buchprüfer(in) und Steuerberater(in)
application	Bewerbung
CV [siːˈviː] (= curriculum vitae)	Lebenslauf
[kəˈrɪkjʊləm ˈviːtaɪ]	
vacancy ['veɪkənsɪ]	freie Stelle
shop assistant	Verkäufer(in)
on-the-job training	Ausbildung am Arbeitsplatz
working conditions	Arbeitsbedingungen
success	Erfolg
→ to succeed	Erfolg haben
→ successful ↔ unsuccessful	erfolgreich erfolglos
jobcentre	Arbeitsamt
offer → to offer s.th. (to s.o.)	Angebot (jdm.) etwas anbieten
careers [kəˈrɪəz] **service**	Berufsberatung des Jobcentre
qualification [ˌkwɒlɪfɪˈkeɪʃn]	Qualifikation
→ qualifications	(Schul-)Abschluss
vocational [vəʊˈkeɪʃənl] **course**	berufliches Ausbildungsprogramm
interview ['ɪntəvjuː]	Vorstellungsgespräch,
	hier: (Beratungs-)Gespräch
careers [kəˈrɪəz] **officer**	Berufsberater(in)
gardener	Gärtner(in)
painter and decorator	Maler(in) und Innendekorateur(in)
to share in s.th.	*hier:* an etwas teilnehmen
assembly [əˈsemblɪ] **line**	Fließband
skilled worker ↔ **unskilled worker**	Facharbeiter(in) Hilfsarbeiter(in)
factory	Fabrik
previous ['priːvjəs]	vorherige(r/s)
engineering [ˌendʒɪˈnɪərɪŋ]	Maschinenbau
advantage ↔ **disadvantage**	Vorteil Nachteil
to train for s.th.	sich für etwas ausbilden lassen
career [kəˈrɪə]	Laufbahn, Karriere, Beruf
banking	Bankwesen
to earn (good) money	(gut) Geld verdienen
finance ['faɪnæns]	Finanzwesen
colleague ['kɒliːg]	Kollege, Kollegin
(bank) manager	Filialleiter(in) (einer Bank)
branch [brɑːnʃ]	Filiale, Zweigstelle
doctor	Arzt
nurse [nɜːs] → male nurse	Krankenschwester Krankenpfleger
technician [tekˈnɪʃn]	Techniker(in)
applicant ['æplɪkənt]	Bewerber(in)

The world of work

2 Finding a job

Finding any job is difficult today. It is also important to find the right job. Some young people enjoy talking to people, answering the phone, listening to people's problems. Some are happier working in an office, **typing** letters, working with cars or machines, **installing** or **repairing equipment**. Others become nurses or **veterinary nurses** because they want to help people or animals. There are plenty of jobs for **social workers** who would like to look after old people, children or **the disabled**.

You need certain **skills** for most jobs, but these skills are not always so specialized. A nurse or **hairdresser** should be able to **get on with** people. A painter and decorator needs more **creativity** than a bus driver or a taxi driver, but a taxi driver needs a better memory. A **builder** must be **handy with tools** but he or she does not need to have the same reading and writing skills as a **civil servant**, a **translator** or an **interpreter**.

People in some jobs need A-Levels or higher qualifications: doctors, **dentists** and **vets** of course, but also **pilots**, **editors** and so on.

Most beginners in any job will need to **follow instructions**. Many **manual workers** have to work **outdoors** in all weathers, but a surprising number of 'indoor' jobs include some outdoor work. So the first question you should ask yourself is: Do I like working indoors or outdoors? Then look at the jobs in the lists below.

Indoors	**Outdoors**
Baker	**Bricklayer**
Clerk	**Farmer**
Electrician	**Firefighter**
Flight attendant	**Fisherman**
Journalist/Reporter	Gardener
Mechanic	**Police officer**
Plumber	**Postman/Postwoman**
Programmer	**Sailor**
Receptionist	**Soldier**
Travel agent	**Traffic warden**

The world of work 10

to type [taɪp] (s.th.) — (etwas) tippen, maschineschreiben
to install [ɔː] s.th. — etwas installieren
to repair s.th. — etwas reparieren
equipment [ɪˈkwɪpmənt] — Ausrüstung, Geräte, Gerätschaften
⚠ *(singular only)*
veterinary [ˈvetərɪnərɪ] nurse — Tierarzthelfer(in)
social worker — Sozialarbeiter(in)
the disabled — Behinderte (als Gruppe)
→ disabled — behindert

skill — Fertigkeit
→ skilled — ausgebildet, qualifiziert; geschickt
hairdresser — Friseur, Friseuse
to *get on with s.o. — mit jdm. gut auskommen
creativity [--'---] — Kreativität, schöpferische Phantasie
to create s.th. — etwas erschaffen/kreieren
builder — Bauarbeiter(in)
handy with tools → tool — handwerklich geschickt   Werkzeug
civil [ˈsɪvl] servant — Beamter, Beamtin
translator → to translate s.th. — Übersetzer(in)   etwas übersetzen
interpreter → to interpret — Dolmetscher(in)   dolmetschen

dentist — Zahnarzt/-ärztin
vet — Tierarzt/-ärztin
pilot [ˈpaɪlət] — Pilot(in)
editor [ˈedɪtə] — Redakteur(in)

to follow instructions — Anweisungen befolgen
manual [ˈ---] worker — körperlich Arbeitende(r)
outdoors ↔ indoors — im Freien, draußen   drinnen

baker — Bäcker(in)
clerk [klɑːk] — Büroangestellte(r)
electrician [--ˈ--] — Elektriker(in)
flight attendant — Flugbegleiter(in)
journalist, reporter — Journalist(in), Reporter(in)
mechanic [mɪˈkænɪk] — KFZ-Mechaniker(in)
plumber [ˈplʌmə] — Klempner(in), Installateur(in)
programmer — Programmierer(in)
receptionist — Empfangsdame/-herr
travel agent — Reisebüroangestellte(r)

bricklayer — Maurer
farmer — Bauer/Bäuerin, Landwirt(in)
firefighter — Feuerwehrmann/-frau
fisherman — Fischer
police officer — Polizist(in)
postman/postwoman — Postbote/-botin, Briefträger(in)
sailor — Seemann (Männer u. Frauen)
soldier — Soldat(in)
traffic warden — Verkehrspolizist(in), Politesse

3 A talk with the school careers teacher

Ms. Hart: Come in, Adrian … Let me see: you're interested in a career in banking

Adrian: That's right, Ms. Hart.

Ms. Hart: **Employers** – especially banks – like their **employees** to have good **GCSE** marks in English and Maths, which should not be a problem for you, Adrian! Now, if you want to start after the summer holidays, you should **apply for a traineeship** now. I saw an **advertisement** in the *Chronicle* yesterday. HSBC is looking for **trainees**. The **trial period** is usually six months, so you'll have plenty of time to find out if you like the job – and if the job likes you. Your **income** wouldn't be very high to start with – the **salary** for a trainee **bank clerk** is about £9,500 a year …

Adrian: Oh …

Ms. Hart: … but you **get a rise** regularly – banks usually **increase** their employees' **wages** every year. And the chances of **promotion** are quite good, too. The **brightest** people are often **promoted** to branch manager while they're still in their thirties.

Adrian: I'm only sixteen …

Ms. Hart: I know, Adrian. But banking is a **profession**, and **professional people** have to **think ahead**. Why are you specially interested in banking?

Adrian: Well, it's a **steady job** with good **prospects** – you don't often hear of bank clerks **on the dole**.

Ms. Hart: That's true. But most banks are open on Saturdays nowadays. Banking is one of the few **office jobs** where you might have to work at the weekend! But you only have a seven-hour **working day** and you get one **afternoon off** during the week. And you don't have to do **overtime** or **shift work**. You should write your **letter of application** right away, Adrian. I think you've already got a CV.

Adrian: That's right, Ms. Hart. We did one as part of our computer training last year. I'll just have to **update** it a bit!

The world of work 10

careers [kəˈrɪəz] teacher	Lehrer(in), der/die für die Berufsberatung zuständig ist
employer [-ˈ--]	Arbeitgeber(in)
→ to employ s.o.	jdn. beschäftigen
employee [--ˈ-]	Arbeitnehmer(in)
GCSE (General Certificate of Secondary Education)	Abschlussprüfung für 16-Jährige (etwa: Mittlere Reife)
to apply for a traineeship [-ˈ--]/job	sich um eine Ausbildungsstelle/Stelle bewerben
advertisement [ədˈvɜːtɪsmənt]	Anzeige
trainee [-ˈ-]	Auszubildende(r), Azubi
trial [ˈtraɪəl] period	Probezeit
income [ˈɪnkʌm]	Einkommen
salary [ˈ---]	(monatliches) Gehalt
bank clerk	Bankangestellte(r)
to *get a rise	eine Gehaltserhöhung bekommen
to increase [-ˈ-] s.th.	etwas erhöhen
→ to increase	sich erhöhen
wages ⚠ (plural)	(Wochen-)Lohn
promotion [-ˈ--]	Beförderung
bright	intelligent, „hell"
to promote s.o. (to s.th.)	jdn. (zu etwas) befördern
profession	Beruf, der eine höhere Ausbildung erfordert
professional people	Menschen mit qualifiziertem Beruf
to *think ahead	an die Zukunft denken
a steady job	ein sicherer Arbeitsplatz
prospects	Aussichten
on the dole (slang)	arbeitslos
= unemployed	
→ the dole	das Arbeitslosengeld
office job	Büroarbeit
working day	Arbeitstag
an afternoon/a morning off	ein freier Nach-/Vormittag
to *do overtime	Überstunden machen
shift work	Schichtarbeit
letter of application	Bewerbung(sschreiben)
to update [-ˈ-] s.th.	etwas auf den neuesten Stand bringen

> A school-leaver was being interviewed for a job.
> "You'll get fifty pounds a week to begin with," said the manager, "and then after six months you'll get seventy pounds a week." "Fine," said the school-leaver. "I'll come back in six months!"

10 The world of work

4 A letter of application

> 36 Walmsley Grove
> Urmston
> Manchester M21 6PE
>
> WILSON ENGINEERING **Co. Ltd.**
> **Personnel Dept.**
> Flag Lane
> Crewe ST6 9UW
>
> 16th April 2006
>
> **Re**: Your advertisement offering engineering **apprenticeships**
>
> Dear Sir/Madam,
>
> I am 16 years old and left school last year with 3 GCSE passes (English, Maths and Technical Drawing). I would like to apply for one of your engineering apprenticeships.
>
> As there were no vacancies for engineering **apprentices** in my area at the time, I tried to find a **full-time job** in a local firm. But as **unemployment** is high in our part of Manchester, and I was unable to find anything, I decided to go to **technical college**. I also took a **part-time job** (evenings only) at a small toy factory to get some **work experience** and to improve my **technical ability**.
>
> Please let me know whether you are able to consider me for an apprenticeship. I can send the usual **references** and am **enclosing** my CV and a **photocopy** of my GCSE **certificate**. I am also sending you a copy of a short article from our local paper about the factory where I am working at the moment.
>
> Yours faithfully,
>
>   Patricia Andrews

VERY SPECIAL FACTORY – **Self-help** project in Urmston

This toy factory in Urmston is **run** by **unemployed** people from the area. Most of them are skilled workers who were **made redundant** when a big local toy factory **closed down** after a long **strike** last year.
Workers **went on strike** for better working conditions (the firm **had a reputation for firing** members of the **trade unions**).
Some of the people **doing voluntary work** at this small self-help factory have been **out of work** and on **unemployment benefit** for long periods. The **manager** is Mr Joe Collins, who **retired** from the old company last year.

The world of work

Co. (= Company) ['kʌmpəni]	Firma, Gesellschaft
Ltd. (= Limited)	GmbH
personnel [,--'-] dept. (= department)	Personalabteilung
re: [riː]	Betr.:, bezüglich:
apprenticeship [ə'prentɪsʃɪp]	Lehre
apprentice	Lehrling
full-time job	Vollzeitbeschäftigung
unemployment	Arbeitslosigkeit
technical college ['---,--]	technische Fachhochschule
part-time job	Teilzeitstelle
work experience	Arbeitserfahrung; Praktikum
technical ability	technisches Können
reference ['---]	*hier:* Empfehlung
to enclose [ɪn'kləʊz] s.th.	etwas beilegen
photocopy ['--,--]	Fotokopie
certificate [sə'tɪfɪkət]	Prüfungszeugnis
self-help	Selbsthilfe
to *run a firm	eine Firma leiten
unemployed	arbeitslos
to *be made redundant [-'--]	den Arbeitsplatz verlieren, arbeitslos werden
to close down	schließen *(Werk, Fabrik)*
strike	Streik
to *go on strike = to strike	streiken
to *have a reputation for s.th.	bekannt für etwas sein
→ reputation	Ruf
to fire s.o.	jdn. feuern
trade union ['juːnjən]	Gewerkschaft
to *do voluntary ['vɒləntrɪ] work	ehrenamtlich tätig sein
→ voluntary	freiwillig
to *be out of work	arbeitslos sein
= to *be unemployed	
to *be on unemployment benefit	Arbeitslosengeld beziehen
manager	Geschäftsführer(in)
to retire	sich zur Ruhe setzen, in Rente gehen
→ retired	pensioniert

> "How many people work in this office?"
> "About half of them."

Exercises

10

a) Write your own CV. First put the letters of the *words in bold italics* in the right order.

Mucilurcru Evita	
Name:	
Date of birth:	_____ 19___
Education and *gritinan*:	Primary school:
	Secondary school:
Krow iceperexen:	Last year I worked
Scoinifaqulati:	Mittlere Reife
Languages:	German,
Interests:	Music,
Efernecers:	

b) Here are ten definitions of new words introduced in this chapter. Write the word on the line beside the definition. Sometimes there is more than one correct answer.

1. The science of machines: _____

2. Person who runs a firm, shop, etc.: _____

3. Young person who is learning a job: _____

4. The money that employees get for their work: _____

5. Not having a job: _____

Exercises 10

6. To put inside an envelope with a letter: _to_ _____

7. He or she books holidays for you: _____ _____

8. To lose your job: _to be made_ _____

9. A building where goods are produced: _____

10. Person who works at the same place as you: _____

c) **Look-alikes. You need one of the pairs of words in the box to complete the sentences below, but be careful to choose the right one!**

> appliance – application   assistant – attendant
> brunch – branch   carrier – career
> employer – employee   personal – personnel
> programme – programmer   receiver – receptionist
> reputation – repetition   tip – type

"I see from your _____ that you are interested in a _____ as a computer _____. Your previous _____ has given you a good reference. Where did you work before that?"

"After I left school I didn't know what I really wanted to do. At first I worked as a shop _____ for a few months. Then I worked at a hotel as a _____ during the summer. But the hotel had a bad _____ , so I left."

"How about computer skills? Can you _____ fast?"

"Yes. I spent a few months working in the _____ department at the local _____ of a big international company. We were using computers all the time."

Technology

Technology

1 Teenagers' views on modern technology

The magazine "Teen Scene" recently asked its readers for their views on technology in the modern world. Here are two opinions:

A positive view

Modern technology is a wonderful thing! We have lots of **electric** and **electronic devices** at home. They make life easier for my parents and more pleasant for me. When Dad bought himself the latest **CD player** and **digital radio**, he gave my little sister the old **hi-fi** from the living-room – it's only four years old – to use in her bedroom. As well as our **video recorder** we now also have a **DVD player** and a big new **flatscreen** TV with **surround sound**. Fantastic!

In the kitchen, as well as the usual **stove, dishwasher, fridge** and **washing machine**, we also have a **microwave oven**, of course. I often use it to make myself something hot to eat when I come home from school before Mum gets back from work. We have plenty of **instant meals** in our big new **freezer**.

Technological progress is so fast nowadays that my Dad says he needs a new computer, so I can have his old one and my younger sister can have mine. She has been asking for a computer of her own for ages, and she's only ten! That's progress!

A less positive view

I'm not so sure that modern technology is such a wonderful thing. After school I spend a couple of hours a day in front of my **computer monitor**. It is well known that such **equipment** – and even an ordinary TV **screen** – **emits** dangerous **radiation**. A lot of new household **gadgets** use **laser** technology, and direct contact with laser **beams** is a known **health risk**. At home, we have a **cordless telephone**, which is very **handy** but, like my **mobile phone**, it also makes use of **wireless waves** about which far too little is known. Some people think that mobiles can even cause **brain tumours**!

And then there is the cost. Almost everything in the modern home – all **household appliances** and even the water pump on our **central heating** system – depends on **electricity**. Our electricity bill arrived yesterday and Dad nearly had a heart attack!

Technology

technology [-'---] | Technologie, Technik
electric [ɪ'lektrɪk] | elektrisch
electronic [ˌɪlek'trɒnɪk] | elektronisch
device [dɪ'vaɪs] | Gerät, Apparat, Vorrichtung
CD player | CD-Spieler
digital ['dɪdʒɪtl] **radio** | Digitalradio
hi-fi ['haɪfaɪ] | Hi-Fi-Anlage
video recorder | Video(aufnahme)gerät
DVD [ˌdiːˌviːˈdiː] **player** | DVD-Spieler
flatscreen | Flachbildschirm
surround sound | Raumklang

stove | Herd
dishwasher | Spülmaschine
fridge = refrigerator | Kühlschrank
washing machine | Waschmaschine
microwave oven ['ʌvn] | Mikrowellenherd
instant ['ɪnstənt] **meal** | Fertiggericht
→ instant coffee | Pulverkaffee
freezer | Tiefkühltruhe, Gefrierschrank

technological [ˌteknə'lɒdʒɪkl] | technologisch
progress ['prəʊgrəs] | Fortschritt(e)
⚠ no plural!

computer monitor | Computer-Bildschirm
equipment [ɪ'kwɪpmənt] | Ausrüstung, Ausstattung, Geräte
⚠ no plural!
→ a piece of equipment | ein Gerät
screen | Bildschirm
to emit [ɪ'mɪt] **s.th.** | etwas ausstrahlen
→ emission | Ausstrahlung, Emission
radiation [ˌreɪdɪ'eɪʃn] | Strahlung, Strahlen
→ harmful radiation | schädliche Strahlen
gadget ['gædʒɪt] | (modernes) Gerät;
 | *auch:* technische Spielerei

laser | Laser
beam | Strahl
health risk → risky | Gesundheitsrisiko   riskant
→ to risk s.th., to *take a risk | etwas riskieren
cordless telephone → cord | schnurloses Telefon   Schnur
handy ⚠ ≠ German: "Handy" | handlich, geschickt, nützlich, leicht
 | zu handhaben

mobile ['məʊbaɪl] **(phone)** *(BE)* | Handy, Mobiltelefon
= cellphone ['selfəʊn] *(AE)*
wireless wave | Radiowelle
brain tumour ['tjuːmə] | Gehirntumor

household appliance [ə'plaɪəns] | Haushaltsgerät
(central) heating | (Zentral-)Heizung
→ to heat (s.th.) → heater | (etwas) heizen/erhitzen   Heizgerät
electricity [ɪˌlek'trɪsəti] | Strom, Elektrizität

123

Technology

Electronic **waste** is already a big problem because people always want the latest gadgets. What happens to all the electronic equipment that people throw away? Surely we could **recycle** such items?

2 Two interviews for "Teen Scene"

*A reporter from "Teen Scene" also asked young people in the street what they thought about some recent technical and **scientific** developments.*

TS: Do you think that **CCTV** has made life in our big cities safer?

Julie: Yes, I always feel safer – especially late in the evening – when I see the camera and the sign: CCTV **IN OPERATION**. I think it makes criminals and terrorists think twice before they attack someone or set off bombs.

Alan: I think there is too much **surveillance** already! We've got police **speed cameras** on most of the roads into town now. Our passports are **scanned** at the checkpoints when we leave the country. The government wants to introduce **ID cards** with all kinds of **genetic** information soon. Enough is enough!

TS: When you go shopping in a supermarket, do you check whether the food you buy is **GM-free**?

Richard: GM-free? What's that?

Fiona: Free of **genetically modified organisms** – **GMOs** for short. Our biology teacher told us that GM foods could put an end to Third-World hunger. These **modifications** make crops more **resistant to disease**. But some people are worried that not enough **research** has been done into the connection between **allergies** and GMOs. I don't think we know enough about the **long-term effects** of **genetic engineering** on the human **immune system** or **the balance of nature** yet. Not enough has been done to **assess** the risks.

Richard: That's right. But if the **benefits** of GM foods are so great, it's surely worth taking the risks.

Fiona: I don't agree! But there are other **controversial** developments and **discoveries** in **medicine** that I find even more worrying. Using **stem cells** taken from embryos for new **medical** treatments, for example. The idea of **cloning**, and using technology to 'design' your baby, seems to me more frightening than whether I eat GM foods or not.

Technology 11

waste = rubbish	Müll, Schrott, Abfall
→ wastepaper basket	Papierkorb
to recycle s.th.	etwas wieder aufbereiten
scientific [ˌsaɪən'tɪfɪk]	(natur)wissenschaftlich
→ science ['saɪəns]	(Natur-)Wissenschaft
CCTV = closed-circuit television	Fernsehüberwachungsanlage
in operation	in Betrieb
→ to operate a machine	eine Maschine bedienen
surveillance [sə'veɪləns]	Überwachung
→ surveillance camera	Überwachungskamera
speed camera	Radargerät zur Geschwindigkeitsmessung
to scan s.th.	etwas einscannen/einlesen
ID (= identity) **card**	Personalausweis
genetic [dʒɪ'netɪk]	genetisch
→ gene [dʒiːn]	Gen
GM-free	frei von Gentechnik
genetically modified	gentechnisch verändert
→ to modify s.th.	etwas verändern/modifizieren
organism ['ɔːgənɪzm]	Organismus
modification [ˌmɒdɪfɪ'keɪʃn]	Veränderung, Modifikation
= change	
resistant to s.th.	resistent/immun gegen etwas
disease [dɪ'ziːz]	Krankheit
research [rɪ'sɜːtʃ] *(no plural!)*	Forschung
allergy ['ælədʒɪ]	Allergie
→ to *be allergic [ə'lɜːdʒɪk] to s.th.	gegen etwas allergisch sein
long-term	Langzeit-, langfristig
effect [ɪ'fekt]	Auswirkung
genetic engineering	Gentechnik
→ engineering [ˌendʒɪ'nɪərɪŋ]	Maschinenbau
immune [ɪ'mjuːn] **system**	Immunsystem
the balance of nature	das Gleichgewicht der Natur
to assess [ə'ses] **s.th.** = to judge s.th.	etwas einschätzen
→ assessment	Einschätzung
benefit ['benɪfɪt] = advantage	Vorteil, Nutzen
↔ disadvantage	Nachteil
controversial [--'--]	umstritten, kontrovers
discovery [dɪs'kʌvərɪ]	Entdeckung
→ to discover s.th.	etwas entdecken
medicine ['medsɪn]→	Medizin
medical	medizinisch, ärztlich
stem cell	Stammzelle
to clone s.th./s.o → clone	etwas/jdn. klonen Klon

Technology

Richard: OK, but what about the use of **DNA** technology to solve crimes even years after they've been committed? I think **breakthroughs** like that are a sign of real progress!

3 The impact of electricity on our lives

No technology has had a greater impact on human life than electricity. Try to imagine a world without it! Yet only a century ago there were still many homes without electricity. Although the electric **light bulb** had been **invented** by Thomas Alva Edison in 1876, it was not until the 1930s or later that electricity for **lighting** became **available** to most people. It was a long time before **labour-saving** electric appliances such as electric **irons**, **vacuum cleaners** and washing machines began to make the housewife's life easier. A refrigerator and, later, a freezer **contributed** to a healthier and more **convenient** lifestyle. People no longer needed to go shopping for fresh food every day. Radios and **gramophones** were followed in the 1950s by televisions. Then came video recorders, personal computers, CD players and DVD systems. The list is endless.

"That looks like an excellent idea, Mr Edison!"

The use of **batteries** and battery packs soon made some devices **portable**. The development of the **microchip** was the next step in the electronic revolution. Microchips soon made pieces of equipment much smaller. More **features** could be **integrated into** devices of the same size. PCs were followed by **laptops**. Laptops were followed by **palmtops**. Most mobile phones can now also be used as a camera, a **fax machine** and a connection to the Internet thanks to **wireless** and **infrared** technology. Strangely enough, the word 'wireless' had lost its old meaning of a 'radio' until it was used again in the context of **telecommunications** and **satellite** technology.

A life without electricity has indeed become unimaginable, as people discover when there is a **power failure**. Computers in offices **crash**, the lights in big supermarkets – many of them without windows – go out and there is chaos. Hospitals switch on their **emergency generators** and airports are forced to close down. Luckily, complete **black-outs** do not happen often in the big cities. But there are frequent **'brown-outs'** where the **demands** on the **electricity supply** are almost too great for the system. This frequently happens in the USA in hot summers, when everybody turns their **air-conditioning** on. Perhaps we should remember this before we buy our next electrical gadget.

Technology 11

DNA = deoxyribonucleic acid	DNS (Desoxyribonukleinsäure)
breakthrough ['--]	Durchbruch
impact ['--]	*hier:* Einfluss, (starke) Auswirkung
light bulb [bʌlb]	Glühbirne
to invent [ɪn'vent] s.th.	etwas erfinden
→ inventor	Erfinder(in)
→ invention	Erfindung
lighting	Beleuchtung
available	verfügbar
labour-saving	arbeitssparend
iron ['aɪən]	Bügeleisen
vacuum ['vækju:m] cleaner	Staubsauger
to contribute [kən'trɪbju:t] to s.th.	zu etwas beitragen
→ contribution [ˌkɒntrɪ'bju:ʃn]	Beitrag
convenient [kən'vi:nɪənt]	bequem, praktisch, zweckmäßig
→ modern conveniences	(moderne) Komforteinrichtungen
gramophone	Plattenspieler
battery ['bætərɪ]	Batterie
portable ['pɔ:təbl]	tragbar
microchip ['maɪkrəʊtʃɪp]	Mikrochip
feature	Eigenschaft, Besonderheit
to integrate s.th. into s.th.	etwas in etwas einbauen/integrieren
laptop	Laptop-Computer
palmtop	Palmtop-Computer
fax machine	Faxgerät
wireless	drahtlos, Funk-, Radio-
infrared	infrarot, Infrarot-
telecommunications ⚠ *(plural)* ['telɪkəˌmju:nɪ'keɪʃnz]	Telekommunikation, Fernmeldewesen
satellite ['sætəlaɪt]	Satellit
power failure ['faɪljə]	Stromausfall
→ power	Strom; Macht, Kraft
→ to fail	*hier:* ausfallen, versagen
to crash	abstürzen
emergency generator ['dʒenəreɪtə]	Notstromaggregat/-generator
black-out ['--]	Stromausfall
'brown-out' ['--]	Abschwächung der Stromversorgung
demand [dɪ'mɑ:nd]	Nachfrage, Bedarf, Beanspruchung
electricity supply [sə'plaɪ]	Stromversorgung
air-conditioning	Klimaanlage

11 Exercises

a) Match the words from the box to the definitions below.

> mobile   electricity   gadget   equipment
> research   radiation   benefit   emit
> clone   washing machine   instant   stove

1. You use this to get your clothes clean: _____
2. To give off (e.g. light, heat etc.): to _____
3. This is quite handy for phoning friends when you are not at home: _____
4. You cook your meals on this: _____
5. Another, less serious word for a small 'appliance': _____
6. Finding out more about something: _____.
7. Ready in a very short time: _____
8. To make a perfect copy of a living creature: to _____
9. The most dangerous aspect of atomic power: _____
10. The opposite of 'disadvantage': _____
11. Important source of power: _____
12. A singular word in English for a collection of technical devices: _____

Exercises

11

b) Find synonyms for the following words and give any related words (noun, adjective or verb) that you know.

Related word

1. danger   = _____   _____

2. change   = _____   _____

3. to judge = _____   _____

4. rubbish   = _____   _____

5. to warm up = _____   _____

c) Pick out the 24 words which appear in this chapter. 11 run horizontally, 5 run vertically and 8 run diagonally from top left to bottom right.

E	L	S	T	E	M	C	E	L	L	S	C	I	E	N	T	I	F	I	C
R	A	M	P	S	C	L	O	T	Y	Z	M	O	L	E	M	I	C	M	E
A	L	L	E	R	G	Y	N	T	E	O	K	I	E	A	B	E	A	M	O
P	E	P	A	M	I	N	T	L	Q	C	R	A	C	M	O	R	S	U	E
P	R	O	G	R	E	S	S	I	A	E	H	P	T	R	E	M	I	N	G
L	D	E	R	E	S	D	T	C	Q	S	Y	N	R	A	O	I	R	E	J
I	R	R	A	T	N	B	I	E	R	N	E	W	O	L	D	W	O	W	S
A	F	R	I	K	A	E	M	C	O	E	P	R	N	L	S	C	A	N	V
N	F	R	I	D	G	E	T	J	I	E	E	L	I	M	O	N	A	V	Q
C	L	A	E	R	E	G	H	I	A	N	W	N	C	R	U	G	H	I	E
E	C	A	M	E	R	A	T	S	C	O	E	M	P	L	D	S	Y	S	H
P	O	T	C	H	Z	Y	B	R	E	A	K	T	H	R	O	U	G	H	A
A	D	E	V	I	C	E	G	R	A	Y	L	I	N	G	S	N	R	U	N
D	N	S	H	R	I	A	R	G	A	W	P	W	O	N	Z	T	E	A	D
S	A	I	N	S	B	U	R	Y	S	X	D	I	S	C	O	V	E	R	Y

129

12 Lifestyle

Lifestyle

1 Are you OK?

Everybody wants to be happy. But is **happiness** still possible in our **hectic** modern **society**? Here are two opinions:

Sarah (19): Life these days is very **competitive**. There's a lot of **pressure** to do well. I suppose everyone is afraid of **failure**. You just have to work hard if you want to be **successful**. First you must have a **goal**, of course, and then do all you can to **achieve** it! Personally, I feel happiest when I'm working – so I don't mind the **stress**. It's become a **habit** now.

David (22): Nearly everyone seems to **be in a hurry**. Some people are so **busy**, they get **stressed out** because they have no time to **relax** and **enjoy life**. But you can work out an **alternative** lifestyle if you really want to. **Wealth** isn't so important to me. I don't need to fly to **exotic** countries when I **go on holiday**. A week walking in the hills near home is much more relaxing. And it's cheaper and **safer**, too! It's best to be **satisfied** with a **simple way of life**, I think. Some people are always **dreaming of** an ideal life in the **future**. But they get so **obsessed** with their dreams that they **spend** all their **time searching for** things they haven't got. So they don't notice all the **positive aspects** of what they *have* got!

2 Do you really need it?

According to statistics, 95 per cent of all British girls between 10 and 19 are **addicted to** shopping. A lot of the money they **spend** goes on **fashion** and **beauty products**.

We are all **consumers**. But what – and how much – we consume depends, more than you might think, on **advertising**.

Advertising is so much a part of our lives that we don't often stop to think what it does to us. What is the **aim** of all those **advertisements**, **special offers**, TV **commercials** and **slogans**? To sell things, of course. But it is more than that. It is also to make people buy things that they cannot **afford**. It is to **persuade** them to spend their money instead of **saving** it for more important things. It is to make them **dissatisfied** with themselves. The **message** is simple:

"All the best people have got it, so you must have it, too."

Lifestyle

lifestyle	Lebensstil
happiness	Zufriedenheit, Glück
hectic	hektisch
society [sə'saıətı]	Gesellschaft
competitive [kəm'petıtıv]	von Konkurrenzdenken geprägt
pressure ['preʃə]	Druck
failure ['feıljə]	Scheitern, Versagen, Misserfolg
successful	erfolgreich
goal [gəʊl] = aim	Ziel
to achieve s.th.	etwas erreichen/erlangen
stress → stressful	Stress stressig
habit	Gewohnheit
to *be in a hurry	es eilig haben
busy ['bızı]	beschäftigt
stressed out	total gestresst
to relax → relaxing	sich entspannen entspannend
to enjoy life	das Leben genießen
alternative [ɔːl'tɜːnətıv]	alternativ
wealth [welθ] ↔ poverty ['pɒvətı]	Reichtum, Wohlstand Armut
exotic [ıg'zɒtık]	exotisch
to *go on holiday	in Urlaub fahren
safe	sicher, gefahrlos
to *be satisfied ['---] **with s.th.**	mit etwas zufrieden sein
simple	einfach, schlicht
way of life	Lebensstil, Lebensart, Lebensweise
to *dream of s.th.	von etwas träumen
the future ↔ the past	die Zukunft die Vergangenheit
obsessed (with s.th.)	besessen (von etwas)
to *spend time	Zeit verbringen
to search for s.th.	nach etwas suchen
positive aspect	positive Seite, positiver Aspekt
addicted (to s.th.)	süchtig (nach etwas)
to *spend money (on s.th.)	Geld (für etwas) ausgeben
fashion	Mode
beauty product	Kosmetikartikel
consumer → to consume s.th.	Verbraucher(in) etwas verbrauchen
advertising ['ædvətaızıŋ]	Werbung, Reklame
aim → to aim at s.th.	Ziel, Zweck auf etwas (ab)zielen
advertisement [əd'vɜːtısmənt]	(Werbe-)Anzeige
special offer	Sonderangebot
(TV) commercial [kə'mɜːʃl]	Fernsehwerbung, Werbespot
slogan	Slogan, Werbespruch
to afford [ə'fɔːd] **s.th.**	sich etwas leisten
to persuade [pə'sweıd] **s.o. to do s.th.**	jdn. überreden, etwas zu tun
to save money	Geld sparen
dissatisfied	unzufrieden
message ['mesıdʒ]	Botschaft

131

Lifestyle

3 Women at work – and at home

The **role** of women has changed a lot over the years. Some people think it should change even more – while others **take a more traditional view**. What do you think? Answer these questions to find out!

	Yes	No	Not sure
1. Do you think it is important to give girls and boys **equal opportunities** at school – and later at work?			
2. Is it right to **bring up** children without making any **difference** between the **sexes**? (e.g. Would you give a little boy a **doll** to play with?)			
3. "It is all right for a woman with children to **work part-time**, but it should be the father's main **responsibility** to **support the family**." Is this a **sexist attitude**?			
4. "If both the man and the woman **go out to work**, the man should **do his share** of the **housework**." Do you agree?			
5. Today's cities are full of **ambitious career women**. But some people think it is unnatural for a woman to want a career or a **business** of her own. Is this just **prejudice**?			
6. "**Housekeeping** and **looking after** small children is a **full-time job**." Do you agree?			
7. Is it a **disadvantage** for young children to be **cared for** by a **child-minder** or an **au pair** instead of their mother or father?			
8. Some women don't want to **go back to work** after they have **had a baby**. Do you think that looking after the home and family can be as **fulfilling** as a paid job?			
9. A **survey** of 2,000 British schoolchildren found that 46 per cent of boys saw themselves as **leaders** – compared with only 18 per cent of girls. Should we try to **counteract** these **gender** differences?			
10. Over 90 per cent of British nurses are **female**. Over 90 per cent of top university professors and engineers are **male**. Is this because women are usually better at certain jobs – and men usually better at others?			

Lifestyle 12

role	Rolle
to *take a traditional [-'---] view [vjuː]	eine konservative Ansicht haben
equal ['iːkwəl] → equality [-'---] opportunity [ˌɒpə'tjuːnəti]	gleich Gleichheit Möglichkeit, Chance
to *bring s.o. up	jdn. großziehen/aufziehen
difference	Unterschied, Unterscheidung
the sexes	die Geschlechter
doll [dɒl]	Puppe
to work part-time	Teilzeit arbeiten
↔ to work full-time	Vollzeit arbeiten
responsibility	Verantwortung, Pflicht
to support the family	die Familie unterhalten/ernähren
sexist	männer-/frauenfeindlich, sexistisch
attitude	Einstellung, Haltung
to *go out to work	arbeiten gehen
to *do one's share of s.th.	seinen Anteil an etwas machen
→ to share s.th.	etwas teilen
housework	Hausarbeit
ambitious [æm'bɪʃəs]	ehrgeizig
career [kə'rɪə] woman	Karrierefrau
→ career	Karriere, Beruf
business ['bɪznɪs]	Geschäft, Betrieb
prejudice ['predʒədɪs]	Vorurteil, Voreingenommenheit
housekeeping	Haushaltsführung
to look after s.o.	sich um jdn. kümmern, auf jdn. aufpassen
it's a full-time job	das kann einen rund um die Uhr beschäftigen
disadvantage ↔ advantage	Nachteil Vorteil
to care for s.o.	für jdn. sorgen
child-minder	Tagesmutter
au pair	Au-pair-Mädchen/-Junge
to *go back to work	wieder arbeiten gehen/berufstätig sein
to *have a baby	ein Kind bekommen
a fulfilling job	eine Tätigkeit, in der man Erfüllung findet
→ to fulfil s.o.	jdn. erfüllen
survey ['sɜːveɪ]	Umfrage
leader	*hier:* Führernatur
to counteract [ˌ-'-'-] s.th.	einer Sache entgegenwirken
gender ['dʒendə]	Geschlecht
female ['fiːmeɪl]	weiblich
male	männlich

133

Lifestyle

a **detached house** two **semi-detached houses** a **row** of **terraced houses** a **bungalow**

4 Housing

In Britain (and America) it is more common to have a house – or a **flat** – of your own than it is in Germany. Not so many people live in **rented accommodation**. On the other hand, although they **own** their homes, people in Britain – and the USA – **move house** more often than they do in Germany. So there are usually a lot of houses and flats **for sale**.

a **tower block**

5 I believe

In this world full of problems, a **belief** in God or a **universal spirit** helps many people to feel their lives have a **meaning**. Whether you are a **Muslim**, a **Buddhist** or a **Hindu**, a **Christian** or a **Jew**, your **religion** can make a big difference to the way you live.

Nancy (17): A lot of people I know only **go to church** if there's a **wedding**, a **christening** or a **funeral** in the family. I like the morning **service** at our church, and the lovely **hymns**, though I don't go every Sunday. I think you can **worship** God, read the **Bible** and **pray** without going to church.

Philip (18): Some of my friends are **atheists**. I'm not sure yet what I believe, so I suppose I'm an **agnostic**. The **teachings** of Christ are fine. But is there really a life after **death**? I find it hard to believe in things like **heaven** and **hell**. If God **exists**, why does he allow so much **evil** in the world he **created**?

Liz (21): People's actions are more important than what they say they believe. I wouldn't respect a person more just because he or she was a **priest** – or even the **Pope**!

Lifestyle 12

detached [dɪ'tætʃt] house	freistehendes Haus, Einzelhaus
semi-detached house	Doppelhaushälfte
row [rəʊ]	Reihe
terraced house	Reihenhaus
bungalow ['bʌŋgələʊ]	Bungalow
tower block	Hochhaus
housing ['haʊzɪŋ] ⚠ *(singular)*	Wohnungen
flat *(BE)* = apartment *(AE)*	Wohnung
→ block of flats	Wohnblock
rented accommodation ⚠ *(singular)*	Mietwohnung(en), Miethaus/-häuser
to own s.th. → owner	etwas besitzen Eigentümer(in)
to move house	umziehen
to *be for sale	zum Verkauf stehen
to believe (in s.th.)	(an etwas) glauben
belief	Glaube
universal [ˌjuːnɪ'vɜːsl]	universell, allgemein
spirit	Geist
meaning	Sinn, Bedeutung
Muslim ['mʊzlɪm]	Moslem/Moslime
Buddhist ['bʊdɪst]	Buddhist(in)
Hindu	Hindu(istin)
Christian ['krɪstʃən]	Christ(in)
→ Jesus Christ [ˌdʒiːzəs 'kraɪst]	Jesus Christus
Jew [dʒuː]	Jude/Jüdin
religion [rɪ'lɪdʒən] → religious	Religion, Glaube religiös
to *go to church	in die Kirche gehen
wedding	Hochzeit
christening ['krɪsnɪŋ]	Taufe
funeral ['fjuːnərəl]	Beerdigung
service	Gottesdienst
hymn [hɪm]	Kirchenlied
to worship ['wɜːʃɪp] God	Gott verehren/anbeten
the Bible ['baɪbl]	die Bibel
to pray [preɪ] → prayer [preə]	beten Gebet
atheist ['eɪθɪɪst]	Atheist(in)
agnostic	Agnostiker(in)
teachings ⚠ *(plural)*	Lehre
death [deθ]	(der) Tod
heaven ['hevn]	(der) Himmel
hell	(die) Hölle
to exist	existieren
evil ['iːvl] *(noun/adj.)*	Böses, Übel; böse, schlecht
to create s.th.	etwas erschaffen/schöpfen
→ creation	Schöpfung
priest [priːst]	Geistliche(r)
the Pope	der Papst

Lifestyle

John (20): Religion is OK as long as it doesn't get **fanatical**. Religious **fundamentalism** causes so many problems! And people that **belong to sects** are often very **narrow-minded**. You have to be very careful what church you **join**. And whatever religion you choose, I think you should try to stay **open to** all the others.

6 Travelling

By road

Simon: Hello, Judy. Did you have a good **journey**?

Judy: Not too bad, I suppose. But I couldn't break any **speed limits**! There was a lot of **traffic** on the **motorway**.

Simon: As usual!

Judy: There was an awful **hold-up** near Bristol. It wasn't the **rush-hour**, so I thought at first there'd been an **accident**. But one of the **lanes** was closed because of **road works**. So I left the motorway at the next **exit**.

Simon: Was it better after that?

Judy: Not much. I don't think I chose a good **route**. The **main roads** were nearly as busy as the motorway. For a long time I was behind an enormous lorry and I couldn't **overtake** because there were so many **bends**. Then there was a **diversion**. I **missed the turning** to Exeter, too. I didn't see the **sign**. And then I **went the wrong way**!

Simon: Poor you! But you got here safely in the end.

Judy: Yes, but I think I'll dream of **roundabouts** and **traffic lights** tonight. Well, at least I didn't have a **breakdown**!

Simon: I'm quite glad I haven't got a **driving licence**. Going by **public transport** is much more relaxing.

Judy: As long as your friends can **pick you up** whenever you need a **lift**, eh, Simon?

By rail: *At the station*

Clerk: Who's next in the **queue**, please?

Passenger: We are! – Two **tickets** to Newcastle, please.

Clerk: **Single** or **return**?

Passenger: Single, please. Which **platform** does the train leave from?

Clerk: Platform 4. The next train's **due** in twenty minutes. I'm afraid you've just **missed** one.

Passenger: Oh well, we'll easily **catch** the next! Is it a **through train**?

Clerk: No – **change** at York. There's a good **connection** – you only have to wait fifteen minutes.

Lifestyle 12

fanatical	fanatisch
fundamentalism [ˌ--'----]	Fundamentalismus
to belong to a sect	einer Sekte angehören
narrow-minded ↔ open-minded	engstirnig aufgeschlossen
to join s.th.	*hier:* einer Sache beitreten
to *be open to s.th.	offen für etwas sein
to travel	reisen
journey ['dʒɜːnɪ]	Reise, Fahrt
speed limit	Geschwindigkeitsbegrenzung
traffic	Verkehr
motorway	Autobahn
a hold-up ['--]	stockender Verkehr
rush-hour	Hauptverkehrszeit, Stoßzeit
accident	Unfall
lane	*hier:* Fahrspur
road works	Straßenarbeiten, Baustelle
exit	(Autobahn-)Ausfahrt
route [ruːt]	Route, Strecke
main road [-'-]	Hauptverkehrsstraße
to *overtake [--'-] (s.o.)	(jdn.) überholen
bend	Kurve
diversion [daɪ'vɜːʃn]	Umleitung
to miss a turning	eine Abzweigung verpassen
sign	(Verkehrs-)Schild
to *go the wrong way	falsch fahren, sich verfahren
roundabout ['---]	Kreisverkehr
traffic lights △ *(plural)*	Ampel
breakdown ['--]	Panne
driving licence ['laɪsəns] *(BE)*	Führerschein
= driver's license *(AE)*	
public transport △ *(singular)*	öffentliche Verkehrsmittel
to pick s.o. up	jdn. abholen/mitnehmen
lift	*hier:* Mitfahrgelegenheit
➔ to *give s.o. a lift	jdn. mitnehmen
by rail ➔ railway *(BE)*	mit der Bahn (Eisen-)Bahn
= railroad *(AE)*	
station	Bahnhof
queue [kjuː] *(BE)* = line *(AE)*	Warteschlange
➔ to queue/to *stand in line	sich anstellen, Schlange stehen
ticket	Fahrkarte, Fahrschein
single	einfache Fahrt
return	Hin- und Rückfahrt
platform	Gleis, Bahnsteig
to *be due [djuː]	*hier:* (laut Fahrplan) erwartet werden
to miss a train/bus/…	einen Zug/Bus/… verpassen
to *catch a train/bus/…	einen Zug/Bus/… kriegen/erreichen
through train	durchgehender Zug, Direktverbindung
to change (trains)	umsteigen
connection	Anschluss, Verbindung

12 Lifestyle

By bike

Christine: I'm really looking forward to this trip. I love **cycling**!
Melissa: So do I. Have you checked your bike yet?
Christine: More or less. I've tested the **brakes** and the lights, and they **work** OK. The **gears** are all right, too, and so is the **chain**.
Melissa: Your back **tyre** looks a bit flat. You'd better **pump it up**.
Christine: Can I have your **bicycle pump**? My brother took mine – and he hasn't given it back yet. And he took some things out of my **saddlebag**, too – to **mend a puncture**, I think.
Melissa: Here's my pump. – I'm going to change the height of my **saddle** a bit – it's too low. I can **pedal** better if it's higher.
Christine: Look at my new **helmet**. What do you think of it?
Melissa: OK – but do we really need helmets? We're going to keep to the **cycle paths** – we won't be **riding** on any main roads.
Christine: Better to be safe than sorry.
Melissa: That's what my dad always says! But he had a **collision** with a **pedestrian** and her dog a few weeks ago. The woman and the dog were OK, but Dad's front **wheel** was **damaged** and his **handlebars** were bent! Luckily it was his old bike – not his **racing bike**.

By air

Mr Körner is a businessman from South Germany. Today he is flying back to Munich from London. There is a connection by **Underground** from central London to Heathrow **Airport**.

He gets to the airport **in good time**, and **checks in**. He has only got a small piece of hand **luggage**, which he can take with him **on board** the **aircraft**. This means he won't have to wait at the **baggage reclaim** when he **arrives** in Munich. He'll be able to go straight to the **multi-storey car park** where he's left his car.

He goes up the **escalator** and looks at the **departure board**. Sometimes **flights** are **delayed**, or – if the weather is really bad – they may even be **cancelled**. But his flight to Munich is due to leave **on schedule**.

Lifestyle 12

cycling → cyclist	Radfahren Radfahrer(in)
brake → to brake	Bremse bremsen
to work = to function	*hier:* funktionieren
gears [gɪəz] ⚠ *(plural)* → gear	Gangschaltung Gang
chain	Kette
tyre	Reifen
to pump a tyre up	einen Reifen aufpumpen
bicycle pump	Fahrradpumpe
saddlebag	Satteltasche
to mend a puncture	einen Reifen flicken
→ to *have a puncture	einen Platten haben
saddle	Sattel
to pedal ['--] → pedal ['--]	(in die Pedale) treten Pedal
helmet ['helmɪt]	Helm
cycle path	Radweg
to *ride (a bicycle)	Rad fahren
collision [kəˈlɪʒn]	Zusammenstoß
→ to collide (with s.o.)	(mit jdm.) zusammenstoßen
pedestrian [-'---]	Fußgänger(in)
wheel	Rad
to damage [ˈdæmɪdʒ] s.th.	etwas beschädigen
handlebars ⚠ *(plural)*	Lenkstange
racing bike	Rennrad
Underground	Untergrundbahn
airport	Flughafen
in good time	frühzeitig rechtzeitig
to check in	einchecken, sich anmelden
luggage [ˈlʌɡɪdʒ] (BE)	Gepäck
= baggage [ˈbæɡɪdʒ] (AE)	
on board	an Bord
aircraft ⚠ *(plural: aircraft)*	Flugzeug, Maschine
baggage reclaim [rɪˈkleɪm]	Gepäckausgabe
to arrive	ankommen
multi-storey car park	(mehrstöckiges) Parkhaus
escalator ['----]	Rolltreppe
departure board [dɪˈpɑːtʃə ˌbɔːd]	Anzeigetafel der Abflüge
flight → to *fly	Flug fliegen
to *be delayed → delay	Verspätung haben Verspätung
to cancel [ˈkænsl] s.th.	etwas streichen/ausfallen lassen
on schedule [ˈʃedjuːl] (AE [ˈskedʒuːl])	planmäßig, pünktlich
= on time	

139

Lifestyle

Mr Körner goes through **passport control** and **security**. Then he goes to the **departure lounge** and waits there for his flight to be called. Soon the **gate** number is **announced**. Twenty minutes later the plane is in the air. All **seat-belts** have been **fastened**. The **captain** has spoken a few words over the loud-speaker, and members of the **crew** are serving a light meal now. They are serving drinks, too. Mr Körner likes a glass of red wine. Cheers!

By sea

Woman: I'd like some leaflets about **ferries** to France.
Travel agent: Where do you want to **sail** from?
Woman: Folkestone, I think. Or is there a shorter **crossing** from Dover?
Travel agent: There isn't much difference. Here are the leaflets, with the **timetables** and **fares** – for Folkestone to Boulogne and Dover to Calais. I've got details about other **destinations**, too, of course. Dieppe, for example, if you decide to sail from Newhaven. Or there's the **Channel Tunnel**, of course. That goes from Folkestone to Calais.
Woman: Thanks. – What a lot of interesting **catalogues** you've got over there. Mediterranean **cruises**! **Trips** round the world – fantastic! Those **ocean liners** look great, don't they?
Travel agent: They're all right if you like long sea **voyages**. No good for me. Just the sight of a **boat** makes me feel **seasick**!

7 Holidays

Many people's idea of a dream holiday may be to **stay** at a **luxury** hotel, **lazing** on a beach in the sun all day at some exotic **resort** in a beautiful country far away from home.

Others are interested in **sightseeing** and **exploring** new places. In these days of **mass tourism**, it is possible to **book** all kinds of different holidays – from **coach tours** to highly **adventurous** activities like climbing the world's highest mountains. Whatever their **choice**, the main thing for most **holidaymakers** is to **escape** from the **nine-to-five lifestyle** they normally lead – and to **experience** something different.

Lifestyle 12

passport control	Passkontrolle
security	Sicherheitskontrolle
departure lounge	Warteraum (vor Abflug)
gate	Ausgang, Flugsteig
to announce s.th.	etwas durchsagen/bekannt geben
→ announcement	Durchsage
seat-belt	Sicherheitsgurt
to fasten ['fɑːsn] s.th.	etwas festmachen/schließen
captain ['kæptɪn]	Kapitän
crew [kruː]	Besatzung, Flugpersonal
ferry	Fähre
travel agent	Reisebürokaufmann/-frau
→ travel agency	Reisebüro
to sail	abfahren (mit Schiff), absegeln
crossing	Überfahrt
timetable	Fahrplan
fare	Fahrpreis
destination	Reiseziel
the Channel Tunnel [ˌtʃænl 'tʌnl]	der Eurotunnel
catalogue ['kætəlɒɡ]	Katalog
cruise [kruːz]	Kreuzfahrt
trip	Reise, Ausflug
ocean liner [ˌəʊʃn 'laɪnə]	Ozeandampfer
voyage ['vɔɪɪdʒ]	Seereise, Seefahrt
boat	Boot
seasick	seekrank
to stay at a place	(vorübergehend) an einem Ort wohnen
luxury ['lʌkʃəri]	Luxus(-)
to laze → lazy	faulenzen faul
(holiday) resort [rɪ'zɔːt]	Urlaubsort, Ferienort
sightseeing	Besichtigungen
→ sight	Sehenswürdigkeit
to explore s.th.	etwas erkunden
mass tourism [ˌmæs 'tʊərɪzm]	Massentourismus
to book s.th.	etwas buchen
coach tour	Busreise
adventurous [əd'ventʃərəs]	abenteuerlich
→ adventure	Abenteuer
choice	Wahl, Entscheidung
→ to *choose [tʃuːz] s.th.	etwas wählen
holidaymaker	Urlauber(in)
to escape (from s.th.)	(einer Sache) entkommen
nine-to-five lifestyle	Büroalltag, Achtstundenalltag
to experience [ɪk'spɪəriəns] s.th.	etwas erfahren/erleben
→ experience	Erfahrung, Erlebnis

Lifestyle

Although **package tours** are very popular, many people want to plan their own route – and to be more **flexible**. **Youth hostelling**, **interrailing** and **backpacking** can also offer a **satisfying** way to see the world and '**get away from it all**'.

8 Do you like reading?

Sarah: In my family, we're all **readers**. When my brother and I were little, my mother used to read us **bedtime stories – fairy tales**, **adventure stories**, and sometimes little **poems** and **rhymes**. Now I usually go to the **library** every week or so and get a new book out. I like **novels** best. If a book's really good, I sometimes get to like the **characters** so much that I feel quite sad when I finish the last **chapter**!

Tom: I used to read a lot of **science fiction**, but now I prefer **thrillers**. I like stories with complicated **plots**, lots of **action** – and lots of **suspense**! When I was about twelve, I read masses of **detective stories**, especially ones **by** Agatha Christie. Her books nearly always have a very special **atmosphere** – and a surprise **ending**, and I always liked that. I haven't really got a favourite **author** now, though. There are so many **best-sellers** these days, by so many different **writers**.

Tricia: My favourite books are historical novels – **about heroes** or **heroines** that really existed, and – if possible! – with **tragic scenes** that make me cry. I'm not so keen on **humorous** books, although I enjoy a good **comedy** on TV.

Ben: I don't do much reading. But sometimes I might buy a book after I've seen the film or the TV **adaptation** of the story. The first book I read that way was 'Tom Sawyer', which I bought with a **book token** I'd been given. My father reads a lot – especially **short stories**.

Lifestyle

package tour ['--,-]	Pauschalreise
flexible ['---]	flexibel, beweglich
youth hostelling ['-,---]	Urlaub in Jugendherbergen
interrailing [,--'--]	Reisen per Interrail
backpacking ['---] → backpack ['--]	Rucksackreisen Rucksack
satisfying ['----] → satisfaction [,--'--]	befriedigend Zufriedenheit
to *get away from it all	den Alltag hinter sich lassen
reader	*hier:* Leseratte
bedtime story	Gutenachtgeschichte
fairy tale → fairy	Märchen Fee
adventure story	Abenteuergeschichte
poem ['pəʊɪm] → poet → poetry	Gedicht Dichter(in) Lyrik
rhyme [raɪm] → to rhyme	Reim sich reimen
library ['laɪbrərɪ]	Bibliothek, Bücherei
novel ['nɒvl]	Roman ⚠ (*nicht:* Novelle)
character ['kærəktə]	Figur, Person (in Roman, Film usw.)
chapter	Kapitel
science fiction → fiction	Sciencefiction Erzählliteratur
thriller	Thriller
plot	Handlung
action	Action, turbulente Handlung
suspense [-'-]	Spannung
⚠ exciting	spannend
detective story	Krimi, Kriminalroman
(written) by	von
atmosphere ['ætməsfɪə]	Stimmung
ending → happy ending	Schluss, Ende Happy End
author ['ɔːθə] = writer	Schriftsteller(in), Autor(in)
best-seller	Bestseller
→ to *sell well	sich gut verkaufen
writer	Schriftsteller(in)
to *be about s.o./s.th.	von jdm./etwas handeln
hero ['hɪərəʊ] ⚠ (*plural:* heroes)	Held
heroine ['herəʊɪn]	Heldin
tragic ['trædʒɪk] → tragedy ['---]	tragisch Tragödie
scene [siːn]	Szene
humourous ['hjuːmərəs]	lustig, humorvoll
→ humour ['--]	Humor
comedy ['kɒmədɪ] → comic	Komödie komisch, lustig
adaptation [,--'--]	Adaption, Bearbeitung
→ to adapt [-'-] s.th.	etwas adaptieren/bearbeiten
book token	Geschenkgutschein für ein Buch
short story [,-'--]	Kurzgeschichte

Exercises

12

a) Thirty words to do with travelling and holidays are hidden in this grid. They run (like a crossword) from left to right and from top to bottom. To help you, the German equivalents are given at the bottom of the page.

A	G	P	O	T	E	X	I	V	R	U	M	I	S	O	G
S	E	A	S	I	C	K	N	O	X	F	A	T	W	J	S
P	L	A	T	F	O	R	M	V	F	L	I	G	H	T	H
E	E	X	R	O	L	W	T	A	D	A	B	M	E	G	A
E	Y	R	A	I	L	O	E	X	I	T	C	A	E	O	N
D	R	I	V	B	I	S	F	R	V	O	H	C	L	U	D
L	A	N	E	A	S	T	I	M	E	T	A	B	L	E	L
I	G	O	L	B	I	Q	B	H	R	I	N	O	Y	V	E
M	A	S	S	T	O	U	R	I	S	M	G	A	V	E	B
I	P	E	I	R	N	E	E	K	I	T	E	T	I	A	A
T	I	C	K	E	T	W	A	L	O	R	N	A	S	C	R
A	W	U	P	B	R	A	K	E	N	A	D	I	T	C	S
T	Y	R	E	W	X	I	D	O	D	F	C	H	A	I	N
T	R	I	P	O	R	B	O	O	K	F	R	A	T	D	O
R	E	T	U	R	N	A	W	P	A	I	Z	Z	I	E	K
O	U	Y	W	E	C	O	N	N	E	C	T	I	O	N	E
V	I	D	E	P	E	D	E	S	T	R	I	A	N	T	P

*Anschluss   Ausflug/Reise   Ausfahrt   Bahn   Bahnhof
Bahnsteig   Bremse   Boot   buchen   Fahrplan   Fahrkarte
Fahrspur   Flug   Fußgänger   Geschwindigkeitsbegrenzung
Hin- und Rückfahrt   Kette   Lenkstange   Massentourismus
Panne   Rad   Reifen   reisen   seekrank   Sicherheitskontrolle
Umleitung   umsteigen   Unfall   Verkehr   Zusammenstoß*

Exercises 12

b) Which is the right word?

1. When are you going _____ holiday?
2. How much do you spend _____ clothes?
3. A child-minder looks _____ their baby.
4. Bringing _____ children isn't always easy.
5. Why are you always _____ a hurry?
6. Lots of girls are addicted _____ shopping.
7. Do you believe _____ God?
8. The Browns' house is _____ sale.
9. I'm always open _____ new ideas.
10. Who was 'Romeo and Juliet' written _____?

after
by
for
in
in
on
on
to
to
up

c) What do you call these people and things?

1. A place where you can borrow books is a _____.
2. A person in a novel is called a _____.
3. The opposite of a tragedy is a _____.
4. A novel about a crime and how it is solved is a _____.
5. A version of a story that is shown as a film is called an _____.
6. An author of novels, plays, etc. can also be called a _____.
7. A story that finishes happily has a happy _____.
8. Books that are very exciting are full of _____.

Festivities and public holidays

1 Celebrations – in Britain and in Germany

Nicola's German exchange partner, Kathrin, is in England for 10 days. It is the end of October, and there are already **Christmas decorations** in some of the shops.

Nicola: How do you **celebrate** Christmas in Germany?
Kathrin: The **festive season** really starts with **Advent**. Children have Advent calendars, and most people have a **wreath** with four Advent **candles** on the table. We bake a lot of biscuits and **gingerbread**, and a lot of people **make things** – like decorations or **presents**.
Nicola: Do German children believe in **Father Christmas**? Over here they **hang up their stockings** on **Christmas Eve**, and Father Christmas comes down the **chimney** in the night. He fills their stockings with presents, and they open them the next morning – on **Christmas Day**.
Kathrin: Father Christmas is the same as **Santa Claus**, isn't he? In Germany we have a similar tradition with **Saint** Nikolaus. He gives children little presents on December 6th.
Nicola: Do you have **Christmas carols**? In England it's the **custom** for **carol singers** to go round to people's houses in the evenings before Christmas, **collecting** money for **charities**.
Kathrin: We do that on January 6th. Children **dress up** as the **Three Kings**. You call January 6th **Twelfth Night**, don't you?
Nicola: Yes, that's right. Is **Boxing Day** a holiday with you?
Kathrin: Oh yes. And **New Year's Day**, too. There are a lot of celebrations and parties on **New Year's Eve**.
Nicola: That's the same here! **Dances** and **balls** are popular on New Year's Eve. But even people who don't go out usually stay up till **midnight** to **see the New Year in** – and **drink a toast**.
Kathrin: Do you have **fireworks** on New Year's Eve, too?
Nicola: No, but we have them on **Guy Fawkes Night** – that's on November 5th. People have parties outside, usually round a big **bonfire**, and a **home-made** 'guy' is burnt on top of it. Some people call Guy Fawkes Night 'Bonfire Night'. You know – Guy Fawkes tried to blow up the Houses of Parliament. At least, he was the one who was caught with all the gunpowder!

Festivities and public holidays

festivity [fe'stɪvətɪ], festivities	Feier, Feierlichkeiten
public holiday	gesetzlicher Feiertag
celebration	Feier, Fest
Christmas	Weihnachten, Weihnachts-
decoration(s)	Schmuck (z.B. am Baum)
→ to decorate s.th.	etwas schmücken
to celebrate s.th.	etwas feiern
festive season	Festzeit
Advent ['ædvənt]	Advent
wreath [riːθ]	Kranz
candle	Kerze
gingerbread ['dʒɪndʒəbred]	Gewürzkuchen, Lebkuchen
→ ginger	Ingwer
to *make things	basteln
present ['--]	Geschenk
Father Christmas *(BE)*	der Weihnachtsmann
to *hang up one's stocking	den Weihnachtsstrumpf aufhängen
Christmas Eve	der Heilige Abend
chimney ['tʃɪmnɪ]	Schornstein
Christmas Day	der erste Weihnachtstag
Santa Claus [klɔːz] *(AE)*	der Weihnachtsmann
saint [seɪnt]	Heilige(r/s) (St.)
(St [sənt] + *name, e.g.* St George)	
Christmas carol ['kærəl]	Weihnachtslied
custom ['kʌstəm]	Sitte, Brauch
carol singer	Sternsinger
to collect money → collection	Geld sammeln Sammlung
charity ['tʃærətɪ]	Wohltätigkeitsverein
to dress up (as s.o.)	sich (als jd.) verkleiden
the Three Kings	die Heiligen Drei Könige
Twelfth Night	der 6. Januar (Ende der Weihnachtszeit)
Boxing Day	der zweite Weihnachtstag
New Year's Day	Neujahr, der 1. Januar
New Year's Eve	Silvester, der 31. Dezember
dance → to dance	Tanz, Ball tanzen
ball [ɔː]	Ball
midnight	Mitternacht
to *see the New Year in	das neue Jahr begrüßen
to *drink a toast (to s.o./s.th.)	(auf jdn./etwas) trinken
fireworks △ *(plural)*	Feuerwerk
→ firework	Feuerwerkskörper
Guy Fawkes [ˌgaɪ 'fɔːks] Night	5. November *(siehe History S. 34)*
bonfire	(Freuden-)Feuer
home-made	selbst gebastelt, hausgemacht

147

13 Festivities and public holidays

2 More holidays and special days

Apart from the usual **anniversaries** and birthdays that people celebrate every year, there are a number of other **special occasions**. Some are the same in Britain and in Germany – others are not.

- **Valentine's Day** (February 14th) is a big day for the makers of **greetings cards** – it has been a tradition in Britain for over 500 years! (Lovers can quickly turn into enemies if Valentine's Day is forgotten. So remember to make a note of it in your **diary**!)

- People eat pancakes on **Shrove Tuesday**, but there is no **equivalent** of 'Fasching' in Britain. However, there are sometimes local **carnivals** with **parades** through the streets at other times of the year. (The Notting Hill Carnival in London, which **takes place** every August, is an example.) **Fancy dress** parties are **held** at **Halloween** (October 31st), which has become a very popular **festival** in Britain.

- **Lent** begins on **Ash Wednesday**. It is still the custom to 'give up' something during Lent – even if it's only sweets or chocolate! **Good Friday** is a holiday, and so is **Easter Monday**. **Easter eggs** are part of the **annual** celebrations, but the tradition of the **Easter bunny** and of painting eggs and hiding them on **Easter Day** is more common in Germany.

- **April Fool's Day** is a popular time for **practical jokes**, and **May Day**, a traditional festival with a young girl as the 'May Queen', is still often celebrated in villages on the first Saturday in May. The official public holiday, however, always falls on the first Monday in May.

- Other **church festivals** include **Whitsun** (sometimes also called **Pentecost**, especially in the USA) and **Ascension Day**. **Remembrance Day** is the second Sunday in November, when the people who died in the two World Wars are remembered.

- There is no **national day** in Britain, but in Northern Ireland **St Patrick's Day** (March 17th) is a public holiday.

- **Bank Holidays** are days when banks are closed and people don't go to work. They are usually on a Monday – to make a long weekend! The last Mondays in May and August are always Bank Holidays. Boxing Day and Good Friday, although they are church festivals, are also counted as Bank Holidays.

Festivities and public holidays

anniversary [ˌ--'---]	Jahrestag
special occasion	besonderer Anlass, besonderes Ereignis
Valentine's ['væləntaɪnz] **Day**	Valentinstag
greetings card → **card**	Grußkarte Karte
diary ['daɪərɪ]	*hier:* Terminkalender, Taschenkalender
⚠ **calendar** ['kæləndə]	⚠ Wandkalender
Shrove [ʃrəʊv] **Tuesday**	Fastnachtsdienstag
equivalent [ɪ'kwɪvələnt]	Entsprechung, Gegenstück
carnival ['kɑːnɪvl]	Karneval
parade [pə'reɪd]	Umzug, Parade
to *take place	stattfinden
⚠ to *sit down	⚠ Platz nehmen
fancy dress	(Masken-)Kostüm, Verkleidung
to *hold a party/a meeting/...	eine Party/eine Besprechung/… veranstalten
Halloween [ˌhæləʊ'iːn]	Tag vor Allerheiligen
festival	Fest
Lent	Fastenzeit
Ash Wednesday	Aschermittwoch
Good Friday	Karfreitag
Easter Monday	Ostermontag
Easter egg	Osterei
annual ['ænjʊəl]	jährlich
Easter bunny	Osterhase
Easter Day	Ostersonntag
April Fool's Day	der 1. April
practical joke	Streich
May Day	*gesetzlicher Feiertag am ersten Montag im Mai*
church festival	Kirchenfest
Whitsun ['wɪtsn] *(BE)*/**Pentecost** ['pentɪkɒst] *(AE)*	Pfingsten
Ascension [ə'senʃn] **Day**	Himmelfahrt(stag)
Remembrance Day	*britischer Volkstrauertag*
national day	Nationalfeiertag
St Patrick's Day	der 17. März *(irischer Nationalfeiertag)*
Bank Holiday	*etwa:* gesetzlicher Feiertag

Festivities and public holidays

3 American celebrations

Dear Markus:

In your last e-mail you asked me to tell you something about holidays in the USA. Well, I guess the biggest day here is the **Fourth of July**, when we celebrate our **independence**! There are lots of fireworks and parades then.

Thanksgiving Day is important, too. That's when we remember the first Thanksgiving celebrated by the **Pilgrims** in 1621. It's a big family occasion. Most families have a big **get-together**, and there's always a big **feast** – with an enormous **turkey** to eat!

One of our biggest days for parties is Halloween, which is popular with everyone – not only children! You've probably heard of '**trick or treat**'. That's what children say when they come to people's doors dressed up in their Halloween **costumes**. Sometimes they **play** really **mean tricks** if they don't get the **treat** they want. So it's important to know about the custom if you're new in the States!

We have a few other holidays – for example, **Martin Luther King Day**, **in memory of** the great civil rights leader, and **Labor Day** at the end of the summer **vacation**. Then there's St Patrick's Day (lots of Americans have Irish blood!), and **Memorial Day in honor of** American soldiers who died. **Presidents' Day** (in honor of all US presidents) is in February.

Christmas over here is just 25th December – the day after is a normal **workday**. Maybe you'd be surprised to see our **Christmas trees** – a lot of people have a **plastic** tree, which they can put away and use again **year after year**! Plastic **holly** and **mistletoe** are popular, too, and some people put up lots of Christmas lights and decorations outside their houses. Do you do that in Germany, too?

Bye now! Nelson

4 What to say on special occasions

 "**Happy birthday**!" "**Many happy returns of the day**!"

 "So you've passed your test! **Congratulations**!"

"Thank you so much for the **invitation**!"

"**Merry Christmas** and a **Happy New Year**!"

 "**Good luck** in your exams!"

 "**With love** and **best wishes**!"

Festivities and public holidays 13

the Fourth of July	Unabhängigkeitstag (USA)
= Independence Day	
independence [ˌ--'--] → independent	Unabhängigkeit unabhängig
Thanksgiving Day	*Feiertag in den USA (letzter Donnerstag im November)*
→ Thanksgiving	Erntedankfest
the Pilgrims	die Pilgerväter
get-together	Treffen
feast [fiːst]	*hier:* Festessen, Festmahl
turkey ['tɜːkɪ]	Truthahn
trick or treat	*Ausspruch der Kinder zu Halloween*
costume ['kɒstjuːm]	Kostüm, Verkleidung
to play a trick (on s.o.)	jdm. einen Streich spielen
mean	gemein, gehässig
treat	etwas Besonderes (oft Süßigkeiten)
Martin Luther King Day	*Feiertag in den USA (3. Montag im Januar)*
in memory of s.o./s.th.	zur Erinnerung/zum Gedenken an jdn./etwas
Labor ['leɪbə] Day *(AE)*	*etwa:* Tag der Arbeit *(1. Montag im September)*
vacation [və'keɪʃn] *(AE)*	Ferien, Urlaub
Memorial [mə'mɔːrɪəl] Day	*Volkstrauertag in den USA (letzter Montag im Mai)*
in honor ['ɒnə] of s.o. *(AE)*	zu jds. Ehre
= in honour of s.o. *(BE)*	
Presidents' Day	*Feiertag in den USA (3. Montag im Februar)*
workday	Arbeitstag
Christmas tree	Weihnachtsbaum
plastic	Kunststoff
year after year	Jahr für Jahr
holly	Stechpalme (immergrüner Strauch mit roten Beeren)
mistletoe ['mɪsltəʊ]	Mistel
Happy birthday!/ Many happy returns of the day! → return	Herzlichen Glückwunsch/Alles Gute zum Geburtstag! Rückkehr
invitation [ˌ--'--]	Einladung
→ to invite [-'-] s.o. to s.th.	jdn. zu etwas einladen
Good luck!	Viel Glück!
Congratulations!	Herzlichen Glückwunsch!, Ich gratuliere!
Merry Christmas!	Fröhliche Weihnachten!
Happy New Year!	Ein gutes neues Jahr!
With love (from)	Herzlichst (Dein/e)
(With) best wishes	Mit freundlichen Grüßen, mit den besten Wünschen

13 Exercises

a) Decide which of these words can be combined with the words below. Then translate the expressions into German.

> Ash Bank Christmas Easter✔ fancy Good
> practical Santa Shrove special Twelfth

1. _Easter_ egg: _Osterei_
2. _____ Eve: _____
3. _____ occasion: _____
4. _____ Wednesday: _____
5. _____ dress: _____
6. _____ joke: _____
7. _____ Tuesday: _____
8. _____ Holiday: _____
9. _____ Claus: _____
10. _____ Night: _____
11. _____ Friday: _____

Now match each expression with the correct definition or clue.

a) the first day of Lent   ___
b) what people wear for Halloween parties   ___
c) the day when Christians remember the death of Jesus   ___
d) something sweet, usually made of chocolate   _1_
e) pancake day in lots of British families   ___
f) something to look out for on April 1st   ___
g) the time when children hang up their stockings   ___
h) the last day of the Christmas season   ___
i) an important event that you want to celebrate   ___
j) usually a Monday – but without work   ___
k) the American equivalent of Father Christmas   ___

Exercises 13

b) Find the right word.

1. The Notting Hill Carnival takes _p_____ in August.   ← k u l c
2. Did Judy send you an _____ to the party?   c l u b i p
3. I'm going to ring Tom and wish him good _____ in his exam tomorrow.   e c l a p
4. You've won the first prize? Wow! _____!   d r a w y o k
5. December 26th is a normal _____ in the USA.   o s a l t o c u r a n t i n g
6. On Thanksgiving Day American families usually eat _____.   t r u h o f
7. Independence Day is on the _____ of July.   y u k t e r
8. Is New Year's Day a _____ holiday in Germany?   a n t i v o t i n i

c) Which is the odd one out?

1. ❏ Whitsun ❏ Lent ❏ Pentecost
2. ❏ anniversary ❏ calender ❏ diary
3. ❏ holly ❏ mistletoe ❏ decoration
4. ❏ dance ❏ carol ❏ ball
5. ❏ Boxing Day ❏ fireworks ❏ bonfire
6. ❏ stocking ❏ bunny ❏ chimney
7. ❏ happy ❏ merry ❏ mean
8. ❏ Ascension Day ❏ Labour Day ❏ Presidents' Day

Skills and tips

1 Writing letters

1. Introducing yourself

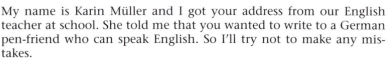

Dear Sayed,

My name is Karin Müller and I got your address from our English teacher at school. She told me that you wanted to write to a German pen-friend who can speak English. So I'll try not to make any mistakes.

I am 16 years old and live in a small village called Bürg in Southern Germany with my parents and my younger brother Michael. And I go to the technical grammar school in Neuenstadt. But **I'm glad to say that** I will be leaving school this summer. I want to become a secretary or a bank clerk if I can get a job in a bank.

My hobbies are music and dancing (we go to a disco in Heilbronn every Saturday), and I also like animals. We have a big black dog called Robin and two cats.

Please write to me soon and tell me something about life in Egypt. **I hope you and your family are well. I'm really looking forward to hearing from you!**

Yours,

Karin Müller

2. A letter to a good friend

Hi there, Karin!

I was so pleased to get your letter! **I'm sorry I haven't written for so long**, and even this is only a quick note to tell you that your trip to England is OK! **Let me know** when your flight arrives. Mum and Dad say you can stay with us before we go to Cornwall together.

You talked about pony trekking in your letter. I've got one or two addresses in Wales, but perhaps you should **get in touch with** the farm where your sister stayed last year. You could phone them or **drop them a line**. It sounds like a wonderful place! It's on Dartmoor, isn't it?

I'll phone my cousin Cathy and ask her if she'd like to come with us. **I hope everything is fine with you**. **Bye for now** and **all the best** to your parents. **Take care** and **write again soon**!

Love,

Samantha

Skills and tips

3. Useful phrases for an informal letter

Dear Linda,	Liebe Linda,
Hi (there), John!	Hallo, John!
I was so pleased to get your letter.	Ich habe mich sehr über deinen Brief gefreut.
Thanks for your letter.	Vielen Dank für deinen Brief.
I'm sorry I haven't written for so long, but …	Es tut mir leid, dass ich so lange nicht geschrieben habe, aber …
I hope you're well. I hope everything is fine with you. }	Ich hoffe, es geht dir gut.
I'm very happy/glad to tell you that …	Es freut mich, dir sagen zu können …
I'm very sorry/sad to say that …	Es tut mir leid, dir sagen zu müssen …
It was nice of you to invite me to …	Es war lieb von dir, mich zu … einzuladen.
I'm looking forward to hearing from you soon.	Ich freue mich darauf, bald von dir zu hören.
Let me know what you're doing.	Erzähl mir, was du machst.
Drop me a line!	Schreib mir ein paar Zeilen!
Please write soon. Write (again) soon. }	Schreib bald wieder!
Let's keep in touch.	Lass uns in Kontakt bleiben.
How can I get in touch with you?	Wie kann ich dich erreichen?/Wie kann ich mit dir Kontakt aufnehmen?
Bye for now,	Tschüss!
See you (soon),	Bis bald,
Say hello to … for/from me.	Schöne Grüße an …
Give my regards/best wishes to …	Liebe Grüße an …
Take care!	Mach's gut!
All the best,	Alles Gute,
Yours,	Dein(e)
Kindest regards,	mit herzlichen Grüßen, herzlichst
Love (from),	liebe Grüße
(an Verwandte bzw. sehr gute Freunde)	

⚠ *Always start the first paragraph with a capital letter*

Skills and tips

4. *Asking for information*

Züttlinger Str.26
D-74196 Bürg
Germany

Happy Days Riding School
attn. Mrs Hawtree
Dobson's Farm
Ashburton
Devon EX18 6PJ

19 May 2006

Dear Mrs Hawtree,

Last year my sister Britta spent a very interesting week at your riding school on Dartmoor.

This summer my English friend and I are planning to go on holiday in Devon and Cornwall. We are both interested in riding and would like to go pony trekking. **Could you please send us** some information about your school **as soon as possible**?

I will be staying with my English pen-friend in London for a week before we come to Devon. We are both 16 years old.

I look forward to hearing from you soon.

Yours sincerely,

Karin Müller

5. *Joining a society or a club*

25 Rillington Place
Gloucester GL3 6EP

Friends of the Earth
56-58 Alma Street
Luton
Beds. LU1 2YZ

25 February 2006

Dear Sir/Madam,

I read your magazine regularly in our school library. I am leaving school this summer, and **would like to join** Friends of the Earth.

If my GCSE results are good, I hope to go to Sixth Form College or Technical College in the autumn. So **please enrol me as a student member**.

As I do not have a bank account of my own yet, I **enclose** a cheque from my mother for £8. **Please let me know** if this is OK.

I very much look forward to hearing from you soon and to receiving my first 'personal' copy of your magazine.

Yours faithfully,

Heather West

Skills and tips

6. Useful phrases for a formal letter

attn. (= attention)	z. Hd.
Dear Mr/Mrs Smith,	Sehr geehrter/Lieber Herr/ Sehr geehrte/Liebe Frau Smith,
Dear Miss Smith *(Anrede an unverheiratete Frau)*	Sehr geehrte/Liebe Frau (*veraltet:* Sehr geehrtes/Liebes Frl.) Smith
Dear Ms [mɪz] **Smith,** *(wenn man nicht weiß, ob eine Frau verheiratet ist oder nicht)*	Liebe Frau Smith,
Dear Sirs, *(Anrede an eine Firma)*	Sehr geehrte Damen und Herren,
Dear Sir,/Dear Madam, *(formale Anrede, wenn das Geschlecht des Empfängers bekannt ist)*	Sehr geehrter Herr,/Sehr geehrte Dame,
Dear Sir/Madam, *(formale Anrede, wenn das Geschlecht des Empfängers unbekannt ist)*	Sehr geehrte Dame/Sehr geehrter Herr,
Sir,	*Anrede in Leserbriefen an Zeitungsredaktionen*
I am writing for information about …	Würden Sie mir Informationen über … schicken?
I would like to have further details about …	Ich wüsste gerne Näheres über …
Thank you for the information you sent me.	Haben Sie für die zugeschickte Information recht herzlichen Dank.
Thank you for sending me …	Besten Dank dafür, dass Sie mir … geschickt haben.
Could you please send me … (as soon as possible)?	Würden Sie mir bitte (so bald wie möglich)… zusenden?
I would like to join …	Ich möchte Mitglied von … werden.
Please enrol me as a member.	Bitte nehmen Sie mich als Mitglied auf.
I enclose my application form/a cheque for …	Anbei finden Sie mein Antragsformular/einen Scheck über …
Please let me know …	Bitte teilen Sie mir mit …
I (very much) look forward to hearing from you soon.	Ich freue mich (sehr) darauf, bald von Ihnen zu hören.
Yours sincerely, [sɪnˈsɪəlɪ] *(in Briefen, die mit* Dear Mr/Mrs … *usw., anfangen)*	mit freundlichen Grüßen
Yours faithfully, [ˈfeɪθfəlɪ] *(in förmlichen Briefen, die mit* Dear Sir/Madam *anfangen)*	mit freundlichen Grüßen/Hochachtungsvoll

⚠ *Always use the postcode and put it at the end of the address.*
⚠ *Always start the first paragraph with a capital letter.*

Skills and tips

2 Saying what you think

1. Expressing an opinion

I think/don't think …	Ich glaube/glaube nicht …
I believe that …	Ich glaube, dass …
I find it strange that …	Ich finde es eigenartig, dass …
I'm sure that …	Ich bin mir sicher, dass …
In my opinion …	Meiner Meinung nach …
I suppose …	Ich nehme an …
I think it's a good idea because …	Ich glaube, es ist eine gute Idee, da …
It seems to me that …	Mir scheint, dass …
I'm for/against (doing) …	Ich bin für/gegen …/Ich bin dafür/dagegen dass …

2. Agreeing/disagreeing

I agree/disagree with you.	Ich bin (nicht) deiner/Ihrer Meinung.
I think you're right/wrong.	Ich glaube, du hast/Sie haben recht/unrecht.
That's quite true.	Das stimmt.
That's not true at all.	Das stimmt überhaupt nicht.
You can't really say that.	Das kann man eigentlich nicht sagen.
That's not the same.	Das ist nicht dasselbe.

3. Introducing a different argument

On the one hand … on the other (hand) …	Einerseits … andererseits …
We should either … or …	Wir sollten entweder … oder …
You have to look at the pros and cons.	Man muss das Für und Wider berücksichtigen.
We must consider the advantages and disadvantages.	Wir müssen die Vor- und Nachteile in Betracht ziehen.
We must take the arguments on both sides into consideration.	Wir müssen die Argumente beider Seiten in Betracht ziehen.

⚠ *Be careful!*

I **think** ….	Ich **meine** …
I **mean** …	Ich **will damit sagen** …
What does this word **mean**?	Was **heißt/bedeutet** diese Wort?
Do you know the **meaning** of that word?	Kennst du die **Bedeutung** dieses Wortes?

Skills and tips

3 False friends

1. Different meanings

actual ≠ aktuell

He **actually** knows the Queen.	Er kennt die Königin **wirklich/ tatsächlich**.

This is a **topical** subject.	Das ist ein **aktuelles** Thema.

also ≠ also

Her father **also** came.	Ihr Vater kam **auch**.
So he did come after all.	Er ist **also** doch gekommen.

bank

She works at a **bank**.	Sie arbeitet in einer **Bank**. *(Geldinstitut)*

But **bank** ≠ **Bank** *in*

There is a new **bench/seat** near the river bank.	Es gibt eine neue (Park-)**Bank** am Flussufer.

become ≠ bekommen

He **became** a pilot.	Er **wurde** Pilot.
 (become + noun = werden)
She **became/got** angry	Sie **wurde** wütend.
 (become/get + adjective = werden)
I **got** a letter from her.	Ich **bekam** einen Brief von ihr.
 (get + noun = bekommen)

After waiting half an hour for his meal at a London restaurant, a German tourist asked the waiter: "When will I become the steak which I ordered?" "Never, I hope, sir!" was the waiter's shocked reply.

---

blame ≠ blamieren

If you **make a fool of yourself,** don't **blame** me!	Wenn **du dich blamierst**, dann **gib** mir bitte nicht **die Schuld**!
Why do I always get the **blame**!	Warum bekomme immer ich die **Schuld**?

brave ≠ brav

It was **brave** of her to jump into the river to save the dog.	Es war **mutig** von ihr, in den Fluss zu springen, um den Hund zu retten.
Be good!	**Sei brav!**

Skills and tips

chips *(BE)* ≠ **Chips**

fish and **chips**   Fisch und **Pommes frites**
(potato) **crisps**   Kartoffel**chips**

⚠ *Im AE heißen „Pommes frites" nicht „chips", sondern „(French) fries", und BE „crisps" heißen im AE „chips".*

critic ≠ **Kritik**

The **film critic** of *The Times* wrote a long **review** of the film.   Der **Filmkritiker** der *Times* schrieb eine lange **Kritik** über den Film.

eventually ≠ **eventuell**

We **eventually** arrived.   Wir kamen **schließlich** an.
We **may possibly** visit Cardiff.   **Eventuell** besuchen wir Cardiff.

handy ≠ **Handy**

I find my **mobile** very **handy**.   Ich finde mein **Handy** sehr **nützlich**.
The extra money will **come in very handy**.   Das zusätzliche Geld wird **eine große Hilfe sein**.

meaning ≠ **Meinung**

Do you know the **meaning** of that word?   Kennst du die **Bedeutung** dieses Wortes?
In my **opinion** …   Meiner **Meinung** nach …

note ≠ **Note**

I'll **make a note** of it.   Ich **schreib's mir auf**.
You don't need to **take notes**.   Ihr braucht keine **Notizen** zu **machen**.
Did you get my **note**?   Hast du meinen **Zettel** bekommen?
What **mark**/**grade** did you get?   Welche **Note** hast du bekommen?
Have you got your **music**?   Hast du deine **Noten**?

photograph ≠ **Fotograf(in)**

My sister is a **photographer** [-'---].   Meine Schwester ist **Fotografin**.
Have you seen her **photographs** ['---]?   Hast du ihre **Fotos** gesehen?

prospect ≠ **Prospekt**

I got this **brochure**/**leaflet** at the tourist information centre.   Ich bekam diesen **Prospekt** im Fremdenverkehrszentrum.
She's stuck in a job with no **prospects**.   Sie steckt in einem Beruf ohne **Aussichten**.

Skills and tips

recipe ≠ (ärztliches) Rezept

The doctor gave him a **prescription**. Die Ärztin gab ihm ein **Rezept**.
But:
Have you got a **recipe** for …? Hast du ein (Koch-)**Rezept** für …?

sensible ≠ sensibel

It was a **sensible** decision. Es war eine **vernünftige** Entscheidung.
He's a **sensitive** boy. Er ist ein **sensibler** Junge.

small ≠ schmal

It is a **small** town with **narrow** streets. Es ist eine **kleine** Stadt/eine **Klein**stadt mit **schmalen** Straßen.
She's got a **thin** face. Sie hat ein **schmales** Gesicht.

spend ≠ spenden

I **spent** a lot of money at the weekend. Ich **habe** am Wochenende viel Geld **ausgegeben**.
We **spent** two weeks in Italy. Wir **haben** zwei Wochen in Italien **verbracht**.

They **donated** £500 to the Red Cross. Sie **spendeten** dem Roten Kreuz £500.

sympathetic ≠ sympathisch

He was very **sympathetic** when he heard my story. Er **zeigte** sehr viel **Mitgefühl**, als er meine Geschichte hörte.
I **like** her parents a lot.
I think her parents are very **nice**. } Ihre Eltern **sind mir** sehr **sympathisch**.

2. Different spellings in British English

address	Adresse	**licence** (*AE:* license)	Lizenz
calendar	Kalender	**litre**	Liter
career	Karriere	**model**	Modell
carnival	Karneval	**per cent** (*AE:* percent)	Prozent
catalogue	Katalog	**photo**	Foto
colleague	Kollege	**rhyme**	Reim
guitar	Gitarre	**second**	Sekunde
kilometre	Kilometer	**wonder**	Wunder

⚠ *German words ending in '-er' like 'Meter' and 'Liter' are spelt the same in American English ('meter', 'liter').*
Many German words containing a 'k' are spelt with a 'c' in English: 'America', 'comma', 'music', etc.

Skills and tips

4 Singular and plural words

1. True and false pairs

'True' pairs are always two things: *a pair of shoes* = **two** shoes.
The noun can be used in the singular or plural with a singular or plural verb, e.g.:

> My left **shoe is** gone! Both **shoes were** in the kitchen yesterday.

Some pairs are 'false' pairs. The plural form (often with the words *a pair of*) is used for only one thing:
a pair of jeans = **one** piece of clothing with two legs.
With false pairs there is no singular form of the noun, and you need a plural verb, e.g.:

> My **trousers are** too small for me. = Meine **Hose ist** mir zu klein.

If you want to use *a/an* or a number with 'false' pairs, you must use the words *pair(s) of*, e.g.:

> His mother bought him **a new pair of trousers** for school and **two new pairs of jeans** to wear at home.

True pairs – two separate things

one glove/two gloves	ein Handschuh/zwei Handschuhe
a pair of shoes/socks/ gloves/rollerblades/ ice-skates/skis	ein Paar Schuhe/Socken/ Handschuhe/Rollerblades/ Schlittschuhe/Ski(er)

False pairs – plural form used for one thing

(a pair of) **trousers** (*AE:* pants)	(eine) Hose
(a pair of) **jeans**	(eine) Jeans-Hose
(a pair of) **shorts**	(eine) kurze Hose
(a pair of) **pyjamas** (*AE:* pajamas)	(ein) Schlafanzug
(a pair of) **tights**	(eine) Strumpfhose
(a pair of) **scissors**	(eine) Schere
(a pair of) **glasses/spectacles**	(eine) Brille
(a pair of) **goggles**	(eine) Schutzbrille/Sportbrille
(a pair of) **binoculars**	(ein) Fernglas

2. Other plural nouns which are singular in German

scales	Waage
stairs	Treppe
handlebars	Lenkstange
clothes	Kleidung

Skills and tips

3. No plural in English – plural in German

The nouns *information*, *advice*, *news*, *homework* and *furniture* are only used as collectives (like *milk* and *bread*) in English, although they have a plural in German. If you use them with *a/an, several/many*, etc. or a number, you need a word like *piece* or *bit* ('a piece of furniture', 'two pieces/bits of advice', etc.).

The **information** was interesting.	Die **Information(en)** war(en) interessant
It was **an** interesting **piece of information**.	Es war **eine** interessante **Information**.
He gave me several **pieces of advice**.	Er gab mir mehrere **Ratschläge**.
I thanked him for his **advice**.	Ich dankte ihm für seinen **Rat**.
Let me give you **a bit of advice**.	Darf ich dir **einen Rat** geben?
The **news** is good.	Die **Nachrichten** sind gut.
That's **an** interesting **piece of news**.	Das ist **eine** interessante **Neuigkeit**.
Is **homework** really necessary?	Sind **Hausaufgaben** wirklich nötig?
I like your **furniture**!	Eure **Möbel** gefallen mir.
I bought several new **pieces of furniture** last week.	Ich habe letzte Woche mehrere neue **Möbel(stücke)** gekauft.

4. Plural noun with a singular verb

The **USA is** a big country.	Die **USA sind** ein großes Land.
Maths / **Physics** / **Gymnastics** **is** my favourite school subject.	**Mathematik** / **Physik** / **Gymnastik** **ist** mein Lieblingsfach.

5. Singular noun with a plural verb

We use a plural verb with grammatically 'singular' nouns (*police, people, crowd*, etc.) that refer to a group of people:

The **police were waiting** for him.	Die **Polizei wartete** auf ihn.
The **crowd are** on their feet as the athletes come into the stadium.	Das ganze **Stadion ist** auf den Beinen, als die Athleten hereinkommen.

Skills and tips

5 Describing what people are like

1. Describing what people look like

blond(e) / fair-haired	blond
dark-haired	dunkelhaarig
bald	kahl, glatzköpfig
pretty	hübsch
beautiful	schön
good-looking	gut aussehend
ugly [ʌ]	hässlich
small, short	klein
tall	groß
smart	schick, flott
well-dressed	gut angezogen
curly-haired	mit lockigen Haaren
straight-haired	mit glatten Haaren
slim	schlank
well-built	stämmig
overweight	übergewichtig
thin	dünn
fat	dick
moustache [məˈstɑːʃ]	Schnurbart
beard	Bart

"I have six legs, two bodies, fifteen eyes, four noses and forty fingers on each hand. What am I?"
"Ugly!"

2. Describing character and qualities

The column on the left gives positive qualities. Their opposites are in the column on the right.

careful	vorsichtig; sorgfältig	careless	leichtsinnig; nachlässig
clever/smart	klug/schlau	stupid	dumm, blöd
friendly	freundlich	unfriendly	unfreundlich
generous [ˈdʒenərəs]	großzügig; wohlwollend	mean	kleinlich, geizig; gemein
helpful	hilfsbereit	unhelpful	wenig hilfsbereit
honest [ˈɒnɪst]	ehrlich	dishonest	unehrlich
interesting	interessant	boring	langweilig
kind	nett, lieb	cruel [ˈkrʊəl]	grausam
hard-working	fleißig	lazy	faul
modest	bescheiden	proud	stolz
nice	nett	nasty	gemein, ekelhaft
optimistic [ˌ--ˈ---]	optimistisch	pessimistic [ˌ--ˈ---]	pessimistisch
out-going	extravertiert	shy	schüchtern
patient [ˈpeɪʃnt]	geduldig	impatient	ungeduldig

164

Skills and tips

polite	höflich	**impolite/rude**	unhöflich
positive	positiv	**negative**	negativ
quiet	ruhig	**loud/noisy**	laut
relaxed	entspannt	**tense**	angespannt
sensible ['---]	vernünftig	**silly**	albern
strong	stark	**weak**	schwach
thoughtful	nachdenklich	**thoughtless**	gedankenlos
unselfish	uneigennützig	**selfish**	egoistisch

3. Describing how people feel

angry	wütend	**funny**	komisch
annoyed	verärgert	**glad**	froh
awful	schrecklich	**happy**	froh, glücklich
bored	gelangweilt	**horrible**	schrecklich
brave	tapfer	**lonely**	einsam
confident	selbstsicher	**nervous** ['--]	nervös
cool	gefasst	**pleased**	erfreut, zufrieden
crazy	verrückt	**surprised**	überrascht
depressed	deprimiert	**terrible**	furchtbar
disappointed	enttäuscht	**tired**	müde
embarrassed	verlegen	**unhappy/sad**	traurig
excited	aufgeregt	**worried**	besorgt

6 Spelling and pronunciation

1. Some words that are pronounced the same but spelt differently:

Peter: John! Sam! Sheila! Where is everybody?
John: Hello, Peter. What's up?
Peter: Oh, **here** you are, John. Why don't the others **hear** me calling?
John: They all went down to the beach a few minutes ago. Do you need some help?
Peter: **Would** you like to fetch some **wood** for the fire?
John: But I promised Sheila I'd **meet** her at the supermarket and help her to buy the **meat** for the barbecue. Can't you ask someone else?
Peter: Who? Sam's sitting in the **sun** playing with his **son**. The others have gone to **see** the **sea**. I expect they're sitting down **there** with **their** feet in the water while I do all the work!
John: **Poor** Peter! Never mind! Shall I **pour** you a cup of tea before I get the food?

[hɪə] = here, hear   [wʊd] = would, wood   [miːt] = meet, meat
[sʌn] = sun, son   [siː] = see, sea   [ðeə] = there, their
[pɔː] = poor, pour

165

Skills and tips

Two robbers too many – watch your spelling!

Two men wanted to rob a bank when it opened at two o'clock. But they were too late. Two other men had the same idea, too. These two men hid in the bank just before the people in the bank went to lunch. Then they started to break into the safe. But they were too slow. When the manager returned at exactly two minutes to two, he saw the other two men waiting outside the bank. So he telephoned the police station to get help. When they saw two police cars arriving, the two men outside the bank ran off. The two men inside the bank wanted to escape, too, but the police were too quick for them. The men were arrested and taken to the police station.

The robbers did not know that there was no money in the safe. It was an old safe, and the bank manager knew that a new safe would be delivered that afternoon, so the old safe was empty.

[nəʊ] = no, know [njuː] = new, knew [tuː] = two, too

[bluː]
The tornado **blew** the **blue** car off the road.

Der Wirbelwind **blies** das **blaue** Auto von der Straße.

[θruː]
The new girl **threw** a stone **through** the school window.

Die Neue **warf** einen Stein **durchs** Schulfenster.

[wiːk], [ˈaʊə]
Manchester United has had a **weak week**.
"But **our hour** will come!" said the manager.

Manchester United hatte eine **schwache Woche**.
„**Unsere Stunde** wird aber kommen!" sagte der Cheftrainer.

[raɪt]
Write the **right** answer on a postcard and send it to Mr **Wright**.

Schreiben Sie die **richtige** Antwort auf eine Postkarte und schicken Sie sie an Herrn **Wright**.

– *What is black and white and red all over?*
– *I don't know. How can something be black, white and red all over?*
– *Well, a book is printed in black and white – but it's re(a)d, too!"*

Skills and tips

2. Same spelling, different pronunciation

row

They were sitting in the front **row** [rəʊ].   Sie saßen in der ersten **Reihe**.

He had a **row** [raʊ] with his girlfriend.   Er hatte **Krach** mit seiner Freundin.

bow

A **bow** [bəʊ] and arrow.   Ein Pfeil und **Bogen**.

Robin Hood **bowed** [baʊd] to the Sheriff of Nottingham.   Robin Hood **verbeugte sich** vor dem Sheriff von Nottingham.

live

We **live** [lɪv] in Britain.   Wir **leben** in Großbritannien.

There was **live** [laɪv] music at the party.   Es gab **Live**-Musik auf der Party.

⚠ *Germans often pronounce the word 'Live' incorrectly and even spell it incorrectly, too! A „Life-Konzert" would be a „Lebenskonzert"!*

7 'Make' or 'do'?

What shall we do?

Jane: It's a wonderful day today. What shall we **do** this afternoon?
Pete: Let's **go for a cycle ride** in the country. We haven't **done** that for a long time.
Matt: But I've got to **do** some German **homework**. We've got a test tomorrow.
Jane: Can't you **do** that after we come back, Matt?
Matt: OK. Shall we **make** some **sandwiches**?
Jane: Good idea. You can **do** that. And I'll take my camera so I can **take a few pictures**.
Pete: Can we **make** some tea to take with us, too?
Matt: Can't you **do** your share of the work and **make** the tea?
Jane: *Do* stop arguing, you two, or we'll never **get** everything **done**!

In English, the verb 'make' often means *machen* in the sense of 'to actually produce', 'to construct', 'to build'. The verb 'do' often means *tun/machen* in the sense of the German verb *erledigen*:

She **made** a model plane.   Sie **baute** ein Modellflugzeug.
He **did** his homework.   Er **machte** *(=löste)* seine Schulaufgaben
We **did** the test.   Wir **machten** *(= schrieben)* den Test.

Skills and tips

to make = machen

She **made the beds**.
Anyone can **make a mistake**.
Don't **make so much noise**.
We **made a mess** in the kitchen.

She **made fun of** me.
It's **made of** wood.

Sie **machte die Betten**.
Jeder kann **einen Fehler machen**.
Macht nicht soviel Krach.
Wir **machten viel Unordnung** in der Küche.

Sie **machte sich lustig** über mich.
Es ist **aus** Holz (**gemacht**).

to do = machen

What did I **do wrong**?
What do you **do (for a living)**?
I've got to **do my homework**.

He **does his share of the work**.

Was habe ich (da) **falsch gemacht**?
Was **machen Sie beruflich**?
Ich muss **meine Hausaufgaben machen**.

Er **macht seinen Anteil der Arbeit**.

to do = tun

I've got nothing to **do** today.
What can I do for you?
You could **do me a big favour**.

Heute habe ich nichts zu **tun**.
Was kann ich für dich/Sie tun?
Du könntest mir **einen großen Gefallen tun**.

⚠ machen ≠ to make

We **went for a cycle ride**.
I **took a photo**.

Wir **machten eine Radtour**.
Ich **machte ein Foto**.

⚠ to make/to do = different constructions in English and German

He **made friends with** her.
Make up your mind.
They **made** me wait.
He **made** that story **up**.
He **made his fortune** in America.
Make sure all the windows are closed before you leave.
Can you **make the tea**?
She **made a fool of herself** in front of the whole class.
Do you think we'll **make it**?

I don't think she **makes a lot of money** at her present job.
What he told me doesn't **make sense**.
He **made** a strange **request**.

That will do!
Do stop **making such a noise**!

I've **done the shopping**.

Er hat **sich mit** ihr **angefreundet**.
Entscheide dich endlich!
Sie **ließen** mich warten.
Diese Geschichte **hat** er **erfunden**.
Er **wurde** in Amerika **reich**.
Sorge dafür, dass alle Fenster zu sind, bevor du gehst.
Kannst du **den Tee kochen**?
Sie **machte sich** vor der ganzen Klasse **lächerlich**.
Glaubst du, das **schaffen** wir **rechtzeitig**?

Ich glaube nicht, dass sie bei ihrer jetzigen Arbeit **viel Geld verdient**.
Was er mir sagte, **ergibt keinen Sinn**.

Er **stellte** eine merkwürdige **Bitte**.

Das reicht!/Das genügt!
Hört **doch endlich** auf, so einen Krach zu machen!

Ich habe **eingekauft**.

Skills and tips

She **did well in her exams**.	Sie **schnitt in der Prüfung gut ab**.	
He **does a paper round**.	Er **trägt Zeitungen aus**.	
If there isn't enough food, some people will have to **do without**.	Wenn das Essen nicht ausreicht, müssen eben einige **ohne auskommen/darauf verzichten**.	
Do you think we'll be able to **do it all**?	Glaubst du, **das alles** werden wir **schaffen können**?	
We'll never **get** it all **done**.	Wir werden das alles nie **schaffen**.	

to make do

We'll just have to **make do** with what we've got.	Wir werden einfach mit dem, was wir haben, **auskommen** müssen.

8 Useful expressions with common verbs

to be ...

less formal	more formal	
He **is in**.	He **is at home**.	zu Hause sein
She **is out**.	She **is not at home**.	nicht zu Hause sein
We**'re out of** bread.	We **don't have any more** bread.	kein ... mehr übrig haben (Das Brot ist alle.)
She**'s away** in Scotland.	She **has gone to** Scotland.	verreist sein
It's difficult. **Are** you really **up to it**?	It's difficult. **Can** you really **do it**?	der Sache gewachsen sein
You**'re up** early!	You**'ve got up** early!	aufstehen, auf sein
We**'re off** now!	We**'re leaving** now!	losfahren
The milk **is off**.	The milk **has turned bad**.	schlecht geworden sein
The match **is off**.	The match **has been cancelled**.	abgesagt werden
The race **is on** today.	The race **takes place** today.	stattfinden
They'll **be back** this evening.	They'll **return** this evening.	zurückkommen
The programme **is over**.	The programme **has finished**.	vorbei sein
What **are** the kids **up to**?	What **are** the children **doing**?	etwas anstellen/treiben
I**'m for** doing the washing-up first.	I **think it would be a good idea** to do the washing-up first.	für etwas sein, dafür sein, dass ...
I**'m against** waiting for them.	I **don't think it would be a good idea** to wait for them.	gegen etwas sein, dagegen sein, dass ...

Skills and tips

to bring ...

Our new boss **has brought about** many changes.	etwas herbeiführen
Bring a couple of friends **along**.	jdn. mitbringen
Both her parents died, so her aunt **brought** her **up**.	jdn. großziehen/aufziehen
I'm glad you **brought that point up**.	etwas erwähnen/ins Spiel bringen

to come ...

After a few days one of the wheels of her new rollerblades **came off**.	sich lösen
Come on! We're late already.	Los!/Gehen wir!
What did you do yesterday evening? – Peter **came round** and we watched TV.	vorbeischauen/-kommen
My dream has **come true**.	wahr werden

to get ...

She **got dressed** immediately.	sich anziehen
He **got up** at 6.15.	aufstehen
I **got on** the bus at the station and **got off** at the airport	einsteigen ausstegen
We hope you **get better** soon.	gesund werden
Get well soon!	Gute Besserung!
Sorry I'm late – I **got lost**.	sich verlaufen
The talk was not very interesting, so we soon **got bored**.	sich langweilen
She doesn't **get on with** her mother.	mit jdm. auskommen
The prisoners **got away**.	entkommen
He **got away with** the robbery.	ungestraft davonkommen
How are you **getting on with** your work?	mit etwas vorankommen
Mum **got to know** Dad in Bristol.	jdn. kennen lernen
I soon **got used to** working outdoors.	sich an etwas gewöhnen
He still hasn't **got over** his grandmother's death.	über etwas hinwegkommen
This weather is **getting me down**.	... macht mich ganz fertig.
Hurry up and **get ready**! We're late.	sich fertig machen
Haven't you **got rid of** that cough yet?	etwas loswerden

to go ...

Let's **go for a walk**.	spazieren gehen
"**Go on**," said the policeman.	Erzählen Sie weiter!
"**Go on** with your work," said the boss.	weitermachen
"Why is there so much noise?" asked the headmaster. "What's **going on** here?"	Was ist hier los?/Was geht hier vor?
"Nothing ever **goes right** for me. Everything I do **goes wrong**."	richtig laufen, klappen schief gehen
Where do the cups **go**?	Wo kommen die Tassen hin?
The workers are **going on strike** next week.	streiken

Skills and tips

The bomb **went off** at 7 a.m.	explodieren
The holidays **went by** so quickly!	vorbeigehen, vorübergehen
My Mum will **go mad** if she hears!	wütend werden

to have …

I **had a shower** after the match.	(sich) duschen
We **had breakfast** in the kitchen.	frühstücken
We always **have tea** at six o'clock.	Abendbrot essen
Can we **have a chat** some time?	ein bisschen plaudern
I'd like to **have a word** with you.	mit jdm. (über etwas) reden
Keep warm if you **have a cold**.	erkältet sein
She **had** her car **repaired/washed** last week.	etwas reparieren/waschen lassen
They **have** little **in common**.	etwas gemeinsam haben
I **have to**/I**'ve got to** leave early today.	müssen

to keep …

I try to **keep fit**.	fit bleiben
Danger! **Keep out**!	Eintritt verboten!
He **kept on trying**.	es immer wieder versuchen
Keep to the rules!	sich an etwas halten
Keep to the footpath across the field and try to **keep up with** the others.	auf dem Fußweg bleiben mithalten, mitkommen

to look …

Look at this picture.	(sich) etwas anschauen
He **looked up** and saw her.	aufblicken
Look up their number in the telephone book.	etwas nachschlagen
The police are **looking into** his alibi.	etwas untersuchen/überprüfen
She's **looking for** a better job.	nach etwas suchen
I'm **looking forward to** going on holiday.	sich auf etwas freuen
Look out!	Pass auf!
Look out for snakes!	nach etwas Ausschau halten
Look after the baby while I'm out.	auf jdn./etwas aufpassen
She **looks down on** everybody.	jdn. verachten
He **looks up to** his teacher.	jdn. respektieren
Look in on your way home.	hereinschauen
He **looks like** his brother.	aussehen (wie)

to put …

He **put down** his book.	etwas hinlegen
The army **put the rebellion down** with great brutality.	einen Aufstand niederschlagen
Put that **down** in your notebook.	etwas aufschreiben
They soon **put out the fire**.	das Feuer löschen
Take off your coat and **put** a pullover **on**.	etwas anziehen

Skills and tips

If you don't like it, you'll just have to **put up with** it.	mit etwas leben, sich mit etwas abfinden
If Mr Smith phones, **put** him **through**.	jdn. durchstellen
She's **put her name down for** tennis lessons.	sich für etwas eintragen
He was **put out** that he wasn't invited.	verärgert sein
Can we **put off** our meeting till next week?	etwas verschieben

to run ...

He **runs** a hotel on the edge of town.	etwas führen/betreiben
The trains do not **run** in the winter.	verkehren, fahren
The children **ran away**.	weglaufen
My ipod isn't working. The batteries have **run down**.	schwach/leer werden
He nearly **ran over** a cat on his way to work.	jdn./etwas überfahren
We **ran out of** petrol last week.	... ging uns aus
You **run the risk of** losing your licence.	Gefahr laufen etwas zu tun
She **ran up to** me.	auf jdn. zulaufen
I **ran into** him yesterday.	jdn. zufällig treffen
He **ran into** a tree last week.	gegen etw. fahren/laufen

to take ...

I **took him for** his brother.	jdn. für jdn. anders halten
Our plane **took off** ten minutes late.	starten
They **took off** their shoes.	ausziehen
He **has taken up** painting as a hobby.	mit etwas anfangen
She **takes after** her mother.	jdm. ähnlich sehen
The referee **took out** his whistle.	etwas zücken/hervorholen
We **took a few photos/pictures**.	Fotos machen
I **took** my friends **out** for a meal.	jdn. einladen/ausführen
How long does the journey **take**?	dauern
Don't take all day!	Beeile dich!
The policewoman **took** our names and addresses.	etwas aufschreiben
The competition **takes place** next week.	stattfinden
Do you still want to **take part**?	teilnehmen
He often **takes** the dog **for a walk**.	mit (dem Hund) spazieren gehen
I **took hold of his hand.** I **took** him **by the hand.**	jdn. bei der Hand fassen
We must **take a chance**.	etwas riskieren
Can't we **take turns**?	sich abwechseln
We **took a wrong turning** in Leeds.	falsch abbiegen
I **took** the clock **apart/to pieces** to see how it worked.	etwas auseinander nehmen
My brother has **taken over** our parents' restaurant.	etwas übernehmen
The firm is **taking on** three new employees.	jdn. einstellen
Take care!	Mach's gut!/Pass auf dich auf!
I'm feeling tired. Shall we **take a break**?	eine Pause machen
He's **taking** an English **course**.	einen Kurs machen

Skills and tips

to turn ...

Turn that TV **off** and	ausschalten
turn the radio back **on**, please!	einschalten
Turn up/down the volume a bit.	hoch-/herunterdrehen
He **turned down** a good job last week.	ablehnen
The ugly prince **turned into** a beautiful frog.	sich in etwas verwandeln
She **turned round** quickly.	sich umdrehen
The weather has **turned** quite **cold/warm**.	kalt/warm werden
I waited for ages, but she didn't **turn up**.	erscheinen
Turn over the page and read from the top.	(eine Seite) umblättern

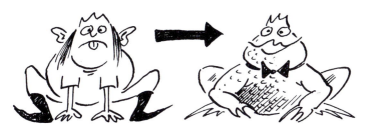

9 Problem words in German

beide, einer von beiden

Beide trugen schwarz.	They **both** wore black.
Beide waren bewaffnet.	They were **both** armed./**Both of them** were armed.
Die Polizei sucht nach **den beiden Verbrechern**.	The police are looking for **the two criminals**.
⚠ *'die beiden' ≠ 'the both'*	
Es gibt eine Belohnung für die Festnahme von **einem der beiden**.	There is a reward for the capture of **either of them**.
Beide Züge halten in Bath. Sie können **beide** nehmen. Nur **einen der beiden**, natürlich!	**Both** trains stop in Bath. You can take **either** of them. *(keine Verwechslung im Englischen möglich!)*

bringen

Du kannst einen Freund **mitbringen**.	You can **bring** a friend **along**.
Kannst du mir eine Zeitschrift (her)**bringen**?	Can you **bring** me a magazine?
Könntest du mich zum Bahnhof (hin)**bringen**?	⚠ Could you **take** me to the station?

⚠ *'take' is always used with movement **away from** a person.*
 *'bring' is always used with movement **towards** a person.*

Skills and tips

fahren, gehen

Ich **gehe** jede Woche ins Kino.	I **go** to the cinema every week.
Ich **fahre** manchmal **mit dem Bus**.	I sometimes **go by bus**.
Der nächste Bus **fährt** um sechs.	The next bus **leaves** at six.
Könntest du mich zum Bahnhof **fahren**?	Could you **take** me to the station?
Meine Mutter **fährt mit dem Auto** zur Arbeit.	My mother **drives** to work/**goes** to work **by car**.
Ich **fahre mit dem Rad** in die Schule aber meine Schwester **geht zu Fuß**.	I **cycle** to school but my sister **walks**.
Wir **fahren** oft mit der Bahn.	We often **take the**/**go by** train.

laufen

Ich **laufe** jeden Tag zur Schule.	I **walk** to school every day.
Wie schnell **bist** du **gelaufen**?	How fast **did** you **run**?
Die Geschäfte **laufen nicht** gut.	Business **isn't going** well.
Der Motor **läuft**.	The engine **is running**.

sagen

Er **sagte** "Guten Morgen". *(with direct speech)*	He **said** "Good morning".
Er **sagte**, er wohne in London. *(with indirect statements)*	He **said** he lived in London.
Sag mir, wo du wohnst. *('sagen' + indirect object ≠ 'say')*	⚠ **Tell me** where you live.
Er **sagte mir** nichts. *('say' is **never** followed by an **indirect object** like this in English)*	⚠ He **told me** nothing. *(indirect object first – use 'tell')* ⚠ He **said** nothing **to me**. *(direct object first – use 'say')*

A young English student rushed into a small German post office just before closing time one evening. He wanted to weigh a parcel but was in such a hurry that he mixed up his German vowels.
He smiled at the young lady behind the counter and said:
"Haben Sie eine Wiege? Ich will etwas wagen!"

Skills and tips

so

Sie spielt nicht **so** gut.	She doesn't play **so/that** well.
Sie spielt nicht **so** gut wie ich.	She doesn't play **as** well as I do.
Das Spiel geht **so**: …	The game goes **like this**: …
Er ist **so** lieb!	He's **so** nice.
So ein Unsinn!/Quatsch!	**What** nonsense/rubbish!
Sie hat **so einen** lieben Hund.	She's got **such a** nice dog.

spielen, Spiel

Wir **spielen** jeden Tag Fußball.	We **play** football every day.
Er **spielt** Schlagzeug.	He **plays** the drums.
Sie **spielte** in dem Stück die Julia.	She **played/acted** Juliet in the play.
Im **Spiel** am Samstag **spielte** die Mannschaft sehr gut.	The team **played** very well in the **match/game** on Saturday.
Es spielt keine Rolle.	**It makes no difference**.

Stück

ein **Stück** Kuchen	a **piece** of cake
ein **(Musik-)Stück** von Mozart.	a **piece** (of music) by Mozart
ein **(Theater-)Stück** von Goethe.	a **play** by Goethe
£ 2 **das Stück**	£2 **each**

10 One word in German, two or more in English

alle/Alles

Alle Kühe fressen Gras.	**All** cows eat grass.
Alle Kühe auf dieser Weide gehören Herrn Smith.	**All the** cows in this meadow belong to Mr Smith.
Wir fahren **alle** zwei Jahre hin.	We go there **every** two years.
Haben wir **alles**?	Have we got **everything**?
Sind **alle** da?	Is **everyone** here?

als

Als ich ihn sah, winkte er.	**When** I saw him, he waved.
Er sah älter aus **als** auf dem Bild.	He looked older **than** in the photo.
Gerade **als** ich ankam, fuhr der Bus los.	Just **as** I arrived, the bus drove off.
Er verkleidete sich **als** Frau.	He dressed up **as** a woman.

bei

The German preposition 'bei' is only rarely translated as 'by' in English:

bei Tag/Nacht	**by** day/night
Sie nahm mich **bei** der Hand.	She took me **by** the hand.

But:

Wir wohnten **bei** Freunden.	We stayed **with** friends.
Gestern war ich **bei** meiner Tante.	I was **at** my aunt**'s** yesterday.

Skills and tips

Ich wohne in Watford **bei** London.
Sie arbeitet **bei** der BBC.
Jetzt ist er **beim Militär**.
Beim Lesen des Artikels …

I live in Watford, **near** London.
She works **at/for** the BBC.
He's **in the army** now.
When reading the article …

besuchen

Er **besucht** sie jede Woche.
Sie **besucht** eine Privatschule.

He **visits** her every week.
She **goes to/attends** a private school.

bis

Wir müssen **bis** 16.00 Uhr in der Schule bleiben.
Er muss **bis** (spätestens) halb zehn am Bahnhof sein. Sein Zug fährt um 9.45 Uhr.

We have to stay at school **until** 4 p.m. *(until = length of action)*
He has to be at the station **by** half past nine. His train leaves at 9.45. *(by = before, at the latest)*

Bus

Wir nahmen den **Bus** zum Bahnhof.

Der **(Reise-)Bus** war sehr bequem.

We took the **bus** to the station. *(bus = Linienbus)*
The **coach** was very comfortable. *(coach = Reisebus)*

erinnern

Sie **erinnert mich** an ihren Bruder.
Ich muss Susi morgen anrufen. Kannst du **mich** daran **erinnern**?
Wir waren vor zehn Jahren hier. **Erinnerst** du **dich** daran?

She **reminds me** of her brother.
I've got to ring Susi tomorrow. Can you **remind me**?
We were here ten years ago. Do you **remember** (it)?

erst

Das Flugzeug landet **erst um** eins.

Erst dann war mir klar, dass …
Aber wir kennen uns **erst** einige Tage!
Das macht es **erst recht** interessant!

The plane does **not** arrive **until** one o'clock. *(compare 'bis')*
It was **only then** that I realized that …
But we've **only** known each other a few days!
That makes it **all the more** interesting!

fertig

Bist du **fertig**? *(Kann's losgehen?)*
Bist du **fertig**? *(am Ende einer Arbeit)*
Ich war **fix und fertig**!

Are you **ready**?
Have you **finished**?
I was **exhausted/tired out**.

früher

Sie kamen **früher**, als ich erwartet hatte.
Wir wohnten **früher** in London.

They arrived **sooner/earlier** than I had expected. *(adverb)*
We **used to** live in London. *(things which you no longer do)*

Skills and tips

Sachsen war **früher** ein Königreich. **Years ago/Formerly/In former times** Saxony was a kingdom.

Früher wurden Schüler **oft** von ihren Lehrern geschlagen. (**In the old days**) pupils **often used to** be hit by their teachers.

Der **frühere** König musste 1918 abdanken. The **former** king was forced to abdicate in 1918. (=*'ehemalig'*)

Sie hatte einen Sohn aus einer **früheren** Ehe. She had a son from a **previous** marriage. (=*'vorherig'*)

⚠ *The phrase 'in former times' is very formal and 'bookish'. The phrase 'used to' is normally the easiest way to translate 'früher' when it is used as an adverb of time: Saxony used to be a kingdom.*

Geschichte

Er erzählte mir eine **Geschichte**. He told me a **story**.
Geschichte ist mein Lieblingsfach. **History** is my favourite subject.

glücklich, Glück

Ich **hatte** sehr viel **Glück**. I **was** very **lucky**.
Was für ein Glück! **What luck!**
Er war sehr **glücklich**, sie zu sehen. He was very **happy** to see her.
Glück kann man nicht kaufen. Money doesn't buy **happiness**.

groß

Napoleon war kein **großer** Mann, aber ein **großer** General. Napoleon was not a **big/tall** man, but he was a **great** general.

hoch

Der Snowdon ist ein **hoher** Berg. Snowdon is a **high** mountain.
Sie starb im **hohen** Alter. She died at a **great** age.
Er verlor die Münze im **hohen** Gras. He lost the coin in the **long** grass.

hören

Wir **hörten** die Explosion. We **heard** the explosion.
Wir **hörten** die Sendung. We **listened to** the programme.
Er **hatte nie** von Einstein **gehört**. He **had never heard of** Einstein.

jeder

Wir gehen **jeden** Tag hin. We go there **every** day.
Das weiß **jeder**. **Everyone/Everybody** knows that. (= *alle Leute*)

Das weiß **jeder Dummkopf**! **Any fool** knows that! (= *jeder x-beliebige als Einzelperson*)

Er gab **jedem (von uns)** einen Apfel. He gave **each of us** an apple.

177

Skills and tips

Karte

Wo fährst du denn im Urlaub hin?
  Zeig's mir auf der **Karte**. Schickst du mir eine **Karte**?
Ich habe **Karten** für's Popkonzert!
Herr Ober! Die **Karte**, bitte!

Where are you going on holiday?
  Show me it on the **map**. Will you send me a **card**?
I've got **tickets** for the pop concert!
Waiter! The **menu** ['menju:], please.

Land

Russland ist ein riesiges **Land**.
Sie besitzt viel **Land**.
Wir wohnen **auf dem Land**.
Leute **aus allen Ländern**
Deutschland besteht aus 15 **Ländern**.

Russia is a huge **country**.
She owns a lot of **land**.
We live **in the country**.
people **from all over the world**
Germany consists of 15 **states/ 'länder'**.

lassen

zulassen, erlauben: 'let' + infinitive without 'to'

Er **lässt mich** manchmal **fahren**.
Die Polizei **ließ sie laufen**.

He sometimes **lets me drive**.
The police **let them go**.

veranlassen, zwingen: 'make' + infinitive without 'to'

Sie **ließen uns** draußen **warten**.

They **made us wait** outside.

etwas (von jdm.) machen lassen: 'have' + object + past participle

Er **ließ** sein Auto **reparieren**.

He **had** his car **repaired**.

other meanings of **lassen**

Sie **ließ** das Buch **fallen**.
Sie **ließ** das Buch auf dem Tisch (**liegen**).
Lass das!

She **dropped** the book.
She **left** the book on the table.

Stop it!

nächste(r/s)

Wo ist die **nächste** Haltestelle?

Wir müssen mit dem **nächsten** Bus fahren.

Where is the **nearest** bus stop?
  (Entfernung)
We have to catch the **next** bus.
  (Reihenfolge)

noch/noch nicht

Es gibt **noch viel** zu tun.
Hast du den Film **noch nicht** gesehen?
Gib mir **noch etwas** Milch, bitte.
Ich habe **noch eine** Frage.
Sie hat **immer noch** einen Brief zu schreiben.
Sind **noch** Plätze frei?

There is **still a lot** to do.
Haven**'t** you seen that film **yet**?

Please give me **a little more** milk.
I've got **another** question.
She **still** has one letter to write.

Are there (**still**) **any** seats left?

Skills and tips

ein paar, ein Paar

Ich borgte mir **ein paar** Pfund, um mir **ein Paar** Handschuhe zu kaufen.	I borrowed **a couple of/a few** pounds to buy myself **a pair of** gloves.
Sie und ihr Freund sind ein glückliches **Paar**.	She and her boyfriend make a happy **couple**.
Ich verreise nur für **zwei, drei** Tage.	I'm only going away for **a couple of** days.

Platz

Das ist mein **Platz**!	This is my **place**! (= seat)
Im Abteil war kein **Platz** frei.	There were no vacant **seats** in the compartment.
Hast du einen **Platz** reserviert?	Have you booked a **seat**?
Nehmen Sie doch **Platz**.	Please **take a seat**./Please **sit down**.
Es gab keinen **Platz** zum Sitzen.	There was no **room/space** to sit.
Hier ist kein **Platz** für die großen Teller.	There's no **room** for the big plates.
Das Hotel ist auf dem **Platz** vor dem Bahnhof.	The hotel is on the **square** in front of the station.
Die Zuschauer stürmten den **Platz**.	The spectators ran onto the **field** (*Fußballplatz usw.*)/**court** (*Tennisplatz*)/**course** (*Golfplatz*).

Preis

Der neue **Preis** beträgt £ 10.	The new **price** [praɪs] is £10.
Sie gewann den ersten **Preis** im Wettbewerb.	She won first **prize** [praɪz] in the competition.

schon

Ich habe meine Hausaufgaben **schon** gemacht.	I've **already** done my homework.
Schon früh konnte er Klavier spielen.	He was able to play the piano **at an early age**.
Schon damals haben alle Leute sein Klavierspiel bewundert.	**Even then** everybody admired the way he played the piano.
Ich warte **schon seit** sechs Monaten auf einen Termin.	I've been waiting for an appointment **for** six months (**now**).

⚠ *'schon' is often left untranslated in sentences like:*

Ich komme (ja) **schon**!	I'm coming!
Sie wohnen **schon** seit Jahren hier.	They've been living here for years.

schwer

Der Koffer war zu **schwer** (*an Gewicht*).	The suitcase was too **heavy**.
Das Problem war zu **schwer** (= *schwierig*).	The problem was too **difficult**.

Skills and tips

sehen

Ich **sah** dich gestern in der Stadt.
Wir **haben** den Film im Fernsehen **gesehen**.
Sie **sieht fern**.
Sie **sahen** sich die Unterschrift genau **an**.
Heute **sah** er entspannter **aus**.

I saw you in town yesterday.
We saw/watched the film on TV.
  ('watch' is more concentrated)
She's watching TV.
They looked at the signature closely.

He looked more relaxed today.

Stock

Sie hatte einen schweren Unfall und geht nun am **Stock**.
Sie wohnt im dritten **Stock**.
Ich wohne in einem **dreistöckigen** Haus.

She had a serious accident and now walks with a stick.
She lives on the third floor.
I live in a three-storey house/a house with three floors.

⚠ *In America the 'ground floor' ('Erdgeschoss') is called the 'first floor', so the 'third floor' ('3. Stock') in a London house would be called the 'fourth floor' in New York!*

Tasche

Er steckte die Hände in die **Taschen**.
Er trug eine schwere **Tasche**.
Sie hatte keine (**Hand-)Tasche** dabei.

He put his hands in his pockets.
He was carrying a heavy bag.
She was not carrying a handbag.
  *(AE often uses **purse** [pɜːs].)*

tragen

Er **trug** eine Maske.
Er **trug** eine Pistole.

He was wearing a mask.
He was carrying a gun.

Uhr

Abends nehme ich immer meine (**Armband-)Uhr** ab.
Eine große **Uhr** hing an der Wand.
Wie viel Uhr ist es?
Es ist vier **Uhr**.

I always take my watch off at night.
There was a large clock on the wall.
What time is it?
It's four o'clock.

viel

Hast du **viel** Gepäck mitgebracht?

Hast du **viele** Taschen?

Did you bring much luggage with you? *('much' + singular noun)*
Have you got many bags? *('many' + plural noun)*

vor

Sie war nervös **vor** der Prüfung.

Er stand **vor** ihr.

She was nervous before her exam. *(time)*
He stood in front of her. *(place)*

Skills and tips

wenn

Ich sag's ihm, **wenn** ich ihn sehe. *(wenn = falls)*
Ich sag's ihm, **wenn** ich ihn das nächste Mal sehe. *(zeitlich)*
Auch wenn er noch recht jung ist, weiß er eine Menge.
Immer wenn ich ihr schreibe, grüße ich sie von dir.

I'll tell him **if** I see him.
I'll tell him **when** I see him next.
Even though/Although he's still quite young, he knows a lot.
Whenever I write to her I send/give her your best wishes.

werden

Es **wird** dunkel.
Er **wurde** rot.
Sie **wird** schnell wütend.
Er **wurde** Polizist.
Er **wurde** verhaftet.

It**'s getting** dark.
He **turned/went** red./He **blushed**.
She **gets** angry easily.
He **became** a policeman.
He **was/got** arrested.

⚠ *Forming the passive with 'get' is common in spoken English.*

wie

Wie machst du das?
Wie machst du das **bloß**?
Wie war das Wetter gestern?
Wie bitte? Ich verstehe dich nicht. *(höfliche Bitte um Wiederholung)*
Wie bitte/Was? Ich verstehe dich nicht! *(weniger höflich oder erstaunt!)*
Wie war das mit dem Auto?
Er lebt **wie** Gott in Frankreich.
Sie ist **so** alt **wie** meine Mutter.

How do you do that?
How on earth do you do/manage it?
What was the weather **like** yesterday?
Sorry/(I beg your) Pardon? I don't understand you.
What? I don't understand you!

What was that about the car?
He lives **like** a king.
She is **as** old **as** my mother.

wohnen

Wo **wohnst** du?
Wo **wohnst** du? *(im Hotel oder bei Besuchen)*
Sie **wohnen** jetzt zusammen und wollen zusammenbleiben.

Where do you **live**?
Where **are** you **staying**?/Who **are** you **staying** *(not 'living'!)* with?
They're **living** together now and they want to stay together.

zuerst

(Zu)erst biegen Sie links ab, dann fahren Sie geradeaus bis zur nächsten Ampel. *(als Erstes)*
Zuerst war ich etwas enttäuscht. *(anfänglich)*

First turn left, then drive straight on until you get to the next traffic lights.
At first I was a bit disappointed.

Skills and tips

11 One word in English, two or more in German

argument

They had a big **argument** last night. Gestern Abend hatten sie einen großen **Streit**.

He put forward several interesting **arguments**. Er brachte einige interessante **Argumente** vor.

before

Be home **before** eleven. Sei **vor** elf zu Hause!
Say goodbye **before** you go. Sag auf Wiedersehen **bevor** du gehst.

change

She has **changed** her e-mail address. Sie hat ihre E-Mail-Adresse **geändert**.
You haven't **changed** a bit. Du hast **dich** überhaupt nicht **verändert**.

Can I **change** in your bedroom? Kann ich **mich** in deinem Schlafzimmer **umziehen**?

Can I **change** this T-shirt? Kann ich dieses T-Shirt **umtauschen**?
You should **change** your doctor. Sie sollten Ihren Arzt **wechseln**.
I think we have to **change** here. Ich glaube, wir müssen hier **umsteigen**.

Today we had coffee **for a change**. Heute tranken wir **zur Abwechslung** Kaffee.

fair

That's not **fair**! Das ist nicht **fair**!
We went to the **fair**. Wir gingen zum **Jahrmarkt/Rummel**.
He's got **fair** hair. Er hat **blondes** Haar.

fault

Why blame me? It's not my **fault**. Warum gibst du mir die Schuld? Es ist nicht meine **Schuld**.

He has many **faults**. Er hat viele **Fehler**.

kind

That was **kind** of you. Das war **nett** von dir.
What kind of car have they got? **Was für** ein Auto haben sie?
I don't like these biscuits. Have you got any other **kind**? Ich mag diese Kekse nicht. Haben Sie eine andere **Sorte**?

know

I **know** him by sight, but I don't **know** his name. Ich **kenne** ihn vom Sehen, aber ich **weiß** seinen Namen nicht.
Mum **got to know** Dad in Bristol. Mutti **lernte** Vati in Bristol **kennen**.

Skills and tips

like

He **looks like** his father.
They **like** their cousin Helen.
What's the weather **like** today?

Er **sieht aus wie** sein Vater.
Sie **mögen** ihre Kusine Helen.
Wie ist das Wetter heute?

own

He **owns** a car.
He has a car **of his own**/**his own** car.

Er **besitzt** ein Auto.
Er hat **ein eigenes** Auto.

place

Edinburgh is an interesting **place**.
Pick me up **at my place**.
We'll meet **at my place**.
The race **takes place** every year.
She's always at the wrong **place** at the wrong time!
He finished in third **place**./He came third.

Edinburgh ist ein interessanter **Ort**.
Hol mich **von meiner Wohnung** ab.
Wir treffen uns **bei mir**.
Das Rennen **findet** jedes Jahr **statt**.
Sie ist immer zum falschen Zeitpunkt an der falschen **Stelle**!
Er belegte den dritten **Platz**.

"Let's enjoy it while we can – this is the place where they're going to build the new leisure centre."

pretty

Sue is very **pretty**.
Sue was **pretty** angry with me.

Sue ist sehr **hübsch**.
Sue war **ziemlich** böse auf mich.

rest

Have a rest.
The rest of the week is free.
The rest of them stayed at home.

Ruh dich aus!
Der **Rest der Woche** ist frei.
Die Übrigen blieben zu Hause.

Skills and tips

trip

We went on a **day trip** to London.
Wir machten einen **Tagesausflug** nach London.

When I **tripped** over a stone my friend said "**Have a nice trip!**"
Als ich über einen Stein **stolperte**, sagte mein Bekannter „**Gute Reise!**"

use

⚠ *Be careful! The two pronunciations of 'used' – [juːzd]/[juːst] – have different meanings!*

I always **use** [juːz] the Underground when I'm in London.
Wenn ich in London bin, **benutze** ich immer die U-Bahn.

I **used** [juːzd] your phone last night.
Gestern Abend **habe** ich dein Telefon **benutzt**.

We **used** [juːst] **to live** in Germany.
Wir **wohnten früher** in Deutschland.

We **are used** [juːst] **to** speak**ing** German.
Wir **sind es gewohnt**, Deutsch **zu** sprechen.

We soon **got used** [juːst] **to** eat**ing** German food.
Wir **gewöhnten uns** bald **ans** deutsche Essen.

wonder

It was a **wonder** that she survived the plane crash. I **wonder** if/whether she'll ever fly again!
Es war ein **Wunder**, dass sie den Flugzeugabsturz überlebte. Ich **bin gespannt**, ob sie jemals wieder fliegen wird!

I **wonder** where she is.
Ich **frage mich**, wo sie (wohl) ist/wo sie bleibt.

It's very foggy. **No wonder** the bus is late! I**'m wondering** whether we should take a taxi instead.
Es ist sehr neblig. **Kein Wunder**, dass der Bus Verspätung hat! Ich **überlege**, ob wir nicht lieber ein Taxi nehmen sollten.

Key to the exercises

1 Geography

a) 1. natural resources – *Bodenschätze* 2. industrialized country – *Industrieland* 3. raw material – *Rohstoff* 4. the English Channel – *der Ärmelkanal* 5. inner city – *Innenstadt* 6. housing estate – *Wohnsiedlung* 7. inland port – *Binnenhafen* 8. service industry – *Dienstleistungsbetrieb* 9. the Channel Tunnel – *der Eurotunnel* 10. dairy farming – *Milchwirtschaft* 11. public transport – *öffentliche Verkehrsmittel*

b) 1. urban 2. poverty 3. wide 4. above sea-level 5. to freeze 6. flat 7. a wet day 8. freshwater

c) 1. border 2. crowded 3. low 4. mist 5. meadow 6. gale 7. hemisphere 8. damage 9. production 10. steel

d)

M	A	**P**				
A	R	E	**A**			
I	R	O	N			
C	**R**	O	P			
C	O	A	S	T		
D	O	C	K	**S**		
D	E	**S**	E	R	T	
C	O	M	P	A	N	**Y**
C	A	**P**	I	T	A	L
E	R	**U**	P	T	I	O	N
H	U	**R**	R	I	C	A	N	E
V	E	G	E	T	A	B	**L**	E	**S**

National Park

2 History

a)

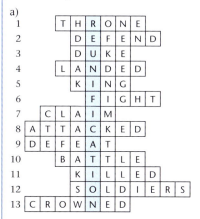

b) 1. centuries – queens – powerful – monarch – rule – Parliament 2. machines – Industrial – goods – factories – coal mines – employ 3. colonists – refugees – freedom – suffer – community 4. pioneers – territory – trains – hunting – reservations

3 Conflicts

a) 1. ethnic minority – *etnische Minderheit* 2. equal rights – *gleiche Rechte* 3. suicide bombing – *Selbstmordattentat* 4. asylum seeker – *Asylsuchender* 5. terrorist attack – *Terroranschlag* 6. skin colour – *Hautfarbe* 7. multi-cultural society – *multikulturelle Gesellschaft* 8. immigration law – *Einwanderungsgesetz* 9. police officer – *Polizeibeamter* 10. armed robbery – *bewaffneter Raub*

b) 1. prejudice 2. force 3. native 4. committed 5. theft

c) murder – to murder s.o./murderer
Verbrechen – criminal

185

Key to the exercises

grausam – cruelty
jdn./etwas hassen – hatred
threat – to threaten s.o.

d) 1. weapon 2. guilty 3. burglary 4. offender 5. jail
6. shoplifting 7. explosion
8. fine 9. vandalism

4 The media

a)

R	E	V	I	E	W		
S	C	R	E	E	N		
C	H	A	N	N	E	L	
P	U	B	L	I	S	H	
H	E	A	D	L	I	N	E
D	I	R	E	C	T	O	R
A	U	D	I	E	N	C	E
P	R	E	S	E	N	T	E	R
P	R	O	G	R	A	M	M	E
N	E	W	S	A	G	E	N	T
C	O	M	M	E	R	C	I	A	L
E	D	U	C	A	T	I	O	N	A	L
E	N	T	E	R	T	A	I	N	M	E	N	T

chat show

b) current affairs: *(politische) Tagesthemen* – popular paper: *Massenblatt* – soap opera: *Seifenoper* – movie theater: *Kino* – role model: *Vorbild* – satellite dish: *Satellitenschüssel* – crossword puzzle: *Kreuzworträtsel* – box-office hit: *Kassenschlager*

c) online – e-mails; log – website – download – print; online provider; connect – net; visit; surf; access; offline; chat rooms

5 Politics

a) 1. monarchy 2. Commons
3. constituency 4. the Supreme court 5. in office
6. Republicans

b) 1. taxpayer 2. government department 3. foreign policy
4. voting system 5. party politics 6. election campaign
7. chancellor 8. majority

c) currency – values – mobility – preident – voter

d) 1. for 2. with 3. to 4. for
5. of 6. in 7. with 8. as

e) to serve s.o. – service
Vorteil – disadvantage
politician – politics/political
regieren – government
to support s.th. – supporter

6 World problems

a)

N	U	C	L	E	A	R		P	O	W	E	R
T	R	A	F	F	I	C						
F	E	R	T	I	L	I	Z	E	R			
G	L	O	B	A	L		W	A	R	M	I	N	G
	P	O	P	U	L	A	T	I	O	N		
O	Z	O	N	E		L	A	Y	E	R		

	D	I	S	E	A	S	E	S				
C	L	I	M	A	T	E		C	H	A	N	G	E
P	O	L	L	U	T	I	O	N				
E	X	H	A	U	S	T		F	U	M	E	S
B	I	L	L	I	O	N						
D	E	C	L	I	N	E						
E	N	V	I	R	O	N	M	E	N	T		

b) 2. bottle bank 3. economic growth 4. water power
5. waste product 6. long-term effect 7. organic food
8. plastic bag 9. developing country

c) 1. to generate s.th. 2. to become extinct 3. to throw s.th. away 4. to waste s.th. 5. rise

7 Education

a) 2. comprehensive 3. boarding
4. General 5. exams 6. leave
7. A-Level 8. results

b) 1. grade 2. notebook
3. period 4. student– 5. high school 6. principal 7. vacation 8. schedule

Key to the exercises

c) 2. lunch break: *Mittagspause* 3. academic standard: *schulisches Niveau* 4. sports ground: *Sportplatz* 5. sixth form: *Oberstufe* 6. grammar school: *Gymnasium* 7. foreign language: *Fremdsprache* 8. main subject: *Hauptfach* 9. Information Technology: *Informatik* 10. doctor's certificate: *ärztliches Attest* 11. Physical Education: *Sport*

d) 1. public school 2. to be cancelled 3. exchange 4. History 5. training course 6. playground 7. to revise 8. rule

8 Relationships and problems

a) 1. uncle 2. grandmother 3. niece 4. brother-in-law 5. grandparents 6. stepfather 7. only child 8. wife

b) 1. up 2. without 3. about 4. at 5. on 6. for 7. of 8. after 9. of 10. with 11. with 12. to 13. over 14. at

c)

D	R	U	N	K					
U	N	K	I	N	D				
S	E	L	F	I	S	H			
H	A	R	M	F	U	L			
J	E	A	L	O	U	S			
D	I	V	O	R	C	E	D		
P	R	E	G	N	A	N	T		
D	E	P	R	E	S	S	E	D	
S	E	P	A	R	A	T	E	D	
I	M	P	A	T	I	E	N	T	
R	I	D	I	C	U	L	O	U	S
I	N	D	E	P	E	N	D	E	N	T
E	M	B	A	R	R	A	S	S	E	D
I	R	R	E	S	P	O	N	S	I	B	L	E

NON-SMOKING AREA

9 Young people's interests

a) 1. sport 2. match 3. play 4. acting 5. audience 6. performance

b) 1. spare 2. cycling 3. meet 4. countryside 5. energetic

6. fit 7. leisure 8. part 9. joined 10. cards

c) rugby athletics cricket open-air journey cinema camping trip sail instructor course facilities challenge drawing competition

10 The world of work

a) Curriculum Vitae training Work experience Qualifications References

b) 1. engineering 2. manager 3. trainee/apprentice 4. salary/wages 5. unemployed/out of work/on the dole 6. enclose 7. travel agent 8. redundant 9. factory 10. colleague

c) application career programmer employer assistant receptionist reputation type personnel branch

11 Technology

a) 1. washing machine 2. emit 3. mobile 4. stove 5. gadget 6. research 7. instant 8. clone 9. radiation 10. benefit 11. electricity 12. equipment

b) 1. risk – risky, to risk s.th. 2. modification – (genetically) modified, to modify (s.th.) 3. to assess – assessment 4. waste – wastepaper basket 5. to heat– heat, (central) heating, heater

Key to the exercises

c)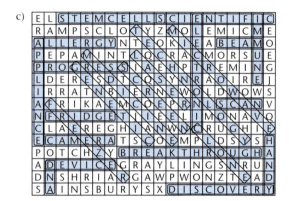

12 Lifestyle

a) [word search grid]

b) 1. on 2. on 3. after
4. up 5. in 6. to
7. in 8. for 9. to 10. by

c) 1. library 2. character
3. comedy 4. detective
story 5. adaptation
6. writer 7. ending
8. suspense

13 Festivities and public holidays

a) 2. Christmas Eve – *der Heilige Abend* 3. special occasion – *besonderer Anlass/besonderes Ereignis* 4. Ash Wednesday – *Aschermittwoch* 5. fancy dress – *Kostüm/Verkleidung* 6. practical joke – *Streich* 7. Shrove Tuesday – *Fastnachtsdienstag* 8. Bank Holiday – *gesetzlicher Feiertag* 9. Santa Claus – *der Weihnachtsmann* 10. Twelfth Night – *der 6. Januar* 11. Good Friday – *Karfreitag*

a) 4 b) 5 c) 11 d) 1 e) 7
f) 6 g) 2 h) 10 i) 3 j) 8
k) 9

b) 1. place 2. invitation 3. luck
4. Congratulations 5. workday
6. turkey 7. Fourth 8. public

c) 1. Lent 2. anniversary
3. decoration 4. carol
5. Boxing Day 6. bunny
7. mean 8. Ascension Day

Irregular verbs

Infinitive	Past tense	Past participle	
to be	was	been	
to beat	beat	beaten	
to become	became	become	
to blow	blew	blown	
to break	broke	broken	
to bring	brought	brought	
to broadcast	broadcast/broadcasted	broadcast/broadcasted	
to build	built	built	
to burn	burnt/burned	burnt/burned	
to catch	caught	caught	
to choose	chose	chosen	
to come	came	come	
to cost	cost	cost	
to cut	cut	cut	
to do	did	done	
to draw	drew	drawn	
to dream	dreamt/dreamed	dreamt/dreamed	
to drink	drank	drunk	
to drive	drove	driven	
to fall	fell	fallen	
to feel	felt	felt	
to fight	fought	fought	
to flee	fled	fled	
to fly	flew	flown	
to freeze	froze	frozen	
to get	got	got	
to give	gave	given	
to go	went	gone	
to grow	grew	grown	
to hang	hung	hung	= *(auf)hängen*
	hanged	hanged	= *(er)hängen*
to have	had	had	

Irregular verbs

Infinitive	Past tense	Past participle
to hit	hit	hit
to hold	held	held
to keep	kept	kept
to know	knew	known
to lead	led	led
to learn	learnt/learned	learnt/learned
to leave	left	left
to lose	lost	lost
to make	made	made
to mean	meant	meant
to meet	met	met
to overtake	overtook	overtaken
to pay	paid [eɪ]	paid [eɪ]
to put	put	put
to ride	rode	ridden
to rise	rose	risen
to run	ran	run
to see	saw	seen
to sell	sold	sold
to set	set	set
to shoot	shot	shot
to sing	sang	sung
to sink	sank	sunk
to sit	sat	sat
to spend	spent	spent
to spin	spun/span	spun
to spread	spread	spread
to stand	stood	stood
to steal	stole	stolen
to stick	stuck	stuck
to sweep	swept	swept
to take	took	taken
to teach	taught	taught
to tell	told	told
to think	thought	thought
to throw	threw	thrown
to understand	understood	understood
to weave	wove	woven
to win	won [ʌ]	won [ʌ]
to write	wrote	written

Index

A

ability 84
  technical ~ 118
to abolish s.th. 38, 44, 66
the Aborigines 46
about: to be ~ s.o./s.th. 142
above sea-level 16
abroad: from ~ 10
absent 88
to absorb s.th. 78
academic: ~ standard 84
  ~ subjects 84
accent 44
to accept s.th. 64
accepted 98
access: to have ~ to s.th. 60
accident 136
accommodation: rented ~ 134
accountant 112
to accuse s.o. of doing s.th. 100
to achieve: ~ an aim 48
  ~ s.th. 130
acid rain 78
act: ~ of war 48
  Act of Parliament 64
  Racial Equality Act 46
acting 106
action 142
active volcano 18
activity: leisure ~ 104
actor 58
actress 58
AD 28
to adapt to s.th. 46
adaptation 142
addict: drug ~ 96
  TV ~ 56
addicted (to s.th.) 130
addiction 96
Administration 68
adult 100
advance 58
advantage 32, 72, 112
Advent 146

adventure story 142
adventurous 140
advertisement 54, 116, 130
advertising 56, 130
advice 96
affairs: current ~ 56
to affect s.o./s.th. 18
to afford s.th. 14, 130
Age: Ice ~, Iron ~ 28
  the Middle ~s 28
agent: travel ~ 114, 140
aggression 44
agnostic 134
ago: 100 years ~ 40
agreement: to come to an ~ 38
agriculture 12
ahead: to think ~ 116
AIDS 80
aim 130
  to achieve an ~ 48
air 14
  to go on the ~ 58
air-conditioning 126
aircraft 138
airport 138
Albania 9
alcoholic 96
A-Level 86
all: to get away from it ~ 142
  ~ day/~ night 24
allergy 124
alternative 130
alternative technology 80
amateur 106
ambitious 132
ancestor 38
ancient 38
the Angles 28
anniversary 148
to announce s.th. 140
annoyed 100
annual 148
to apologize 98
appearance 98
appliance: household ~ 122
applicant 112
application 112
  letter of ~ 116

to apply: ~ for a place 86
  ~ for a traineeship/job 116
  ~ for political asylum 48
to appoint s.o. 70
apprentice 118
apprenticeship 86, 118
appropriate (to s.th.) 86
to approve of s.th. 100
April Fool's Day 148
area 10, 16
  non-smoking ~ 96
  residential ~ 14
argument 98
aristocracy 32
armed: to be ~ 30
  ~ robbery 50
army 28
to arrest s.o. 34, 50
to arrive 138
arrow 30
arson attack 48
Art 86
article 54
Ascension Day 148
Ash Wednesday 148
aspect: positive ~ 130
to assassinate s.o. 38
assembly: regional ~ 66
  ~ hall 88
  ~ line 112
to assess s.th. 124
assistant: shop ~ 112
asylum: to apply for political ~ 48
  ~ seeker 48
atheist 134
athlete 108
athletics 104
atmosphere 76, 142
attack 48
  arson ~ 48
  bomb ~ 48
to attack s.o./s.th. 28, 46
attempt 48
to attend a school 84
attendant: flight ~ 114
attitude 132
  negative ~ 46
to attract s.o. 54
attraction 104
attractive 54

191

Index

at night 24
audience 58, 106
aunt 94
Austria 9
Austrian 9
author 142
authority 96
autumn 24
au pair 132
available 54, 126
average 90
to avoid s.th. 80
awful 96
awkward 98

B

baby: to have a ~ 132
background 46
backpacking 142
bad-tempered 100
bag: plastic ~ 80
baggage reclaim 138
baker 114
balance: the ~ of nature 124
balances: system of checks and ~ 70
ball 146
ballet 106
bank: ~ clerk 116
  Bank Holiday 148
  bottle ~ 80
banking 112
baron 28
base 20
based on: to be ~ s.th. 58
battery 126
battle 30
battle-axe 30
battlefield 32
bay 16
the BBC 56
BC 28
to be into s.th. 104
beach 16
beam 122
beat: on the ~ 50
to beat s.o. up 46
beauty product 130
bedtime story 142
to behave (well/badly) 90

behaviour 100
Belgian 9
Belgium 9
belief 134
to believe (in s.th.) 134
to belong to a sect 136
below freezing point 22
belt: black ~ 106
bend 136
benefit 124
  to be on unemployment ~ 118
best: ~ wishes 150
  the ~ of both worlds 46
  to do what you think ~ 100
best-seller 54, 142
the Bible 134
bicycle: ~ pump 138
  ~ shed 88
bike: racing ~ 138
bill 64
billion 76
Biology 86
birth control 80
birthday: Happy ~! 150
bishop 64
black-out 126
black belt 106
to blame s.o. (for s.th.) 46, 98
blizzard 18
block: tower ~ 134
bloody 30
blossom 20
to blow
  ~ s.th./s.o. up 34, 50
  ~ up 98
board: departure ~ 138
  on ~ 138
boarding school 84
boat 140
bomb attack 48
bombing: suicide ~ 48
bonfire 146
to book s.th. 140
book token 142
border 10
  ~ controls 72
Bosnia-Herzegovina 9
Bosnian 9
bottle: ~ bank 80
  returnable ~ 80

bounds: out of ~ 88
bow 30
bowling 104
box-office hit 58
Boxing Day 146
boyfriend 96
boy scout 104
brain tumour 122
brake 138
branch 68, 112
break: lunch ~ 88
to break: ~ a treaty 38
  ~ the law 50
breakdown 136
breakfast TV 56
breakthrough 126
breeze: a strong ~ 22
bricklayer 114
bridge 108
bright 116
  a ~ start to the day 22
to bring
  ~ s.o. to trial 34
  ~ s.o. up 100, 132
Britain 10
British 9
  the ~ Isles 10
Briton 9
broadcast: outside ~ 56
brother-in-law 94
brothers and sisters 94
brown-out 126
brutal 32, 48
Buddhist 134
to build up 76
builder 114
building 14
bulb: light ~ 126
Bulgaria 9
to bully s.o. 46
bungalow 134
bungee jumping 104
bunny: Easter ~ 148
burglary 50
to burn (s.th.) 32, 76
business 132
  it's none of my ~ 96
  to set up ~ 12
  Business Studies 86
busy 130
by: (written) ~ 142
  ~ hand 10
by-product 76
Byelorussia 9

192

Index

C

cafeteria 88
caffeine 96
camera: speed ~ 124
  web ~ 60
cameraman 58
to camp 30
campaign: election ~ 68
camping 104
canal 12
to cancel s.th. 138
  to be cancelled 90
candidate 64
candle 146
canoeing 108
canyon 20
capacity 78
capital 14
captain 140
  form ~ 90
carbon dioxide 76
card: greetings ~ 148
  ID ~ 124
  to play ~s 108
to care: ~ about s.o. 100
  ~ for s.o. 132
career 86, 112
  ~ woman 132
careers: ~ officer 112
  ~ service 112
  ~ teacher 116
caretaker 88
carnival 148
carol: Christmas ~ 146
  ~ singer 146
cartoon 56
car park: multi-storey ~ 138
case 50
castle 32
catalogue 140
to catch
  ~ a train/bus/... 136
  ~ s.o. (doing s.th.) 98
Catholic 34
cattle ranch 18
caught: to be ~ between two cultures 46
to cause s.th. 78
cave 20
CCTV 124
CD player 122
to celebrate s.th. 146

celebration 146
cell: stem ~ 124
the Celts 28
centigrade: degree ~ 22
central heating 122
centre: leisure ~ 106
century 28
ceremony 66
certificate 118
  doctor's ~ 88
  General Certificate of Secondary Education 84
  school leaving ~ 90
chain 138
challenge 108
chancellor 70
change 34
  climate ~ 78
to change (trains) 136
channel: TV ~ 56
  the English Channel 10
  the Channel Tunnel 10, 140
chapter 142
character 142
charge
  to be in ~ of s.th. 64
  to save ~s 60
charity 66, 80, 146
chat room 60
chat show 56
to cheat 90
checks and balances: system of ~ 70
to check in 138
chemical 12
Chemistry 86
child: an only ~ 94
child-minder 132
childish 98
chimney 36, 146
choice 56, 140
choir practice 88
to choose s.th. 86
christening 134
Christian 134
Christmas 146
  ~ carol 146
  ~ Day 146
  ~ Eve 146
  ~ tree 150
to chuck s.o. 96

church: to go to ~ 134
  ~ festival 148
  the Church of England 28
cigarette 96
cinema 58, 106
circulation: to come into ~ 72
citizen 38, 44, 66
city: inner ~ 14
  the City of London 14
civil: ~ servant 114
  Civil Rights Movement 44
  the (American) Civil War 28
civilization 36
claim: to have a ~ to s.th. 30
clash 44
class: ~ test 90
  ruling ~ 32
classroom 88
to clear up 22
clerk 114
  bank ~ 116
cliff 20
climate 16
  ~ change 78
cloning 124
close: to put s.o. under ~ supervision 50
to close down 118
cloth 34
cloud: not a ~ in the sky 22
cloudy 22
club: to join a ~ 88
Co. (= Company) 118
coach 108
coach tour 140
coal 10
coal-mining 12
coal mine 34
coalition 66
coast 10
coastline 16
co-educational 84
coin 72
the Cold War 28
colleague 112
to collect money 146
collecting stamps 104

193

Index

college 86
   sixth form ~ 86
   technical ~ 118
collision 138
colonial 40
colonist 36
colony 36
colour: skin ~ 44
   ~ magazine 54
to come: ~ into being 40
   ~ to an agreement 38
   ~ to power 66
   ~ to the throne 34
comedy 56, 142
commentator 56
commercial: TV ~ 56, 130
commercial radio 58
Commission: The European ~ 72
to commit a crime 50
common: the Common Market 72
   the House of Commons 64
to communicate s.th. 54
community 36, 44
   the European Community 72
commuter 14
company 12
competition 108
competitive 130
to complain about s.th./s.o. 100
comprehensive school 84
compulsory 86
computer: personal ~ 60
   ~ monitor 122
   ~ technology 58
concert 104
to condemn s.o. to death 34
conditions: living ~ 14
   working ~ 112
to confirm s.o./s.th. 70
conflict 44
conformity 72
Congratulations! 150
Congress 68
to connect s.th. (to s.th. else) 60
connection 60, 136

to conquer s.th. 30
conquest: the Norman Conquest 28
the Conservative Party 66
constituency 64
constitution 70
constitutional 64
to consume s.th. 76
consumer 130
continent 8
to contribute to s.th. 126
contribution 60
control: birth ~ 80
   border ~ 72
   passport ~ 140
   to be under (s.o.'s) ~ 32
   to get out of ~ 78
controversial 124
convenient 126
cooperation: economic ~ 72
copy 54
to copy (from s.o.) 90
cordless telephone 122
corridor 88
corrupt 66
cost of living 14
costume 150
cotton 10
   ~ plantation 38
counselling 50
to counteract s.th. 132
country 8
   in the ~ 14
countryside 16, 104
course 106
   training ~ 86
   vocational ~ 112
   ~ work 84
court 50
   ~ of justice 70
   the Supreme Court 68
cousin 94
to crash 126
   ~ into s.th. 48
crazy: to be ~ about s.o./s.th. 96
to create s.th. 134
creativity 114
crew 140
cricket 104

crime 50
   to commit a ~ 50
criminal 50
critic 48
to criticize s.o./s.th. 100
Croat 9
Croatia 9
Croatian 9
crop 12
crossing 140
crossword puzzle 54
crowded 14
to crown s.o. (king/queen) 32
cruel 32
cruelty 48
cruise 140
the Crusades 28
culture 40, 44
   caught between two ~s 46
currency: single ~ 72
current affairs 56
curriculum 86
custom 38, 44, 146
to cut down on s.th. 80
CV 112
cycle path 138
cycling 104, 138
Cypriot 9
Cyprus 9
Czech 9
   the Czech Republic 9

D

daily paper 54
dairy farming 12
dam 18
damage 18, 78
   to do ~ to s.th. 46
to damage s.th. 138
dance 146
dancing 104
   line ~ 106
   tap ~ 106
Dane 9
Danish 9
daren't 96
dark: to get ~ 24
date *(meeting)* 96
date *(time)* 30
daughter 94

Index

day: all ~ 24
  a ~ out 90
  during the ~ 24
  in those ~s 34
  to the present ~ 28
  to win the ~ 32
  working ~ 116
dead 32
death: to condemn s.o. to ~ 34
decision 64
the Declaration of Independence 36
to declare s.th. as (unconstitutional/...) 70
decline 78
to decline 12
decoration(s) 146
decorator: painter and ~ 112
deep 20
to defeat s.o. 30
defence: self-~ 106
to defend s.o./s.th. 30
degree (centigrade) 22
delayed: to be ~ 138
delegate 68
to deliver s.th. 54
demand 12, 126
democracy 66
Democrats: the ~ 70
  the Liberal ~ 66
demonstration 44
Denmark 9
dentist 114
department
  government ~ 64
  personnel ~ 118
departure: ~ board 138
  ~ lounge 140
deposit 80
depressed 100
desert 16
destination 140
to destroy s.th. 32
destruction 76
detached house 134
detective story 142
detention: to get ~ 90
to develop 10
developing country 78
device 122
devolution 66
diary 148

to die 30
difference 132
digital: ~ radio 122
  ~ TV 56
diploma 72
director 58
disabled 114
disadvantage 132
to disagree (with s.th.) 64
disaster 18
to discover s.th. 20, 28
discovery 124
discrimination 44
discussion 98
disease 36, 78, 124
dish: satellite ~ 56
dishwasher 122
dissatisfied 130
distance 16
distant 24
district 14
diversion 136
diversity 72
divided: to be ~ into s.th. 10
diving 106
divorced 96
DNA 126
to do
  ~ as you please 100
  ~ damage to s.th. 46
  ~ one's share of s.th. 132
  ~ overtime 116
  ~ voluntary work 118
  ~ what you think best 100
  ~ without s.th. 96
  ~ written exams 90
docks 12
doctor 112
  ~'s certificate 88
document 36
documentary 56
dole: on the ~ 116
doll 132
donation 80
to double 76
down: to cut ~ on s.th. 80
to download s.th. 60
downpour 24
to draw (s.th.) 108

to dream of s.th. 130
to dress up (as s.o.) 146
to drink a toast 146
to drive
  ~ s.o. from a place 38
  ~ s.o. off s.th. 46
  ~ s.th. 34
driving licence 136
drizzle 22
to drop a subject 90
drought 24
drug addict 96
drugs: to take ~ 96
drunk 98
due: to be ~ 136
duke 30, 66
dull 22
during the day 24
dustbin 80
Dutch 9
duty 66
DVD 58
  ~ player 122

E

e-mail 60
to earn (good) money 112
the earth 76
  our Earth 24
earthquake 18
Easter
  ~ bunny 148
  ~ Day 148
  ~ egg 148
  ~ Monday 148
eastern 10
economic: ~ and monetary union 72
  ~ cooperation 72
  ~ growth 78
economy: the local ~ 14
ecosystem 78
editor 114
  letter to the ~ 54
education 84
educational 56
effect: greenhouse ~ 78
  long-term ~ 78, 124
  special ~s 58
effort: to make an ~ 80, 100
egg: Easter ~ 148

195

Index

to elect s.o. 64
election: ~ campaign 68
  general ~ 64
electric 122
electrician 114
electricity 80, 122
  ~ supply 126
electronic 122
electronics 12
embarrassed 96
embarrassing 98
emergency generator 126
to emigrate 36
to emit s.th. 122
emphasis: put ~ on s.th. 84
empire 40
to employ s.o. 34
employee 116
employer 116
to enclose s.th. 118
endangered species 80
ending 142
enemy 30
energetic 104
energy 76
  solar ~ 80
engine 36
  steam ~ 36
engineering 112
  genetic ~ 124
  heavy ~ 12
the English Channel 10
to enjoy life 130
enormous 16
to enroll 106
entertainment 56
environment 76
environment-friendly 80
episode 56
equal 132
  ~ rights 44
equality 46
  Racial Equality Act 46
equator 24
equipment 14, 80, 114, 122
equivalent 90, 148
eruption 18
escalator 138
to escape (from s.th.) 140

to establish s.th. 32
estate 32
  housing ~ 14
  industrial ~ 12
Estonia 9
ethnic: ~ group 46
  ~ minority 46
Euro 72
Europe 8
European 8
  the ~ Commission 72
  the ~ Community 72
  the ~ Union 72
Eve: Christmas ~ 146
  New Year's ~ 146
event 28, 68
eventually 78
evil 134
exam: oral ~ 86
  practical ~ 86
  school leaving ~s 90
  to do written ~s 90
  to set an ~ 84
  to take an ~ 84
examination 84
  written ~ 84
excess: to take s.th. to ~ 96
exchange 90
excursion 90
to execute s.o. 34
executive branch 68
exercise 104
exercise book 88
exhausted 30
exhaust fumes 78
to exist 24, 134
exit 136
exotic 130
expanse 18
expectation: to live up to s.o.'s ~s 100
expelled: to be ~ 90
experience: work ~ 118
to experience s.th. 140
experienced 108, 112
to explore s.th. 36, 140
explosion 48
to export s.th. 10
extensive 20
extinct: to become ~ 80
extra work 90
extreme sports 104
eye: in the public ~ 68

F

facilities 108
factory 10, 34, 112
fail 90
to fail (an exam) 86
failure 130
  power ~ 126
fair: to play ~ 108
fairy tale 66, 142
fall of snow 22
to fall in love with s.o. 96
familiar 46
family
  member of the ~ 94
  one-parent ~ 96
  the First Family 68
  the Royal Family 66
famine 36, 80
fanatic 34
fanatical 136
fancy dress 148
fantasy 58
fare 140
farm 14
farmer 114
farming: dairy ~ 12
farmland 12
fashion 130
to fasten s.th. 140
Father Christmas 146
favour: to be in ~ of s.th. 70
fax machine 126
fear 48
to fear s.o./s.th. 32
feast 150
feature 16, 126
federal 70
fee: to pay a ~ 84
to feel like doing s.th. 100
female 132
ferry 140
fertile 12
fertilizer 76
festival 148
  chruch ~ 148
  pop ~ 104
festive season 146
festivity 146
fiction: science ~ 142
field 14

196

Index

fierce 38
to fight (for s.th.) 30
film 56
  ~ industry 58
  ~ star 58
  horror ~ 58
  silent ~ 58
filmmaker 58
finance 112
to fine s.o. 50
Finland 9
Finn 9
Finnish 9
fire: to set ~ to s.th. 32
to fire s.o. 118
firefighter 114
fireworks 146
firm 112
the First Family 68
the First World War 28
fisherman 114
fit: to keep ~ 108
flat *(adj.)* 18
flat *(noun)* 134
flatscreen 122
to flee 32
flexible 142
flight 138
  ~ attendant 114
flooded 22
to flow 16
flower: to be in ~ 20
flowering 20
fog: patches of ~ 22
to follow instructions 114
fond: to be ~ of s.o./s.th. 100
food: organic ~ 80
force 44
  the ~s of nature 18
to force s.o. to do s.th. 38
forecast: weather ~ 22
foreign: ~ language 86
  ~ policy 72
foreigner 44
  hatred of ~s 48
forest 16, 76
form
  ~ captain 90
  sixth ~ 86
to form a government 64

fort 30
fossil fuel 76
to found s.th. 28
the Fourth of July 150
France 9
free trade 72
freedom 36
freezer 122
freezing point: below ~ 22
French 9
freshwater 20
fridge 122
friend: to make ~s 108
frontier 36
fruit 12
fuel: fossil ~ 76
fulfilling 132
full-time job 118, 132
fumes: exhaust ~ 78
fun: to be ~ 108
function 68
fundamentalism 136
funeral 134
the future 78, 130

G

gadget 122
to gain s.th. 106
galaxy 24
gale 22
game: ~ show 56
  team ~ 104
Games 88
gang 46
gap: generation ~ 104
gardener 112
gas 76
  natural ~ 12
gate 140
GCSE 84, 116
gears 138
gender 132
general
  General Certificate of Secondary Education 84
  ~ election 64
  General Science 86
to generate s.th. 80
generation 94
  ~ gap 104

generator: emergency ~ 126
genetic 124
  ~ engineering 124
genetically modified 124
Geography 86
German 9
Germany 9
to get
  ~ married 94
  ~ dark 24
  ~ annoyed 100
  ~ away from it all 142
  ~ on well with s.o. 100
  ~ on with s.o. 114
  ~ out of control 78
  ~ to know about s.th. 98
  ~ to know s.o. 94, 104
get-together 150
ghetto 46
gingerbread 146
to give s.th. up 32, 96
glacier 18
global warming 78
globe 24
glue-sniffing 98
glued to the set: to be ~ 56
GM-free 124
GMO 124
to go
  ~ to school 84
  ~ back to work 132
  ~ on holiday 130
  ~ on strike 118
  ~ on the air 58
  ~ out to work 132
  ~ out with s.o. 96
  ~ the wrong way 136
  ~ to church 134
  ~ to university 86
  ~ wrong 98
goal 130
godmother 94
good
  Good luck! 150
  in ~ time 138
  to be ~ at s.th. 84
goods 34
Good Friday 148
gorge 20
to govern 70

197

Index

government 36, 64
    to form a ~ 64
    ~ department 64
governor 70
grade 84
Grade A 90
gradient 20
grammar school 84
gramophone 126
grandparents 94
great-aunt 94
great-grandmother 94
Great Britain 9
Greece 9
Greek 9
greenhouse effect 78
greetings card 148
grim 34
ground 16
    hunting ~ 38
    sports ground 88
grounds 88
group: ethnic ~ 46
    minority ~ 44
grown-up 100
growth 76
    economic ~ 78
guide: TV ~ 56
guilty (of a crime) 50
the Gunpowder Plot 34
Guy Fawkes Night 146
gym 88, 108

H

habit 130
to hail 24
hailstone 24
hairdresser 114
hairstyle 100
half-sister 94
hall: assembly ~ 88
Halloween 148
hand: by ~ 10
to hand work in 90
handlebars 138
handling stolen goods 50
handy 122
    ~ with tools 114
to hang
    ~ s.o. 34
    ~ up one's stocking 146

hang-gliding 104
hangover 98
happiness 130
Happy birthday! 150
Happy New Year! 150
hardship 36
to harm s.th./s.o. 78
harmful 96
to hate s.o./s.th. 100
hatred 44
    ~ of foreigners 48
have to have a baby 132
head: ~ teacher 84
    Head of State 40, 66
headline 54
headmaster 88
health 78
    ~ risk 122
healthy 96
heart 18
heart-broken 96
to heat s.th. 80
heating: central ~ 122
heatwave 24
heaven 134
heavy: ~ engineering 12
    ~ rain 22
hectic 130
hedge 14
height 20
    to be at one's ~ 40
hell 134
helmet 138
help: special ~ 90
hemisphere 24
hero 38, 142
heroine 142
hi-fi 122
high: ~ security jail 50
    ~ tide 20
    ~ treason 34
    ~ wind 22
to hijack a plane 48
hiking 104
hill 18
Hindu 134
to hire s.th. 60
historic 30
History 86
hit: box-office ~ 58
to hit (s.o.) 50
hitch-hiking 104
to hold a party/a meeting/... 148

hold-up 136
holiday: to go on ~ 130
    Bank Holiday 148
    public ~ 146
holidaymaker 140
holly 150
home-made 146
homeless 78
home page 60
honour: in ~ of s.o. 150
horizon 24
horror film 58
hostage 48
hostility 48
house
    detached ~ 134
    semi-detached ~ 134
    terraced ~ 134
    to move ~ 134
    the Houses of Parliament 34
    the House of Commons 64
    the House of Lords 64
    the House of Representatives 68
household appliance 122
housekeeping 132
housework 132
housing 78, 134
    ~ estate 14
huge 16
humorous 142
Hungarian 9
Hungary 9
hunting ground 38
hurricane 18
hurry: to be in a ~ 130
husband 94
hymn 134

I

the Ice Age 28
ice-rink 108
ice-skating 108
Iceland 9
Icelander 9
Icelandic 9
to identify with s.o./s.th. 66
identity 72
    sense of ~ 46

Index

to idolize s.o. 58
ID card 124
to ignore s.o./s.th. 98
immigrant 36, 46
immigration 48
immune system 124
impact 126
impatient 100
to import s.th. 10
in: ~ good time 138
   ~ honour of s.o. 150
   ~ memory of s.o./s.th. 150
   ~ those days 34
   to be ~ charge of s.th. 64
   to be ~ favour of s.th. 70
income 116
to increase 76
   ~ s.th. 116
incredible 76
independence 36, 150
   the Declaration of Independence 36
   the War of Independence 28
independent 40, 100
   ~ specialist school 84
individuality 72
industrial 10
   ~ estate 12
   ~ production 76
   the Industrial Revolution 10, 28
industrialized country 10
industry 10
   film ~ 58
   seafood ~ 14
   service ~ 12
inferior 46, 98
influence 40
to influence s.o./s.th. 54
influential 68
influx 48
infrared 126
inhabitant 14
to inherit s.th. 64
to injure s.o. 48
inland 16
   ~ port 12
inner city 14
innocent 50

to install s.th. 114
instant: ~ meal 122
   ~ messenger service 60
institution 66
   young offender ~ 50
instruction: to follow ~s 114
instructor 108
instrument: to play an ~ 106
to integrate s.th. into s.th. 126
integrated 46
interactive 60
interest 104
interpreter 114
interrailing 142
interview 54, 112
into: to be ~ s.th. 104
to invade (a country) 28
invader 30
invasion 30
to invent s.th. 34, 126
invention 28, 34
invitation 150
Ireland 9
   Northern ~ 10
   the Republic of ~ 10
Irish 9
iron 12
   electric ~ 126
   the Iron Age 28
irresponsible 100
island 8
Isle: the British ~s 10
issue 72
Italian 9
Italy 9
ITV 56
IT (= Information Technology) 84

J

jail: high security ~ 50
janitor 88
jealous 96
Jew 134
job
   a part-time ~ 118
   a steady ~ 116
   full-time ~ 118, 132
   office ~ 116

jobcentre 112
to join: ~ (an organazation/a club/...) 72, 88, 104, 136
   ~ s.th. (to s.th.) 12
joke: practical ~ 148
journalist 54, 114
journey 104, 136
judge 64
judo 106
justice: court of ~ 70

K

to keep: ~fit 108
   ~ s.th. going 66
   ~ up with s.o. 98
to kick (s.o.) 50
kidnapping 48
to kill s.o. 28, 48
kilometre: square ~ 16
king 28
   the Three Kings 146
kingdom 30
   the United Kingdom 10
kit 88
knight 28
to know
   to get ~ about s.th. 98
   to get ~ s.o. 94, 104

L

laboratory: science ~ 88
Labor Day 150
labour-saving 126
Labour Party 66
lake 18
land
   to work on the ~ 14
   tribal ~ 38
to land 30
landscape 16
lane 136
language: foreign ~ 86
   official ~ 40
   world ~ 40
laptop 126
laser 122
to last 78
Latvia 9
to laugh at s.o. 98

199

Index

law 34
    to break the ~ 50
    to make/reject/pass
    a ~ 64
layer: ozone ~ 78
to laze 140
lazy 90
leader 32, 64, 132
to learn to do s.th. 108
to leave: ~ home 100
    ~ school 86
legislative branch 68
leisure: ~ activity 104
    ~ centre 106
Lent 148
lesson 84
    private ~s 90
letter
    ~ of application 116
    ~ to the editor 54
level 20
the Liberal Democrats 66
library 88, 142
licence: driving ~ 136
life: ~ peer 64
    social ~ 100
    to live your own ~ 100
    to lose one's ~ 30
    way of ~ 46, 130
lifestyle 80, 130
    nine-to-five ~ 140
lift: to get a ~ 136
light: traffic ~s 136
lighting 126
lightning 22
    to be struck by ~ 22
light bulb 126
limit 78
    speed ~ 136
limited 64
line: assembly ~ 112
    railway ~ 36
    ~ dancing 106
liner: ocean ~ 140
link 40, 60
to link: ~ s.th. (to s.th.) 10
    ~ s.th. (together) 72
to listen to (s.th. on) the radio 58
Lithuania 9
live *(adj.)* 56

to live: ~ up to s.o.'s expectations 100
    ~ your own life 100
living: cost of ~ 14
    standard of ~ 76
    ~ conditions 14
local: the ~ economy 14
    ~ paper 54
    ~ radio 58
locomotive 36
to log into the (World Wide) Web 60
long-term effect 78, 124
to look
    ~ after oneself 100
    ~ after s.o. 132
Lord: the House of ~s 64
to lose: ~ one's life 30
    ~ s.th. 32, 108
lounge: departure ~ 140
love: to fall in ~ with s.o. 96
    ~ at first sight 96
    With ~ (from) 150
low 16
    ~ tide 20
Ltd. (= Limited) 118
luck: Good ~! 150
luggage 138
lunch break 88
Luxembourg 9
Luxembourger 9
Luxembourgian 9
luxury 140

M

Macedonia 9
machine 34
machinery 10
made
    to be ~ up of s.th. 8
    to be ~ redundant 118
magazine 54
main: ~ road 136
    ~ subject 90
mainland 8
majority: to have the ~ 70
majority vote 64
to make: ~ music 106
    ~ an effort 80, 100
    ~ a law 64
    ~ a treaty 38

    ~ friends 108
    ~ a speech 68
    ~ things 146
    ~ trouble 46
male 132
Malta 9
Maltese 9
manager 112, 118
manual worker 114
manufacturing 12
Many happy returns of the day! 150
to map s.th. 20
march: protest ~ 44
to march 30
mark 88
    order ~ 90
to mark a paper 90
market: single ~ 72
    the Common Market 72
marriage 94
married 94
    to get ~ 94
martial arts 106
Martin Luther King Day 150
mass: ~ production 12
    ~ tourism 140
massacre 38
match 108
material: raw ~ 10, 78
material *(adj.)* 28, 76
Maths 86
May Day 148
meadow 14
meal: instant ~ 122
mean 150
meaning 134
to measure s.th. 20
mechanic 114
the media 54
medical 124
medicine 124
to meet: ~ friends 108
    ~ s.o. 96
meeting 88
to melt 18
member 40, 64
    Member of Parliament 64
    ~ of staff 88
    ~ of the family 94
    ~ state 72

Index

Memorial Day 150
memory: in ~ of
  s.o./s.th. 150
to mend a puncture 138
Merry Christmas! 150
message 60, 130
messenger: instant ~
  service 60
method 34
microchip 126
microwave oven 122
the Middle Ages 28
midnight 146
might: military ~ 48
migrant 48
mild 18
mile 16
military might 48
the Milky Way 24
mine: coal ~ 34
minister 64
minority: ethnic ~ 46
  ~ group 44
miserable 34
to miss
  ~ a train/bus/… 136
  ~ a turning 136
mist: sea ~ 22
mistletoe 150
mixed: ~ ability 84
  ~ school 84
mobility 72
model: role ~ 58
modification 124
modified: genetically
  ~ 124
Moldavia 9
monarch 28, 64
monarchy 64
monetary: economic and
  ~ union 72
money: pocket ~ 100
monitor: computer ~
  122
monopoly 58
Montenegrin 9
Montenegro 9
monthly (magazine) 54
mood 100
moon: the ~ rises 24
moor 14
mother tongue 40
motive 48
motorway 136

mountain range 16
mountaineering 108
mountainous 16
mouth 12
move: to be on the ~ 36
to move: ~ house 134
  ~ in with s.o. 96
movement: the Civil
  Rights Movement 44
movie theater 58
mugging 50
muggy 24
multi-cultural society 46
multi-storey car park
  138
murder 48
Music 86
music: to make ~ 106
musical 106
Muslim 134

N

narrow-minded 136
national: ~ day 148
  ~ paper 54
  National Park 16
  ~ pride 72
native 38, 46
  Native American 38
  ~ speaker 40
natural: ~ gas 12
  ~ resources 10, 76
nature
  the balance of ~ 124
  the forces of ~ 18
navy 28
negative attitude 46
nephew 94
the net: to surf ~ 60
  to visit a (web)site on
  ~ 60
the Netherlands 9
network 60
New Year's Day 146
New Year's Eve 146
news 54
newsagent 54
newspaper 54
newsreader 56
newsstand 54
nicotine 96
night: all ~ 24
  at ~ 24

nine-to-five lifestyle 140
nobleman 30
noise 14
to nominate s.o. 68
non-smoking area 96
non-white 40, 46
the Norman Conquest
  28
Northern Ireland 10
the North Pole 24
Norway 9
Norwegian 9
note 72
notebook 88
notice-board 88
novel 142
nuclear 76
  ~ power 76
nurse 112
  veterinary ~ 114

O

to obey (s.o.) 32
obsessed (with s.th.) 130
occasion: special ~ 148
ocean liner 140
odd: the ~ fall of snow
  22
off: to have an afternoon
  ~ 116
offence 50
offender 50
  young ~ institution
  50
offer 112
  special ~ 130
office: ~ job 116
  in ~ 68
  to run for ~ 68
officer: careers ~ 112
  police ~ 50, 114
official 64
  ~ language 40
offline 60
oil rig 12
on: ~ board 138
  ~ schedule 138
  ~ the beat 50
  ~ the dole 116
  ~ the net 60
  ~ the radio 58
  ~ trial (for s.th.) 50
to be based ~ s.th. 58

201

Index

on (continued)
    to be ~ 56
    to be ~ the move 36
    to cut down ~ s.th. 80
    to get ~ well with s.o. 100
    to get ~ with s.o. 114
    to go ~ strike 118
    to go ~ the air 58
    to work ~ the land 14
    to go ~ holiday 130
    war ~ terror 28, 48
on-the-job training 112
once 40
one-parent family 96
online: to be ~ 60
    ~ provider 60
an only child 94
open: ~ spaces 18
    to be ~ to s.th. 136
to open s.th. up 36
open-air concert 104
operation 12
    in ~ 124
opportunity 72, 132
the Opposition 64
to oppress s.o. 44
optional 86
oral exam 86
orchestra 88, 106
order mark 90
organic food 80
organism 124
origin 40, 46, 72
out: a day ~ 90
    ~ of bounds 88
    to be ~ of work 118
outbreaks of rain 22
outdoors 114
outdoor sports 106
outer space 24
outlook 22
outside broadcast 56
oven: microwave ~ 122
overcrowded 34
to overrule s.th./s.o. 70
to overtake (s.o.) 136
overtime: to do ~ 116
to own s.th. 134
owner 34
ozone layer 78

P

package tour 142
to paint (s.th.) 108
painter and decorator 112
palmtop 126
paper: *(newspaper)* ~ 54
    to mark a ~ 90
parade 148
Park: National ~ 16
Parliament 28, 64
    Act of ~ 64
    Member of ~ 64
    the Houses of ~ 34
part: to take ~ in s.th. 106
part-time: to work ~ 132
    ~ job 118
party 64
    the Conservative Party, the Labour Party 66
    ~ politics 66
to pass: ~ (an exam) 86
    ~ a law 64
passageway 20
passport control 140
past 40
patches of fog 22
path: cycle ~ 138
patriot 66
to pay a fee 84
PC 60
peace 32
peaceful 38, 44
to pedal 138
pedestrian 138
peer: life ~ 64
peninsula 8
Pentecost 148
people 32
    the ~ 66
to perform s.th. 106
performance 106
period 28
    trial ~ 116
permanent 40
persecution 36
personality 98
personal computer 60
personnel dept. (= department) 118

to persuade s.o. to do s.th. 130
pesticide 76
petrol: to save ~ 80
phone: cordless telephone 122
photo 54
photocopy 118
photography: trick ~ 58
physical 16
    Physical Education 86
Physics 86
to pick s.o. up 136
piece (of music) 106
the Pilgrims 36, 150
pilot 114
pioneer 38
pipeline 12
pit 12
place
    to apply for a ~ 86
    to take ~ 34, 148
plague 28
plain 16
planet 24, 78
plant 20
to plant s.th. 14
plantation: cotton ~ 38
plastic 150
    ~ bag 80
plastics 12
platform 136
play 106
    radio ~ 58
    TV ~ 56
to play
    ~ an instrument 106
    ~ a trick (on s.o.) 150
    ~ cards 108
    ~ fair 108
playground 88
please: to do as you ~ 100
plot 142
    the Gunpowder Plot 34
to plot s.th. 50
plotter 34
plumber 114
pocket money 100
poem 142
point of view 98
Poland 9
Pole 9

Index

Pole: the North ~ 24
police 50
  ~ officer 50, 114
policy 64
  foreign ~ 72
Polish 9
political
  ~ union 72
  to apply for ~ asylum 48
politician 66
politics 64
  party ~ 66
to pollute s.th. 36
pollution 76
poor housing 78
the Pope 134
popular 98
popular paper 54
population 14, 68, 76
pop festival 104
port: inland ~ 12
portable 126
Portugal 9
Portuguese 9
positive aspect 130
postman/postwoman 114
to pour 22
poverty 14, 80
power 32, 64
  nuclear ~ 76
  ~ failure 126
  sea ~ 28
  to come to ~ 66
  water ~, wind ~ 80
to power s.th. 34
powerful 32
practical: ~ exam 86
  ~ joke 148
practice: choir ~ 88
to practise (s.th.) 106
prairie 16
to pray 134
to predict s.th. 78
pregnant 96
prehistoric 28
prejudice 44, 132
prepared: to be ~ to do s.th. 98
present 146
  to be ~ 88
  to the ~ day 28
to present s.th. 56

presenter 56
president 68
Presidents' Day 150
the press 54
pressure 130
  to put s.o. under ~ 100
previous 112
pride: national ~ 72
priest 134
primary school 84
prime minister 64
prince 66
princess 66
to print: ~ s.th. 54
  ~ s.th. out 60
priority: to take ~ 48
prison 50
  to throw s.o. into ~ 34
private: ~ lessons 90
  ~ school 84
privilege 100
prize 108
to produce: ~ a film 58
  ~ s.th. 10, 34
producer 58
product: beauty ~ 130
  waste ~ 76
production
  industrial ~ 76
  mass ~ 12
  ~ (of a play) 106
profession 116
professional people 116
programme 56
programmer 114
progress 28, 78, 122
to promote s.o. (to s.th.) 116
promotion 116
proportional representation 66
prospects 116
to protect s.o./s.th. (from s.th.) 38, 80
protest march 44
to protest (against s.th.) 44
Protestant 34
proud: to be ~ of s.th. 46
provider: online ~ 60
public: in the ~ eye 68
  ~ holiday 146

  ~ school 84
  ~ transport 14, 136
the public 54, 66
to publish s.th. 54
to pull s.th. down 14
pump: bicycle ~ 138
to pump a tyre up 138
puncture: to mend a ~ 138
to punish s.o./s.th. 32, 90
punishment 50
pupil 84
pursuit 104
to put
  ~ down a revolt 32
  ~ s.o. under pressure 100
puzzle: crossword ~ 54

Q

qualification 112
qualifications 72, 86
quarrel 48
queen 28
queue 136

R

race 40, 44
racial
  ~ discrimination 44
  Racial Equality Act 46
racing bike 138
racism 44
radiation 122
radio 54
  commercial ~ 58
  digital ~ 122
  local ~ 58
  to listen to (s.th. on) the ~ 58
  ~ play 58
  ~ station 58
rafting: white-water ~ 104
rage: all the ~ 106
rail: by ~ 136
railway line 36
rain: acid ~ 78
  outbreaks of ~ 22
rainbow 24
ranch: cattle ~ 18
range: mountain ~ 16

203

Index

rape 50
raw material 10, 78
to re-elect s.o. 68
to re-sit an exam 86
to re-use s.th. 80
re: 118
to react against s.th. 44
reader 54, 142
rebellion 32, 96
rebellious 38
receptionist 114
reclaim: baggage ~ 138
to recognize s.o./s.th. 46, 72
recorder: video ~ 122
to recycle s.th. 124
recycling 80
redundant: to be made ~ 118
referee 108
reference 118
referendum 72
refinery 12
refugee 36, 48
regional assembly 66
register 90
regulations: rules and ~ 72
to reject a law 64
relation 94
relationship 94
~ building 48
relative 94
to relax 130
religion 34, 44, 134
Religious Studies 86
Remembrance Day 148
rented accommodation 134
to repair s.th. 114
repeat 56
to replace s.th. 72, 78
report: (newspaper) ~ 84
(school) ~ 54
to report s.th. 50
reporter 114
to represent s.o. 36
representation: proportional ~ 66
representative 36, 66
the House of Representatives 68

republic 64
the Republic of Ireland 10
the Republicans 70
reputation: to have a ~ for s.th. 118
research 124
resentment 48
reservation 38, 46
reservoir 18
residential area 14
to resist (s.th.) 34
resistant to s.th. 124
resort 140
seaside ~ 18
resources: natural ~ 10, 76
to respect s.o. 100
responsibility 132
responsible: to be ~ (for s.o./s.th.) 100
to restore s.th. 32
result 84
to result in s.th. 76
to retire 118
to retreat 32
return 136
Many happy ~s of the day! 150
returnable bottle 80
reunification 28
revenge 38
review 54
to revise (for an exam) 90
revolt 32
revolution 28
the Industrial Revolution 10, 28
rhyme 142
to ride (a bicycle) 138
ridiculous 98
rig: oil ~ 12
right 64
Civil Rights Movement 44
equal rights 44
rise 76
to get a ~ 116
to rise: the moon rises 24
risk 104, 122
rival 46
river 16

road: main ~ 136
~ works 136
robbery: armed ~ 50
rock-climbing 108
rocky 16
role 132
~ model 58
Romania 9
the Romans 28
rough 22
roundabout 136
route 136
row 134
rowing 108
the Royal Family 66
rubbish: to sort (one's) ~ 80
rude 98
rugby 104
to ruin one's life 96
rule 72, 88
to rule (s.o.) 28, 66
ruler 40
ruling class 32
to run
~ a firm 118
~ a machine 34
~ for office 68
~ out 78
to be run by the state 84
rural 14
rush-hour 136
Russia 9

S

saddle 138
saddlebag 138
safe 130
to make the world a safer place 48
to sail 108, 140
sailor 114
saint 146
salary 116
sale: to be for ~ 134
sandy 16
Santa Claus 146
satellite 126
~ dish 56
satisfied: to be ~ with s.th. 130
satisfying 142

204

Index

to save: ~ charges 60
  ~ money 130
  ~ petrol 80
  ~ s.o./s.th. (from s.th.) 80
the Saxons 28
to scan s.th. 124
scandal 54, 66
scattered showers 22
scene 58, 142
scenery 16
schedule: on ~ 138
school: boarding ~ 84
  comprehensive ~ 84
  grammar ~ 84
  mixed ~ 84
  primary ~ 84
  private ~ 84
  public ~ 84
  secondary ~ 84
  state ~ 84
  to be at a ~ 90
  to go to ~ 84
  to leave ~ 86
  ~ leaving certificate 90
  ~ leaving exams 90
  ~ uniform 90
science: ~ laboratory 88
  General Science 86
  ~ fiction 58, 142
scientific 124
scout: boy ~ 104
screen 58, 122
scuba-diving 108
sea 8
  ~ mist 22
  ~ power 28
sea-level: above/below ~ 16
seafood industry 14
seaport 12
search: in ~ of s.th. 36
to search for s.th. 130
seasick 140
seaside resort 18
season 24
  festive season 146
seat 64
seat-belt 140
second: the Second World War 28
second-class citizen 44
secondary school 84

secretary 112
sect: to belong to a ~ 136
security 78, 140
  high ~ jail 50
to see the New Year in 146
seeker: asylum ~ 48
segregation 44
self-defence 106
self-government 40
self-help 118
selfish 100
semi-detached house 134
the Senate 68
senator 68
sensational 54
sense of identity 46
to separate s.th. 70
separated 96
  to be ~ from s.th. 10
Serb 9
Serbia 9
Serbian 9
serial 56
serious paper 54
servant: civil ~ 114
to serve s.o./s.th. 66
service: (church) ~ 134
  careers ~ 112
  instant messenger ~ 60
  ~ industry 12
session 108
set: to sit in front of the (TV) ~ 56
to set: ~ an exam 84
  ~ fire to s.th. 32
  ~ up business 12
  the sun sets 24
  to be set in a place 58
to settle 36, 46
settler 36
severe 50
the sexes 132
sexist 132
shabby 14
shade: in the ~ 24
share: to to do one's ~ of s.th. 132
to share: ~ in s.th. 112
  ~ s.th. 80
shed: bicycle ~ 88

sheep 14
shield 30
shift work 116
shipbuilding 12
shipyard 12
shocked 48
to shoot s.o. 32
shop assistant 112
shoplifting 50
shore 18
shortage 78
short story 142
show: game ~, chat ~, variety ~ 56
shower: scattered ~s 22
Shrove Tuesday 148
shy 96
sick: to be ~ 98
sight 24
  love at first ~ 96
sightseeing 140
sign 136
to sign s.th. 28
silent film 58
simple 130
singer: carol ~ 146
single: ~ (ticket) 136
  ~ currency 72
  ~ market 72
to sink 24
to sit: ~ an exam 86
  ~ in front of the (TV) set 56
situation 112
sixth form 86
  ~ college 86
size 16
skateboarding 104
skiing 106
skill 114
skilled worker 112
skin colour 44
to skip a lesson 90
sky: not a cloud in the ~ 22
to slaughter an animal 32
slave 38
slavery 38, 44
sleet 22
slogan 130
slope 20
Slovak 9
Slovakia 9

205

Index

Slovakian 9
Slovenia 9
slum 14
smoke 36
to smoke 96
snorkelling 106
snow: fall of ~ 22
snowboarding 106
soap (opera) 56
soccer 104
social: ~ life 100
~ worker 114
society 66, 130
multi-cultural ~ 46
soil 12
on one's own ~ 48
solar: ~ energy 80
~ system 24
soldier 30, 114
to sort (one's) rubbish 80
sound: surround ~ 122
to turn the ~ off 56
source 78
southern 10
space: open ~s 18
outer ~ 24
Spain 9
Spaniard 9
Spanish 9
spare time 104
speaker: native ~ 40
special: ~ effects 58
~ help 90
~ occasion 148
~ offer 130
species: endangered ~ 80
speech: to make a ~ 68
speed: ~ camera 124
~ limit 136
spell: sunny ~s 22
to spend: ~ money (on s.th.) 98, 130
~ time 130
to spin (s.th.) 34
spirit 134
sports 84
extreme ~ 104
outdoor ~ 106
~ ground 88
water ~ 108
sportsman 108
sportswoman 108
to spread 22, 36, 78

spring 24
square kilometre 16
squash 104
St Patrick's Day 148
staff: member of ~ 88
staffroom 88
stage 106
stamp: collecting ~s 104
stand: he can't ~ s.th. 100
standard: academic ~ 84
~ of living 76
star 24
film ~ 58
to starve 76
state 66
Head of State 40, 66
member ~ 72
~ (of the US) 68
~ school 84
station 136
radio ~ 58
to stay: ~ at a place 140
~ down 90
steady: a ~ job 116
steam 34
~ engine 36
steel 12
steep 20
stem cell 124
stepmother 94
stereotyped 44
to stick to s.th. 106
stocking: to hang up one's ~ 146
stolen goods: handling ~ 50
stony 16
store 30
storm 22
story: adventure ~ 142
bedtime ~ 142
detective ~ 142
short ~ 142
stove 122
stream 16
stress 130
stressed out 130
to stretch (over s.th.) 20
strict 90, 100
strike 118
to go on ~ 118
struck: to be ~ by lightning 22

struggle 44
Studies: Business ~ 86
Religious ~ 86
studio 58
to study a subject 86
subject 66
acacemic ~ 84
main ~ 90
substance 96
suburb 14
to succeed s.o. 30
success 112
successful 130
successor 30
to suffer (s.th.) 36
suicide bombing 48
summit 16
sun: the ~ sets 24
Sunday paper 54
sunny spell 22
supervision: to put s.o. under close ~ 50
supplement 54
supply 78
electricity ~ 126
to supply s.th. 18
to support
~ s.o./s.th. 64, 80
~ the family 132
the Supreme Court 68
to surf the net 60
surface 20
surfing 106
to surrender 38
to surround s.th. 16
surround sound 122
surveillance 124
survey 132
to survive (s.th.) 38, 78
suspended: to be ~ 90
suspense 142
suspicious of s.o./s.th. 44
swampland 18
Swede 9
Sweden 9
Swedish 9
to sweep 18
Swiss 9
to switch: ~ off 56
~ over (to ...) 56
Switzerland 9
sword 30
sympathetic 100

206

Index

sympathy 46
system: immune ~ 124
 solar ~ 24
 two-party ~ 66
 ~ of checks and balances 70

T

tabloid 54
to take: ~ an exam 84
 ~ a traditional view 132
 ~ drugs 96
 ~ s.th. to excess 96
 ~ part (in s.th.) 106
 ~ place 34, 148
tale: fairy ~ 66, 142
to talk things over with s.o. 98
tap dancing 106
tax 36, 66
taxpayer 64
teacher: careers ~ 116
 head ~ 84
teachings 134
team 108
 ~ game 104
to tease s.o. (about s.th.) 98
technical: ~ ability 118
 ~ college 118
technician 58, 112
technological 122
technology 84, 122
 alternative ~ 80
 computer ~ 58
 IT (= Information Technology) 84
telecommunications 126
telephone: cordless ~ 122
television 54
to tell s.o. off 98
temperature 22
tension 46
term
 (school) ~ 84
 ~ (of office) 68
terraced house 134
territory 36
terror: war on ~ 28, 48
terrorism 48

terrorist 28, 48
 ~ attack 48
test: class ~ 90
to test s.th. 84
textiles 10
Thanksgiving Day 150
theater: movie ~ 58
theatre 106
theft 50
things: to make ~ 146
 to talk ~ over with s.o. 98
to think ahead 116
to threaten s.o. 30, 46
the Three Kings 146
thrill 104
thriller 56, 142
throne 30
 to come to the ~ 34
through train 136
to throw
 ~ s.o. into prison 34
 ~ s.th. away 80
thunder 22
ticket 136
tide 20
 high ~, low ~ 20
time: in good ~ 138
 spare ~ 104
timetable 86, 140
toast: to drink a ~ 146
token: book ~ 142
tolerance 44
tolerant 34
tongue: mother ~ 40
tool: handy with ~s 114
topic 54
tornado 18
to torture s.o. 34
tour: coach ~ 140
 package ~ 142
to tour around (a country) 104
tourism: mass ~ 140
tournament 108
tower block 134
trade 10, 40
 free ~ 72
 ~ union 118
tradition 38, 66
traditional: to take a ~ view 132
traffic 76, 136
 ~ lights 136

~ warden 114
tragedy 48
tragic 142
trail 38
train: through ~ 136
 wagon ~ 38
to train for s.th. 112
trainee 116
traineeship 116
training
 on-the-job ~ 112
 vocational ~ 50
 ~ course 86
translator 114
transmission 58
transport: public ~ 14, 136
to transport s.th. 80
to travel 36, 136
travel agent 114, 140
treason: high ~ 34
treat 150
to treat s.o. (well/badly/...) 32, 46, 100
treaty: to make/break a ~ 38
tree: Christmas ~ 150
trend 98
trial: on ~ (for s.th.) 50
 to bring s.o. to ~ 34
 ~ period 116
tribal land 38
tribe 38
trick: to play a ~ (on s.o.) 150
 ~ or treat 150
 ~ photography 58
trip 104, 140
trouble 98
 to make ~ 46
to trust s.o. 100
to try: ~ s.o. 34
 ~ s.th. out 96
tumour: brain ~ 122
tunnel: the Channel Tunnel 10, 140
Turk 9
Turkey 9
turkey 150
Turkish 9
to turn
 ~ the sound off 56
 ~ up the volume 56
turning: to miss a ~ 136

207

Index

TV: breakfast ~ 56
  digital ~ 56
  to watch ~ 56
  ~ addict 56
  ~ guide 56
  ~ play 56
Twelfth Night 146
twins 94
two-party system 66
to type (s.th.) 114
tyre 138

U

ugly 14
Ukraine 9
Ukrainian 9
umpire 108
unattractive 98
uncle 94
uncomfortable 98
unconstitutional 68
under: to be ~ (s.o.'s) control 32
  to be ~ close supervision 50
  to put s.o. ~ pressure 100
Underground 138
understanding 44
unemployed 118
unemployment 118
  to be on ~ benefit 118
uniform: school ~ 90
union: economic and monetary ~ 72
  political ~ 72
  the European Union 72
  the Union (= the USA) 38
  trade ~ 118
united 72
  the United Kingdom 10
universal 134
universe 24
university: to go to ~ 86
unkind 46, 98
unsettled 22
up: it's ~ to you 80
to update s.th. 60, 116
urban area 12
to use s.th. up 76

V

vacancy 112
vacant: situations ~ 112
vacation 150
vacuum cleaner 126
Valentine's Day 148
valley 16
values 72, 98
vandalism 50
variety show 56
vast 16
vegetables 12
vehicle 78
vet 114
veterinary nurse 114
to veto s.th. 70
via 60
vice versa 72
victim 48
victory 32
video 58
  ~ recorder 122
view: point of ~ 98
  to take a traditional ~ 132
viewer 56
the Vikings 28
village 14
violence 44
violent 50
to visit a (web)site on the net 60
vital: to be ~ to s.o./s.th. 72
vocational: ~ course 112
  ~ training 50
volcano 18
volume: to turn up the ~ 56
voluntary: to do ~ work 118
vote: majority ~ 64
to vote for/against s.o. 64
voter 64
voting system 66
voyage 140

W

wages 116
wagon train 38
war: act of ~ 48
  to be at ~ 36
  ~ on terror 28, 48
  the (American) Civil War 28
  the Cold War 28
  the First/Second World War 28
  the War of Independence 28
warden: traffic ~ 114
warlike 38
warming: global ~ 78
washing machine 122
waste 76, 124
  ~ product 76
to waste s.th. 80
to watch TV 56
water 80
  ~ sports 108
waterfall 18
wave 22
  wireless ~ 122
way
  to go the wrong ~ 136
  ~ of life 46, 130
  the Milky Way 24
wealth 14, 130
weapon 30, 50
weather forecast 22
weatherman 22
to weave (s.th.) 34
web: the World Wide Web 60
  ~ camera 60
website 60
wedding 94, 134
weekly (magazine) 54
western 10
wet: a ~ day 24
wheat 12
wheel 138
whirlwind 18
whist 108
white-water rafting 104
Whitsun 148
wide 16
wife 94
wild 18
wilderness 16, 36
wildlife 80
to win 108
  ~ the day 32
wind: high ~ 22
  ~ power 80
windsurfing 104